On the Laying Out, Planting, and Managing of Cemeteries

is not in ... closely la... or contrary to their interests.

... ...

Your most obt servt.

A. C. ...

is not immediately had, or in contrary to their interest.

I am

Sir,

Your most Obt. Servt.

S. C. _____

ON THE

LAYING OUT, PLANTING, AND MANAGING

OF

CEMETERIES;

AND ON

THE IMPROVEMENT

OF

CHURCHYARDS.

WITH SIXTY ENGRAVINGS.

By J. C. LOUDON, F.L.S., &c.

AUTHOR OF THE ARBORETUM BRITANNICUM, ETC., AND CONDUCTOR OF THE
GARDENER'S MAGAZINE.

LONDON:

PRINTED FOR THE AUTHOR;

AND SOLD BY

LONGMAN, BROWN, GREEN, AND LONGMANS.

1843.

LIST OF ENGRAVINGS.

LONDON: Printed by A. SPOTTISWOODE, New-Street-Square.

PREFACE.

CONSIDERING the laying out of cemeteries as coming within the province of the landscape-gardener, we have directed the attention of gardeners to the subject on various occasions and in various works, but more especially in the *Gardener's Magazine*, from its commencement in 1825 to the present time.

Our own attention was first forcibly directed to the subject of cemeteries in the year 1813; when, during a residence of between five and six months in Poland, we visited the public cemetery at Warsaw, and saw there the coffins of the higher classes inserted in cells in the boundary wall, and hermetically sealed with stucco (the name of the deceased being traced with an iron instrument on the plaster while yet wet, so as to leave a deep and lasting impression obtained at little cost), while the poor were buried in trenches in the open ground, without coffins. In the neighbourhood of the military hospitals, outside the same city, we saw cart-loads of naked dead soldiers (for the battle of Bautzen had then just taken place) shot into large square pits, more than one of which were sometimes filled in the course of a day; and, a little farther in the country, we saw the bodies of the aged poor, whose relatives could not afford either a coffin or the churchyard fees, dropped from the parish coffin into holes dug by the road side. (p. 45. *note*.) The strong impression made by these scenes has induced us ever since to pay particular attention to cemeteries and churchyards wherever we have been, either abroad or at home; and we have since seen all the more remarkable cemeteries on the Continent, from Stockholm to Naples, and all the large new cemeteries in Britain. None of them, however, have ever appeared to us to be fully calculated to answer the end in view, and we have long designed to write a short work on cemeteries, but have always neglected to do so, till our attention was recalled to the subject by the circumstance mentioned in p. 1., which has given rise to the present publication.

If we had to write the present work over again, we should probably enlarge on two evils prevalent in all the new cemeteries about London, and, we believe, also in most, if not all, of the provincial cemeteries : that of not sealing up the coffins in the catacombs, but merely closing the cell with open ironwork; and that of interring a number of bodies in the same grave, without leaving a sufficient depth of earth over each coffin to absorb the greater part of the gases of decomposition. (See p. 37. and p. 67.) We cannot help considering the practice of exposing the coffins to view in catacombs as disgusting; and there is undoubted proof (p. 4., and p. 45. *note*) of its being dangerous to the living, as it is only requisite to stand for a minute or two beside a grave which has been opened down to the last-deposited coffin, to experience the suffocating effect of the effluvia of decomposition, which escapes even from a coffin which has perhaps been only deposited a week or two, and the wood of which is of course perfectly sound. (See p. 27. *note*.) We refer to the grave-diggers for a description of the horrible and almost intolerable sufferings which they experience in reopening family graves, the effect of which may also be seen in their pale and ghastly countenances.

Because the graves in the new cemeteries are not yet crowded together as they are in the old churchyards, and because there is abundance of room in the vaults, it is commonly thought that the new places of interment are free from all the horrors of the old burying-grounds. Undoubtedly there is a great difference between them; but, as far as relates to catacombs, vaults, and brick graves, and to the practice of reopening family and common graves, down to the last-deposited coffin, the improvement has been very trifling, and a thorough reformation is required. Unless this takes place, it is not difficult to foresee that the new cemeteries will soon cease to be wholesome places of recreation, more especially such as are on level ground, or are surrounded by high walls and thick belts of plantation, which exclude the action of the wind on the interior surface. We have suggested (p. 43. to 49.) the kind of reformation that we think requisite; viz., hermetically sealing up all coffins deposited in vaults, catacombs, or brick graves, in certain cases by embedding them in Roman cement; and leaving a stratum of 6 ft. of earth, never on any account to be disturbed, over every coffin, except in the case of two coffins, as of a mother and child, deposited at the same time. To insure the non-disturbance of this stratum of 6 ft. of soil, we have suggested the use of a protecting stone. (p. 37.) In order to protect the skeleton in the case of the last-deposited body, in family or common graves, as well as in the case of graves in which only one interment has been made, we have also recommended (p. 6.) placing a protecting cover or permanent guard, of stone, slate, or even tiles, of the length and breadth of the coffin lid, directly over the coffin, there to remain for ever. In this way we would effectually secure the non-disturbance of human bones after they had been once committed to the soil; and this, we consider, ought to be a grand object in the management of burying-grounds.

We sincerely hope that this subject, and also other improvements which we have suggested, will be duly considered by the directors of cemeteries, as well as by Mr. Mackinnon (see p. 43, 44.) in his new bill now before parliament.

J. C. L.

Bayswater, March 28. 1843.

CONTENTS.

LAYING OUT CEMETERIES,

AND ON THE

IMPROVEMENT OF CHURCHYARDS,

ETC.

THE circumstance of being employed by the Directors of a Cemetery Company at Cambridge to form a plan for their guidance in arranging the ground, and in working and managing the cemetery afterwards, led us to study the principles on which all the arrangements connected with cemeteries are, or ought to be, founded, and the following pages contain the general results of our enquiries. The subjects discussed are :

I. The Uses of Cemeteries.
II. The Laying out, Planting, and Architecture of Cemeteries, with a view to these uses.
III. The Working and Management of Cemeteries.
IV. Certain Innovations suggested, relative to the Selection of Ground for Cemeteries, and the Mode of performing Funerals, &c.
V. A Design for a small Cemetery on level Ground, of moderate extent, exemplified in a cemetery now being formed at Cambridge, illustrated by a plan, sections, and an isometrical view.
VI. Design for a Cemetery on hilly Ground, with an isometrical view.
VII. The present State of the London Cemeteries, considered as cemetery gardens.
VIII. The Improvement and Extension of Country Churchyards, illustrated by plans.
IX. A List of Trees, Shrubs, and perennial herbaceous Plants, adapted for Cemeteries and Churchyards.

I. THE USES OF CEMETERIES.

As, to know the best mode of applying the principles of design to any particular object, it is necessary to know the purposes for which that object is intended, we shall commence by considering the *uses* for which cemeteries or burial-grounds are required.

The *main object* of a burial-ground is, the disposal of the remains of the dead in such a manner as that their decomposition, and return to the earth from which they sprung, shall not prove injurious to the living; either by affecting their health, or shocking their feelings, opinions, or prejudices.

A *secondary object* is, or ought to be, the improvement of the moral sentiments and general taste of all classes, and more especially of the great masses of society.

With respect to the first and most important object, the decomposition of the dead, without the risk of injury to the living, there is, as we think, but one mode in which this can be effected, to which there can be no objection on the part of the living ; and that is, interment in a wooden coffin in the free soil, in a grave 5 or 6 feet deep, rendered secure from being violated, in which no body has been deposited before, or is contemplated to be deposited thereafter.

Various circumstances, however, into which it is needless to enquire, have given rise to burying several bodies in the same grave in the free soil, and to modes of sepulture by which the decomposition of the body, or at least its union with the earth, is prevented ; such as the use of leaden or iron coffins, and depositing them in vaults, catacombs, and other structures, in which they can never, humanly speaking, except in the case of some great change or convulsion, be mingled with the soil, or, in the beautiful language of Scripture, be returned to the dust from which they sprung.   Though we are of opinion that the modes of burial which prevent the body from mixing with the soil, which, for the sake of distinction, we shall call the sepulchral modes, cannot, on account of the danger to the living, be continued much longer in a highly civilised country, yet, in considering the conditions requisite for a complete cemetery suited to the present time, the various modes of sepulchral burial at present in use must be kept in view.   The expense of the sepulchral mode, however, confines it to the comparatively wealthy ; and hence by far the greater part of burial-grounds always was, and is, necessarily devoted to interments in the free soil.   In some churchyards where there is abundance of room, only one coffin is deposited in a grave ; but in most cases, and particularly in the burial-grounds of large towns, the graves are dug very deep, and several coffins, sometimes as many as a dozen, or even more, according to the depth of the grave, are deposited one over another, till they reach within 5 or 6 feet of the surface. Interments in this manner are of two kinds.   The first are made in family graves, in which the different members of the same family are deposited in succession, in the order of their decease ; and to such graves there is always a grave-stone or some kind of monument.   The second are what are called common graves, to which there is no monument, and in which the bodies of the poor and of paupers are deposited, in the order in which they are brought to the cemetery ; probably two or three in one day, or possibly as many in one day as will fill the grave.   Unless this mode were adopted in the public cemeteries, they would, from their present limited extent, very soon be filled up.   Such graves, whether public or private, in the newly formed cemeteries, when once filled with coffins to within 6 ft. of the surface, are understood never to be reopened ; but, in the old burial-grounds, they are in many cases opened after being closed only four or five years, and sometimes much sooner.

When the parties burying cannot afford to purchase a private or family grave, the practice is, in some burial-grounds, to bury singly in graves of the ordinary depth of 6 or 7 feet, and these graves are reopened for a similar purpose in six or seven years ; but, as this is attended with the disinterment of the bones, it is a very objectionable mode.   In a burial-ground properly arranged and managed, a coffin, after it is once interred, should never again be exposed to view, nor a human bone be disturbed.   At present this is only the case in the cemeteries of the Jews, where there is a separate grave for every coffin, and where the graves are never reopened.   It is also the case in the cemeteries of the Quakers ; though not, we believe, from religious principle, as in the case of the Jews, but rather from that general regard to decency and propriety which is a characteristic of that sect of Christians, and perhaps, as in the case of the Moravians, in consequence of their comparatively limited number.

As *data* to proceed upon with reference to interments in the free soil, it is necessary to state that the muscular part of the body either decays rapidly, or dries up rapidly, according to the circumstances in which it is placed; but that the bones do not decay, even under circumstances the most favourable for that purpose, for centuries.

The face of a dead body deposited in the free soil is generally destroyed in three or four months, but the thorax and abdomen undergo very little change, except in colour, till the fourth month. The last part of the muscular fibre which decays is the upper part of the thigh, which in some subjects resists putrefaction for four or five years. In general, a body is considered unfit for dissection after it has been interred eight or nine weeks. In a very dry and warm soil, especially where the body is emaciated, the juices are rapidly absorbed ; and, no moisture coming near it, the solids contract and harden, and a species of mummy is produced. This may be observed in the vaults of various churches in Britain where the soil and situation are remarkably dry ; and it has given rise to those appalling scenes which may be witnessed in the vaults of Bremen, Vienna, Rome, Naples, Palermo, Malta, and other places. (See *Necropolis Glasguensis*, p. 48. to 55. ; and Stephens's *Incidents of Travel*, as quoted in the *Saturday Magazine*, vol. xx. p. 141.)

Bones are chiefly composed of phosphate of lime deposited in gelatine, an animal tissue ; and, unless acted on by powerful acids, they will endure, either in the soil or in the atmosphere, for many centuries. They are even found in the fossil state, and after ages of exposure often contain more or less of the original animal tissue, particularly if they have been embedded in clayey soil. In the ante-hominal part of the creation, there are bones daily discovered which have existed 6000 years at least. Dr. Charles Loudon informs us that he has seen numerous human bones in certain caves near to Naples, which are supposed to be those of the Grecian colonists who settled there before the Christian era, or perhaps those of an older race who inhabited Magna Græcia.* Dr. Loudon has seen several skeletons dug out of the ruins of Pompeii, the bones of which were as dry and entire as the bones of skeletons which we see in dissecting-rooms, though they must have lain there nearly 1800 years under the lava, which, around them, seemed to be a dry greyish kind of earth. Even while writing this, we read in the newspapers (*Morn. Chron.*, Jan. 10.) of the workmen, while digging a deep sewer in Lad Lane in the city, having cut into what is supposed to have been a cemetery of the Romans, and dug up a number of human bones.

With respect to *prejudices*, there is, as every one knows, a decided prejudice in favour of being buried in dry soil, and against the placing of decomposing substances, such as quicklime, in coffins ; and it is one of our principles to respect existing prejudices as well as vested rights. With regard to the use

---

* The desire to preserve the bones from decay seems natural to man, both in a rude and a civilised state. Dr. Dieffenbach informs us that the New Zealanders expose the bodies of their dead, in a sort of canoe-shaped coffin, among the foliage of trees, for several months, till the flesh is sufficiently decomposed ; the bones are then washed and cleaned, and finally deposited in some secret spot in a wood, or in a limestone cavern, of which there are many, or in some chasm of the rocks difficult of access. The bodies of hereditary chiefs are dressed and ornamented, and preserved in mausoleums of elaborately carved work ; but, even in this case, after a time, the tohunga, or priest, removes the bones to a place in the forest often known only to himself. (*Travels in New Zealand*, ii. p. 63.) The monks of the Convent of Mount Sinai, Mr. Stephens informs us, bury their dead for about three years, after which they take them up, clean the bones, and deposit them in one great pit ; except those of the archbishops, which are preserved separately in an adjoining sepulchre, some in baskets, some on shelves, and others tied together and hanging from the roof. (*Incidents of Travel.*)

of quicklime; independently of the existing prejudices against its introduction
in coffins, it is found to cause the solution of the softer parts of the body,
which, unless the coffin is watertight, and this is rarely the case with the
coffins either of the poor or of the middling class, oozes out to such an
extent that the undertaker's men can scarcely carry the coffin, on account of
the flow of matter and the odour.

The health of the living is chiefly affected by a certain description of
gas, respecting which it is necessary to enter into some detail. The decomposition of the muscular part of the human body takes place with
different degrees of rapidity in different soils, and at different depths in
the same soil. It is most rapid in sandy soils somewhat moist, within 3
or 4 feet of the surface, and in a warm climate; it is next in rapidity in chalky
soils; much slower in clayey soils; and slowest of all in peaty soil, saturated
with astringent moisture. In general, dry soil, and a moderate distance of
5 or 6 feet below the surface, are favourable both to decomposition and human
prejudices. In such soil, in the climate of London, the muscular part of the
human body will have become a black mould in between six and seven
years; but, practically speaking, the bones may be considered as indestructible. In the progress of decay, the first change which takes place immediately after death is, the escape of a deleterious gas from the mouth
and nostrils, but generally in so small a quantity as not to be perceptible
for three or four days. In some cases, it is perceptible in a much shorter
period; and in all a gas accumulates within the body, which escapes sooner or
later according to the progress of the putrescent process. If the body is
buried in the free soil, in a wooden coffin, to the depth of 5 or 6 feet, the gas
escapes into the soil, and is, in part at least, absorbed by it, and consequently does not contaminate the air above the surface; but, if a leaden
coffin is used, and the body is deposited in a vault, catacomb, or brick
grave, the gas escapes within the coffin, and either remains there till
the coffin decays, or escapes through crevices in the lead, and through
small holes bored on purpose by the undertaker in the outer wooden
coffin and leaden inner coffin, and concealed by the name-plate. (*Report on
the Health of Towns, Walker, &c.*) By the last mode the gas begins to escape
before the corpse is taken from the house; and its effect is often felt there,
as well as when the service is being read over it in the chapel, and even after
it is deposited in a vault, the catacombs of which, though apparently hermetically sealed, are seldom air-tight. Sometimes the body, especially of
a corpulent person, swells so much before it is removed from the house,
that it is ready to burst both the inner and the outer coffin; and in that case
it requires to be tapped, and the gas burnt as it escapes, or the operation
performed close to an open window. Even in some of the public catacombs
of the new London cemeteries explosions have been known to take place,
and the undertaker obliged to be sent for in order to resolder the coffin; which
shows the disgusting nature of this mode of interment, and its danger to the
living. To inhale this gas, undiluted with atmospheric air, is instant death;
and, even when much diluted, it is productive of disease which commonly ends
in death, of which there is abundant evidence in Walker's *Grave-Yards* and
the Parliamentary Report quoted. The gas abounds to a fearful extent in
the soil of all crowded burial-grounds, and has been proved to be more or
less present in the soil thrown out of graves where bodies have been interred
before. Even in the new London cemeteries, when interments are made in
family graves, or common graves, which have been filled in with earth, such is
the smell when the grave-diggers arrive within 2 or 3 feet of the last deposited
coffin, that they are obliged to be plied constantly with rum to induce them
to proceed. This is more particularly the case when graves are dug in strong
clay, because the gas cannot escape laterally as in a gravelly or sandy soil, but
rises perpendicularly through the soil which has been moved. The remedy
for this evil is, never to allow a family grave, or a common grave, in which an
interment has been made, to be excavated deeper than within 6 ft. of the last

deposited coffin ; and, to make sure of this, there ought to be a protecting stone, or slate, to be hereafter described, deposited when the grave is being filled, at the height of 6 ft. above the last coffin, under a severe penalty. It is only by some regulation of this kind, that burying several coffins in deep graves can be conducted without injuring the health of grave-diggers; and without the gas, which escapes from the earth brought up, endangering the health of those who may be occasional spectators.

In the years 1782 and 1783, when the disinterment of the burying-grounds of Les Innocents in Paris took place under the direction of some eminent French chemists, these philosophers endeavoured to analyse this gas, but were unable to procure it. Fourcroy, speaking in their name, says :—" In vain we endeavoured to induce the grave-diggers to procure any of this elastic fluid. They uniformly refused, declaring that it was only by an unlucky accident they interfered with dead bodies in that dangerous state. The horrible odour and the poisonous activity of this fluid announce to us that if it is mingled, as there is no reason to doubt, with hydrogenous and azotic gas holding sulphur and phosphorus in solution, ordinary and known products of putrefaction, it may contain also another deleterious vapour, whose nature has hitherto escaped philosophical research, while its terrible action upon life is too strikingly evinced. These Paris grave-diggers know," Fourcroy adds, " that the greatest danger to them arises from the disengagement of this vapour from the abdomen of carcasses in a state of incipient putrefaction." (See *Annales de Chimie*, vol. v. p. 154., as quoted in Walker's *Grave-Yards*, p. 86. ; and Ure's *Dictionary of Chemistry*, art. Adipocere.)

While this inflation from gas is going forward, the aqueous part of decomposition, a " fetid sanies," exudes from the body, and sometimes, when interment is delayed too long, to such an extent as to drop from the coffin before it is taken out of the house. This exudation, as already observed, is greatly accelerated and increased by putting quicklime into the coffin. In the free soil this fetid sanies is diffused by the rain in the subsoil, and carried along in the water of the subsoil to its natural outlet, or to the wells which may be dug into it ; and thus, while the gas of decomposition poisons both the earth and the air, the fluid matter contaminates the water.*

---

* Speaking of the infectious agency in the houses in the neighbourhood of that part of London called Fleet Ditch, Dr. Lynch observes :—" The great primary cause is, that the privies are in general under the staircase of the wretched hovels of the poor, and the sulphuretted hydrogen, and the carbonated hydrogen, and the noxious gases there generated, are the same gases as are generated from the dead bodies in a state of decomposition; for the evacuations from the body are decomposed animal and vegetable matter, and a dead body is the same, it is decomposition of the dead body, or a general state of disorganisation, and that produces exactly the same kind of gases. There have been instances mentioned, where people have fallen down dead from a rush of those gases in a concentrated form." (*Report on Health of Towns*, &c., p. 161.)

If the public were fully aware of the dangerous nature of the gases which proceed from the decomposition of dead bodies in crowded churchyards, and in vaults and catacombs, and of the poisonous nature of the water of decomposition,

1. They would not live in houses bordering on churchyards, which, though already full, are still used as burying-grounds.

2. They would not drink the water of wells dug in the vicinity of burial-grounds, whether in town or country ; because, though the filtration of the soil will purify the water from matter suspended in it, it will not free it from what is held in solution

3. They would not attend service in any church or chapel whatever, in

With regard to the *destruction of human bones*, we assume that to be impracticable, otherwise than by means which are altogether out of the question. The most favourable soil for their decomposition is a coarse gravel, subject to be alternately moist and dry; but, though such a soil, so circumstanced in regard to water, might be found naturally, or might be composed by art, yet these cases may be considered as equally impracticable.* Instead, therefore, of endeavouring to destroy the human skeleton, let us limit our endeavours to preventing it from being desecrated by disinterment and exposure. This may be effected in various ways; but by far the most simple, effectual, and economical, as it appears to us, would be to place over the coffin, after it was deposited in the grave, a stone or slate of the same dimensions as the coffin, or even as many flat 12-inch tiles, say six, as would extend from head to foot. As the coffin and the muscular part of its contents decayed and sunk down, the stone, slate, or tiles, would follow it and press close on the bones. In consequence of this arrangement, when the ground was at any future period opened to the depth of the stone, slate, or tile, guard, it would be known that a skeleton was beneath, and the operator would cease to go farther; or, at all events, it should be rendered illegal for him to do so. If a name and date were graven in the stone, being protected from atmospheric changes, it would remain uninjured for ages, and, like the foot-marks which geologists have found in the red sandstone, might, in some far distant age, become part of the geological history of our globe. We prefer stone or tile guards, to guards of metal, because iron would soon rust, and cease to be a guard, and lead or any equally durable metal would offer a temptation to stealing. A layer two or three inches thick of stucco, Roman cement, or a plate of asphalte or oropholithe, might be used as a substitute; but stone, slate, and tiles are decidedly preferable. The slate might even be introduced within the coffin, without rendering it heavier to carry than if a lead coffin were used. Burying in a coffin made entirely of stone or slate we do not consider so likely to prevent desecration as a stone or slate guard; because there is a temptation to dig up the lower part of the stone coffin, and use it as a drinking-trough for cattle, or a cistern for a flower-garden, which is done in various places in the vicinity of old abbeys. A stone hollowed out on the under side might be better than a flat stone; because the depending edges would

---

the vaults of which there were coffins, or in the floors of which interments had taken place. They would absent themselves from all such places, even if there were no immediate danger, in order, by such means as were in their power, to contribute to the discountenance of a practice by all parties allowed to be attended with disgusting and injurious results.

4. Nor would they live in houses in which the privies were not either rendered water-closets, or placed detached from the house.

5. Nor in a house adjoining an open sewer.

6. Nor would they keep a dead body in the house more than five days, or at the most a week.

* If the bones were to be destroyed in the case of a single grave, a hint might be taken from the following passage in Fellowes's *Asia Minor*. " The outward marks of respect are scarcely visible in their burial-grounds, little more being left to mark the place of interment than a row of stones indicating the oblong form of the grave; but a pipe or chimney, generally formed of wood or earthenware, rises a few inches above the ground, and communicates with the corpse beneath; and down this tube libations are poured by the friends of the deceased to the attendant spirit of the dead." (Vol. xi. p. 16.) Were the libations withheld for five or six years, till the muscular part of the body was completely destroyed, and then diluted muriatic acid employed as a libation, the result would probably be obtained in the course of a year or two.

be a kind of side protection to the skeleton; and might, together with the name graven on the upper side, procure more respect from those who should fall upon it accidentally in future ages, in excavating for improvements.

The *space of ground required* for a single interment, and for the interments incident to any given population, requires next to be taken into consideration. If all interments took place in the free soil, if a grave were allowed for each coffin, and the grave were never afterwards to be opened, that is, not opened for several generations, then the space required for cemeteries would be considerable. Thus, supposing graves without head-stones or ornaments of any kind to occupy a surface of 7 ft. by 3 ft. 6 in., and the average area of those having grave-stones or monuments to be 10 ft. by 5 ft., then, making an allowance for grass paths between the graves, and for gravel roads, we may take 8 ft. by 4 ft. as the average space on which to calculate the capacity of a garden or ornamental cemetery. This will give 1361 graves to an acre; and, estimating the deaths in a town population at 3 per cent per annum, this acre would suffice for a population of 1000 souls for 45 years; or for a population of 45,000 for one year. Taking the population of London to be 1,500,000, this would require 33 acres annually, or the whole of that part of Middlesex not covered by London and its suburbs (128,540 acres) in the course of 3895 years. The average number of deaths annually in England and Wales has been ascertained to be about 336,000, which, at 1361 interments to an acre, would require 247 acres annually; or, supposing three interments in each grave 82 acres per annum. On the supposition that ground once occupied by graves was for ever afterwards to be held sacred, and not subjected to cultivation of any kind; the mode of interment which would require so large a sacrifice of surface annually may be considered as impracticable; and, for our present purpose, this is the view that we shall take of it. We shall, however, hereafter show how separate graves may be procured, not only for those who cannot afford gravestones, but even for paupers; and these graves never again opened for generations. In the meantime, the mode of burying several coffins in one grave, provided these coffins are of wood, and layers of soil not less than 6 ft. in thickness interposed, and the graves, when once filled, not opened for generations, appears the best adapted for the present state of things. Supposing that on an average three interments take place in each grave or vault before it is finally closed, this will give upwards of 4000 interments to the acre; and, as the eight public cemeteries recently formed in the neighbourhood of the metropolis, and the unoccupied part of the new burial-grounds recently formed by different sections of the Dissenters, contain upwards of 300 acres inclusive of the space occupied by roads and buildings, this will probably supply the demand for two centuries to come, even allowing the population to increase.

The *security of the grave* was, till within these few years, an important part of the considerations requisite to be had in view in constructing cemeteries. In some cases it was effected by surrounding the enclosure by high walls, or other effective fences; sometimes by constructing central watch-towers for stationary watchmen within; sometimes by employing perambulating watchmen; at others by burying in a grave 15 or 20 feet deep; by burying in a walled grave, covered with an iron grating built into the walls all round, some feet beneath the surface soil, and keeping the surface loose, and planted with flowers or shrubs (which, as the grave could not be disturbed without first taking these up, would by their withered state, when replanted, have told what had been attempted); and sometimes by the very extraordinary mode of letting down over the coffin a ponderous cast-iron box, to remain over it for six or eight weeks, till the body was considered to be so far decomposed as to be unfit for the purposes of the anatomist. The iron box, or case, which had remained whelmed over the coffin, but without touching it, was then disinterred, and drawn up by machinery, and the wooden coffin was covered with soil, and the grave completed a second time in the usual manner. Even the poorest families, in some parts of Scotland, went to this extraordinary expense. Fortunately a law has been passed which renders these precautions unnecessary, and we shall therefore take no farther notice of them.

The secondary object of cemeteries, that of *improving the moral feelings*, will be one of the results of the decorous attainment of the main object; for it must be obvious that the first step to rendering the churchyard a source of amelioration or instruction is, to render it attractive. So far from this being the case at present, they are in many instances the reverse, often presenting, in London and other large towns, a black unearthly-looking surface, so frequently disturbed by interments that no grass will grow upon it * ; while, in the country, the churchyard is commonly covered with rank grass abounding in tall weeds, and neglected grave-stones. Cemeteries in this state "lose their monitory virtue when thus obtruded upon the notice of men occupied with the cares of the world, and too often sullied and defiled by those cares." No wonder that, under such circumstances, the burial-grounds, more especially of towns, are shunned and avoided, rather than sought after as places for meditation. Even under the most favourable circumstances, the associations which are generally attached to churchyards are gloomy and terrific.

> ———— " The Grave! dread thing,
> Men shiver when thou 'rt named: Nature, appall'd,
> Shakes off her wonted firmness. Ah! how dark
> The long extended realms and rueful wastes,
> Where nought but silence reigns, and night, dark night!
> . . . .   The sickly taper,
> By glimmering through thy low-brow'd mirky vaults,
> Furr'd round with misty damps and ropy slime,
> Lets fall a supernumerary horror,
> And only serves to make thy night more irksome."

"Why," says Washington Irving, "should we thus seek to clothe death with unnecessary terrors, and to spread horrors around the tomb of those we love? The grave should be surrounded by every thing that might inspire tenderness and veneration for the dead, or that might win the living to virtue. It is the place, not of disgust and dismay, but of sorrow and meditation." "Nothing can make amends," says Coleridge, "for the want of the soothing influences of nature, and for the absence of those types of renovation and decay which the fields and woods offer to the notice of the serious and contemplative mind. To feel the force of this sentiment, let a man only compare, in imagination, the unsightly manner in which our monuments are crowded together in the busy, noisy, unclean, and almost grassless churchyard of a large town, with the still seclusion of a Turkish cemetery in some remote place, and yet further sanctified by the grove of cypress in which it is embosomed." (*Coleridge's Friend.*)

"Let us be careful, however, in our anxiety to escape from gloom and horror, not to run into the opposite extreme of meretricious gaudiness. Death and the grave are solemn and awful realities; they speak with a powerful and intelligible voice to the heart of every spectator, as being the common lot of all. To say nothing of the bad taste, therefore, anything obtrusively picturesque, anything savouring of fashionable prettiness, any far-fetched conceits

---

* The persons living in the houses which abut on the burial-ground of Bartholomew the Less, Dr. Lynch states, are in the habit of emptying their chamber-pots into it; and the surface of the burial-ground of Bartholomew the Great, adjoining, is so covered with the excrementitious matter floated over from the cesspools of privies, that it is difficult to walk across it. There is no hope of curing any person living in this quarter, when attacked by disease, but by removal. (*Dr. Lynch*, in *Report*, &c. p. 161.)

or tortured allegories, jar upon the feelings of every well-regulated mind, and excite ideas the very opposite to those of sympathy and tenderness. Our cemeteries, then, should bear a solemn and soothing character, equally remote from fanatical gloom and conceited affectation. " (*Picton*, in *Arch. Mag.* iv. p. 430.)

"Where is it, would we ask," says the learned and eloquent author of *Necropolis Glasguensis*, " that the innate desire which is felt in every bosom to live in the recollection of his companions, the pleasing hope that he may still be a remembered denizen of this fleeting world, is more likely to be realised than at the spot where his ashes are laid ? Where is it that the ' *Extincta amabitur*,' such as Cicero professed to his daughter Tullia, and which is still the pledge of friendship offered at the couch of the dying, is more likely to be experienced in all its force and all its purity, than at the tomb where all that remains of worth and loveliness is lying ? Where is it, indeed, that the heart is likely to be so feelingly moved, or the memory to be so powerfully roused, as at a parent's grave or at a sister's tomb?" (p. 27.) After deploring the present state of Scottish churchyards, and contrasting them with some in England and Wales, our author has the following touching paragraphs on the Cemetery of Père la Chaise, which, as they exhibit the *beau idéal* of what a general cemetery ought to be, in order to realise our ideas of its moral influence on the living, we shall quote as preferable to anything that we could say on the subject.

" Who, that has ever visited the romantic Cemetery of Père la Chaise, would not wish that there were, in this our native land, some more attractive spot dedicated to the reception of the dead, than those vast fields of rude stones and ruder hillocks, to which we are ever and anon called, when attending the obsequies of a kinsman or companion ; that in fact there were here some such garden cemetery as that in the neighbourhood of Paris, whither the widowed heart might occasionally resort to hold spiritual communion with the departed partner of earthly joy or woe ; whither the weeping orphan might at times repair, to recall the worth and the virtues of his beloved parent. Within the extensive and delightfully variegated enclosure alluded to, situated on Mount Louis, it is perhaps unnecessary to state that all the disagreeable sensations which are here coupled with a churchyard are dispelled by the beauty of the garden, the variety of its walks, by the romantic nature of its situation, and, above all, by the commanding view of Paris and its environs which it affords. In that vast grove of the dead, each has his own grave, and each his own mausoleum. In place of the clumsy mound or large white stone that so generally covers the ashes of our countrymen, is to be found a little flower-garden surrounded by cedar, spruce, cypress, and yew trees, round which the rose and the honeysuckle are seen entwining; while, instead of a solitary and deserted churchyard, the eye meets at every turn with some pensive or kneeling figure weeping over the remains of a relative, or worshipping his God at the tomb of excellence and virtue.

" The most common burial-places, and perhaps the most affecting, in this cemetery, consist of a square or parallelogram of ground, of about three or four yards broad, enclosed by a neat little railing of iron or wicker-work. Within this spot there is always a sepulchral urn, a small pillar, or a cross, to tell the name and the quality of him who lies below. The remaining portion is filled with flowers, and embellished with pots of rare plants. The more ambitious monuments consist of obelisks, pyramids, temples, and marble sarcophagi, decorated with figures and *bassi rilievi;* while a third consist of crypts and family sepulchres in some degree similar to those of ancient Rome. Amid the green glades and gloomy cypresses which surround and overshadow the vast variety of sepulchral ornaments of Père la Chaise, the contemplative mind is not only impressed with sentiments of solemn sublimity and religious awe, but with those of the most tender and heart-affecting melancholy. Vain man is recalled from the distracting turbulence and folly of the world, to the salutary recollection 'of that undiscovered country from which no traveller returns.' The gay and the giddy are reminded that their 'gibes and jokes' must ere while for ever cease, and are led to reflect that they too must die; and, as 'by the sadness of the countenance the heart is made better,' the religious man, instructed on the narrowness of the boundary which separates him from those who were the 'sun and centre' of his nearest and dearest regards on earth, looks forward not only without fear, but with joy and exultation, to the period when, that boundary being for ever broken down, they shall, in their happy experience, find that, as they were loving and beloved in their lives, 'in their deaths they were not divided.' In the mazes of Père la Chaise, we feel walking as in the porch of eternity, and our heart is at once impressed with a sense of the evanescence and the value of time. There, the instability of all human affairs is emphatically and eloquently taught by the dread silence of the tomb, and unequivocally beheld in the mere change which a few years have produced on the garden itself; for, within the stately mansion whose ruins are now on every side surrounded by melancholy tombs, did the favourite confessor of Louis XIV., the most powerful and most persecuting Jesuit of his time, erst pass his hours of pastime and of pleasure; and the disciples of Jansenius and Molina now repose, in freedom and in peace, in that place to which, when alive, they did not dare even to approach; while the fierce disputes which they mutually excited through the Christian world are fallen, like themselves, into neglect and oblivion!*

" In Scotland it is of every-day occurrence, to find the lie given to the most pompous monuments, a few months after their erection, by the moss overgrowing and obscuring the epitaph which vows and intends unceasing remembrance of the dead. In the Cemetery of Mount Louis, however, the feeling of recollection is exemplified to live a very long time after the engraving of the sepulchral stone and the wonted period prescribed to outward mourning. It is there the custom for surviving friends to visit the tombs of their relatives, and, as a token of recollection and respect to their memory, to weave a garland of flowers, and hang it on their monument. At every turn the eye is arrested by the tender proof of some late friendly visitation. Flowers, as yet fresh and unfaded, are seen scattered over the not yet verdant sod. The greenhouse myrtle flourishes in the parterre dedicated to affection and love; the chaste forget-me-not blooms over the ashes of a faithful friend; the green laurel shades the cenotaph of the hero; and the drooping willow, planted by the hand of the orphan, weeps over the grave of the parent. Every thing is there tasteful, classical, poetical, and eloquent. In that asylum of death, there is nothing found save that which should touch the heart or soothe the afflicted soul, nothing save that which should awaken tender recollections or excite religious feelings. In one word, the Cemetery of Père la Chaise is the spot, of all others, dedicated to the genius of memory; and the one where a more powerful sermon is daily preached than ever fell from the lips of a Fenelon, a Massillon, or a Bossuet. Here the bodies of the

---

" * It is from this confessor, Père la Chaise, that the cemetery derives its appellation. By an edict in 1804, prohibiting burial in churches and inhabited places, the garden and pleasure-grounds of the late confessor were converted into a burial-ground, chiefly for those persons of a higher circle who could afford to purchase a grave and rear a monument; and, at this moment [1831], the whole of this extensive enclosure is nearly covered with tombs and monuments. [We have seen a Report on this cemetery, made to the French Government, dated 1842, by which it appears to be so much crowded as to require enlargement, and also that much ground has been lost in consequence of its not having been laid out originally on some systematic plan. In this Report the want of walks and roads, and of drainage, is particularly deplored, as well as the dilapidated and decaying state of the monuments.]

people of every nation, of every condition, of every age, and of every religion, are found congregated. The Russ sleeps next to the Spaniard, the Protestant next the Catholic, the Jew next the Turk. Individuals the most dissimilar when alive, in faith, in feeling, in practice, are here reconciled amid the peace-making dust of the sepulchre." (*Necropolis Glasguensis*, p. 32.)

" A garden cemetery and monumental decoration are not only beneficial to public morals, to the *improvement of manners*, but are likewise calculated to *extend virtuous and generous feelings*. Affliction, brightened by hope, ever renders man more anxious to love his neighbour. At the brink of the grave we are made most feelingly alive to the shortness and uncertainty of life, and to the danger of procrastinating towards God and man whatever it is our bounden duty to perform. There, too, the conscience is taught the value of mercy, and best feels the recompense which awaits the just in Heaven. There, the man whose heart the riches, titles, and dignities of the world have swollen with pride, best experiences the vanity of all earthly distinction, and humbles himself before the mournful shrine, where

> ' Precedency 's a jest ; vassal and lord,
> Grossly familiar, side by side consume.'

There, the son whose wayward folly may have embittered the last days of a father will, as he gazes on his grave, best receive the impulse that would urge him, as an expiation of his crime, to perform a double duty to his surviving parent. There, in fact, vice looks terrible, virtue lovely; selfishness a sin, patriotism a duty. The cemetery is, in short, the tenderest and most uncompromising monitor of man ; for,

> ' When self-esteem, or other's adulation,
> Would cunningly persuade us we were something
> Above the common level of our kind,
> The grave gainsays the smooth-complexion'd flattery,
> And with blunt truth acquaints us what we are.'

A garden cemetery is the sworn foe to preternatural fear and superstition. The ancients, from their minds being never polluted with the idea of a charnel-house, nor their feelings roused by the revolting emblems of mortality, contemplated death without terror, and visited its gloomy shrine without fear. With them death was tranquillity, and the only images that were associated with it, were those of peaceful repose and tender sorrow. The names of their burial-places indicate no association with terror, and call forth no feeling of fear. The *Cœmeterion* of the Greek suggests only the idea of a bed of slumber ; the *Bethaim* of the Jew speaks but of the mansion of the living. Amid the tombstones of Thermopylæ, we would conceive that the Grecian heart beat no less boldly at midnight than at mid-day ; while we know that the timid female, during the slumber of Jerusalem, could fearlessly wander to the silent sepulchre.* Whence then did the preternatural terrors connected with death arise, which so powerfully swayed the hearts of the middle and more modern

---

" * Among the works of ancient art there is not to be found a single image of a revolting nature connected with death. D'Israeli states that, ' to conceal its deformity to the eye, as well as to elude its suggestion to the mind, seems to have been a universal feeling ; and it accorded with a fundamental principle of ancient art, that of never offering to the eye a distortion of form in the violence of passion which destroyed the beauty of its representation ; such is shown in the Laocoon, where the mouth only opens sufficiently to indicate the suppressed agony of superior humanity, without expressing the loud cry of vulgar suffering.'

ages ; those slavish terrors which, in the ages of ignorance, appeared almost to make the resurrection an unhoped for, rather than a hoped for, event; terrors altogether at antipodes to those just fears that call upon man, ere death, to make up his peace with Heaven ? This slavish and more than vulgar error was chiefly engendered through the monkish artifice of associating man's latter end with all that was disgusting and horrible, and of inspiring the world with the idea, that, to gain heaven, it was not necessary to exist rationally on earth. Amid the general gloom thus created by penances and pilgrimages, by midnight masses and bloody flagellations, the troubled imaginations of Europe, as D'Israeli says, ' first beheld the grave yawn, and death, in the Gothic form of a gaunt anatomy, parading through the universe. The people were affrighted as they viewed every where hung before their eyes, in the twilight of their cathedrals and their pale cloisters, the most revolting emblems of death. Their barbarous taste perceived no absurdity in giving action to a heap of dry bones, which could only keep together in a state of immovability and repose; nor that it was burlesquing the awful idea of the resurrection, by exhibiting the incorruptible spirit under the unnatural and ludicrous figure of mortality, drawn out of the corruption of the grave.' If supernatural terror sprang from such causes, it was from the gloomy, naked, and deserted cemetery that superstition drew her chief influence. Thence flitted the phantoms which terrified the vulgar, and which even carried dread to the thrones of kings and emperors. Solitude peopled itself with ghosts and spectres ; silence disturbed itself with hollow groans ; while Nature, reversing her laws, allowed the dead to collect their scattered mouldering bones, and to appear, at the witching hour of night, wrapt in a winding-sheet. The monsters which man's imagination thus created, he turned from with horror ; they broke his rest in the silence of the winter's night; he heard their cry in the howl of the winds, their threat in the roar of the tempest. If the corrupters of Christianity still attempt to terrify rather than to console humanity, and if superstition still exercises her fatal spell, does it not become the duty of every wellwisher to his species, to pour into the tomb the light of religion and philosophy, and thereby to dissipate the vain phantoms which the false gloom of the grave has tended to call forth. The decoration of the cemetery is a mean peculiarly calculated to produce these effects. Beneath the shade of a spreading tree, amid the fragrance of the balmy flower, surrounded on every hand with the noble works of art, the imagination is robbed of its gloomy horrors, the wildest fancy is freed from its debasing fears. Adorn the sepulchre, and the frightful visions which visit the midnight pillow will disappear ; and if a detestation for annihilation, mingled with the fondest affection for those who are departed, should lead men still to believe that the dead hold communion with the living, the delightful illusions which will result from this state of things will form a pleasing contrast to the vile superstitions that preceded them. Let the fancied voice of a father pierce, in the silence of the night, the ear of the son who lives unmindful of his parent's early counsels ; or let the shade of a warning mother appear in the lunar ray, to the thoughtless and giddy eye of her who threatens to sacrifice her beauty and her virtue at the shrine of flattery. These fancies, the children of a pious sorrow, will neither debase the human mind, nor check the generous impulses of the human heart." (*Necropolis Glasguensis*, p. 62.)

The remaining point to be noticed is, the influence which a cemetery or a churchyard is calculated to have in *improving the taste*. That churchyards have had very little influence of this kind hitherto, we readily acknowledge; but that they are calculated to have a great deal, may be argued from the universality of churches and burying-grounds, and from their being visited by every individual perhaps more frequently than any other scene, except that of his daily occupation. A church and churchyard in the country, or a general cemetery in the neighbourhood of a town, properly designed, laid out, ornamented with tombs, planted with trees, shrubs, and herbaceous plants, all named, and the whole properly kept, might become a school of instruction in architecture, sculpture, landscape-gardening, arboriculture, botany, and in those important parts of general gardening, neatness, order, and high keeping. Some of the new London cemeteries might be referred to as answering in some degree these various purposes, and more particularly the Abney Park Cemetery; which contains a grand entrance in Egyptian architecture; a handsome Gothic chapel; a number, daily increasing, of sculptural monuments; and one of the most complete arboretums in the neighbourhood of London, all the trees and shrubs being named. In summer there are a number of beds filled with flowers of various kinds, and the whole is kept with great neatness and order. We do not, however, approve of various points in the arrangement of the trees and shrubs in this cemetery, nor of the form of the beds containing the flowers, though we admit that the management in these particulars is better than it is in most of the other cemeteries. But this subject will be considered more in detail in division VII.

Churchyards and cemeteries are scenes not only calculated to improve the morals and the taste, and by their botanical riches to cultivate the intellect, but they serve as *historical records*. This is the case with the religious temples and burial-grounds, in all ages and in all countries. The country churchyard was formerly the country labourer's only library, and to it was limited his knowledge of history, chronology, and biography; every grave was to him a page, and every head-stone or tomb a picture or an engraving. With the progress of education and refinement, this part of the uses of churchyards is not superseded, but only extended and improved. It is still to the poor man a local history and biography, though the means of more extended knowledge are now amply furnished by the diffusion of cheap publications, which will at no distant time, it is to be hoped, be rendered still more effective by the establishment of a system of national education. " A garden cemetery and monumental decoration," our eloquent author observes, " afford the most convincing tokens of a nation's progress in civilisation and in the arts which are its result. We have seen with what pains the most celebrated nations of which history speaks have adorned their places of sepulture, and it is from their funereal monuments that we gather much that is known of their civil progress and of their advancement in taste. Is not the story of Egypt written on its pyramids, and is not the chronology of Arabia pictured on its tombs? Is it not on the funeral relics of Greece and Rome that we behold those elegant images of repose and tender sorrow with which they so happily invested the idea of death? Is it not on the urns and sarcophagi of Etruria that the lover of the noble art of sculpture still gazes with delight? And is it not amid the catacombs, the crypts, and the calvaries of Italy, that the sculptor and the painter of the dark ages chiefly present the most splendid specimens of their chisel and their pencil? In modern days, also, has it not been at the shrine of death that the highest efforts of the Michael Angelos, the Canovas, the Thorwaldsens, and the Chantreys, have been elicited and exhibited? The tomb has, in fact, been the great chronicler of taste throughout the world. In the East, from the hoary pyramid to the modern Arab's grave; in Europe, from the rude tomb of the druid to the marble mausoleum of the monarch; in America, from the grove which the Indian chief planted round the sepulchre of his son, to the monument which announces to the lovers of freedom the last resting-place of Washington." (*Necropolis Glasguensis*, p. 63.)

Such are the various important uses of the cemetery and the churchyard, which it was necessary to take into consideration, before devising either a design for laying out a cemetery, or a system of rules and regulations for its working and management.

II. The Laying out, Building, and Planting of Cemeteries.

HAVING shown the uses of cemeteries, we shall next consider the mode in which the ground should be laid out or arranged, with reference to these uses.

The *situation* of cemeteries, as they are at present used, that is, interring several bodies in one grave, and placing coffins in vaults, ought always to be at a distance from human dwellings ; but if only one coffin were to be placed in each grave, and that grave never again opened, but the cemetery when filled used as a public garden, its situation might be regulated solely by convenience ; and, in general, the nearer the town, the more desirable it would be, both as a burial-ground and a promenade. Cemeteries, as at present used, ought to be in an elevated and airy situation, open to the north, but with a south aspect, that the surface may be dried by the sun ; rather than with a north aspect, where the surface would be moist during the winter months. If the surface be even, it will be more convenient for interments than if it were irregular, whether by broken ground, rocks, or undulations. It should be as near the great mass of the population for which it is intended, as a due regard to their health will permit, in order to lessen the expense of carriage, and shorten the time of the performance of funerals and of visits by the living to the tombs of their friends ; it ought to be conspicuous at a distance, because, from its buildings and tombs, it will generally be an ornament to the surrounding country, and an impressive memento of our mortality ; and the outer boundary ought to be regular and simple, in order that it may be short, and consequently less expensive than if it were circuitous.

The *soil*, for reasons which we have already noticed, ought to be dry to the depth of 20 or 30 feet, or capable of being rendered so by underground drains. It ought not to be generally rocky, at least where deep graves are to be dug. As in decomposition a considerable quantity of moisture (sanies) is exuded, the greatest care ought to be taken not to form a cemetery over a stratum of soil which contains the water used in the neighbourhood for drinking. Not to mention numerous instances in London, as noticed in the *Report on the Health of Towns*, there is a churchyard near Kirkaldy in Fifeshire with a perpetual spring immediately without the boundary wall, the water of which, passing through a stratum under the graves, is said to be contaminated ; and the burial-ground of St. Peter's Church, Brighton, cannot be used as such, on account of the proximity of the chalky stratum which contains the water that supplies the wells of the lower part of the town.

In situations where, from the flatness of the country or the nature of the soil, there is not an opportunity of draining to a great depth, care ought always to be taken to carry off as much as possible of the surface water by shallow underground drains placed under the roads, and under the gravel walks and green paths which separate the lines of graves. No drains can be made under those parts of the surface in which graves are to be dug, for obvious reasons. Many details of this kind, which need not be entered into, will readily occur to the practical man.

The prejudices of the living, in every country, are in favour of a gravelly, sandy, or chalky soil ; and in such soils draining is not required. In strong clayey soil, like that of most of the London cemeteries, decomposition does not take place for a very long period, the fleshy part of the bodies being changed into adipocere.

The *extent* of a cemetery must, of course, depend on the population for which it is intended ; the probable increase or decrease of that population ; and whether one, or more than one, interment is to be made in the same grave. The data on which to form the necessary calculations are, that the average outside dimensions of a grave are 7 ft. by 3 ft. 6 in. ; that the average dimensions of a grave, where a number of them are supposed to have grave-stones, are 8 ft. by 4 ft. ; and that the average deaths in a healthy population in the country are 2 per cent, and in crowded towns and cities 3 per cent, per annum. Thus, 20 graves will be required per annum for a rural population of 1000, and 200 per annum for a population of 10,000. An acre will give 1361 graves, which will afford a supply for nearly seven years; and three acres will serve for twenty-one years. At this latter period the town will probably have increased on the side next the cemetery, when the additional ground should be taken at a greater distance, and the old ground, when fully occupied, may be sprinkled over with trees, to be eventually used as a place of recreation for the living. The calculation, however, will be considerably different, if we suppose that all the graves are to be without head-stones, and consequently no longer than is necessary to admit the coffins. For this purpose, the average width of the grave at one end may be 2 ft., and at the other 20 in., and the length 6 ft. Taking the greater width, this will give 12 square feet to each grave, which will give 3630 graves to an acre. These graves in the London cemeteries are dug 15 ft. in depth, and ten coffins of poor persons are deposited in them. The common charge is 25s. for each coffin, or at the rate of the enormous sum of 45,375l. per acre. In some cemeteries as many as fifteen coffins are deposited in one grave, the depth in that case being 20 or 25 feet. We could name a cemetery in which forty-five coffins, we are assured, have been deposited in one grave.

The situation, soil, and extent being fixed on, the next consideration is the *boundary fence*, which ought to be such as to insure security from theft, and favour solemnity by excluding the bustle of every-day life, while a view of distant scenery is admitted to produce a certain degree of cheerfulness, and dissipate absolute gloom. In an open part of the country, where there are few buildings or public roads, an iron railing may be employed as a ring-fence; but, in a populous neighbourhood, a wall 10 or 12 feet high, strengthened by buttresses carried up above the coping, so as to give the wall an architectural character, may be preferable. The buttresses may be of two kinds: ordinary ones, merely for strengthening the wall, or forming piers to panels of open iron railing; and, in the case of cemeteries not laid out in beds or panels, higher and more massive piers rising conspicuously above the others, at regular distances, to receive stones having cut in them the numbers and letters used as indexes to lines for ascertaining the situations of graves, in the manner which will be hereafter described. The numbers and letters alluded to are at present in most cemeteries painted on the brickwork, which has a mean temporary appearance; or they are put on stones or labels of cast iron inserted in the soil, and rising only an inch or two above it, which are liable to be disturbed by the moving of ground. Though we entirely disapprove of this mode of laying out a cemetery, yet, as it is generally practised, we have thought it right to keep it in view. Where economy is an object, a hedge and sunk wall may be used as a boundary, and the best plant for the hedge is the common holly. There ought to be one main entrance; and, if the situation admits of it, a second entrance, for the admission of workmen, carts, &c., necessary for carrying on the executive part of the cemetery.

In *laying out the interior*, the system of roads and walks, the drainage, the situation of the chapel or chapels, and the arrangement of the graves, and of the marks which in large cemeteries, as at present laid out, are necessary at the angles of the squares, require to be taken simultaneously, and also separately, into consideration. There ought to be at least one main road, so as to allow of a hearse having ready access to every part of the grounds; and from this road there ought to be gravel walks into the interior of the compartments formed by the roads, walks, and the boundary wall; and, from these gravel paths, ramifications of narrow grass paths, so as to admit of examining the graves in every part of the grounds, without walking over any of them, and thus insure respect for the dead. We have already observed that all the drains that require to be made must be under these roads, walks, and paths, so as not to interfere with the graves; and the ranges of situations for graves must be determined before the roads, walks, and green alleys are fixed on, otherwise there might be a waste of ground. To be convinced of the bad effects of the neglect of surface drainage in a cemetery, it is only necessary to walk on the grass of that at Kensal Green during winter or spring.

The first point to be attended to, according to the present system, unless the cemetery should be a small one of only an acre or two, is, to devise a system for *throwing the interior into imaginary squares or parallelograms,* which shall be indicated by numbers and letters on the boundary fence, and by marks inserted in the ground at their points of intersection. In cemeteries of moderate dimensions, more particularly if the form be rectangular, the marks at the intersections of the squares may be dispensed with; these intersections being readily ascertained when it is desired to find out the precise situation of any grave, by stretching lines across the cemetery from the letters and figures on the boundary fence. For example, suppose *fig.* 1. to represent a cemetery of five acres, with the

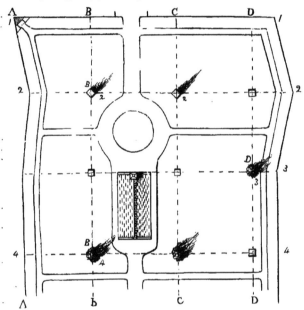

Fig. 1.   *Mode of Laying out a Cemetery in imaginary Squares.*

letters A, B, C, &c., marked at regular distances on the end walls, and figures 1, 2, 3, &c., at the same distances on the side walls ; then, by stretching one line from B to B, and another from 2 to 2, the intersections of the strings will give the point B 2, C 2, &c.: but supposing the surface of the cemetery to be very hilly, or that it is thickly studded with tombs or trees, then, as the lines could not be readily stretched so as to give the points B 2, C 2, &c., with perfect accuracy, a stone or mark of cast iron is inserted when the cemetery is first laid out, in each of the intersecting points, with the letter and figure on it, as shown in the diagram *fig.* 1. at B 2, C 2, D 3, &c. At every other point of intersection throughout the cemetery, there is a sunk stone or iron inserted, with the letter which stands at the ends of the long lines, and the figure which stands at the ends of the cross lines, as shown on a large scale in *fig.* 2. Thus in the diagram *fig.* 1., we should have the squares, A1, B1, C1, D1, &c.; and A 2, B 2, C 2, &c. The use of these squares is to enable the sexton to ascertain and point out, at any future time during the existence of the cemetery, the precise spot where any interment has taken place. For example, required to see the grave of T. W. On turning to the index of the register book of names, T. W. is found to have been interred in the square B 4. Now, on turning to the map book of the cemetery, in which every imaginary square into

Fig. 2. *Showing the manner of marking the Stones at the Angles of the Squares.*

which the cemetery is parcelled out is laid down on a large scale, the position and dimensions of the grave will be found delineated according to the scale; and then, by taking the dimensions from two of the sides of the square and applying them to the ground, the exact position of the grave is found, even though the grave mound should be obliterated. Now it must be evident that it would be exceedingly inconvenient to have the stone marks fall into positions where buildings were to be erected, or roads or walks to be laid out; and hence the propriety, as we have said above, of determining the position of the intersections of the squares, before any other part of the laying out is proceeded with. This is the more necessary in cases where the intersecting points are to be marked by trees of particular kinds, or by an obelisk, or other monumental stone. By using an obelisk or other pillar with four sides, pointing diagonally to the four squares, as at B 2 and C 2 in the diagram *fig.* 1., these stones would not only serve to indicate the intersections of the squares, but to record the names of those buried in each square, if the parties interested thought fit to incur the expense. It is not necessary that all the squares or parallelograms should be of the same size; on the contrary, their dimensions may be varied, so as to suit the ground, the boundary, and all the different circumstances connected with the general arrangement. In some cases the intersections of the squares might be indicated by trees, as shown at B 4, D 3, &c.

It must be confessed, however, that this system of laying out a cemetery into imaginary squares is a very unsatisfactory one, for the following reasons: — 1. It neither admits of a permanent system of surface drainage, nor of grass paths among the graves. 2. From there being no obvious principle of order or arrangement in conformity with which the graves are placed, the general aspect of the interior of the cemetery is confused and unsatisfactory; the graves and tomb-stones seeming to be put down at random as in common churchyards. 3. A very slight error in mapping the graves may render it difficult, if not impossible, to identify a particular grave, either to point it out to the relations of the deceased; or, when the square is nearly full, for the purpose of avoiding an old grave in digging a new one. Let any one who doubts this examine the map books in the principal London cemeteries, and ask to see one of the graves indicated in the plan. 4. Unless a head-stone is put to the grave, or some other permanent mark, it is impossible for any person but the sexton to identify it; which circumstance can by no means be rendered satisfactory to the relations of the deceased. 5. No provision is made for paths among these graves, so that, when the squares are nearly full, there will be no mode of getting to any one grave, but by walking over a number of others; which is not only a species of desecration, but, when there are several of the graves having head-stones, must be exceedingly inconvenient.

A much better system, in our opinion, is to lay out the ground in what may be called double beds with green paths between, in the manner to be described in a future paragraph, which has an orderly appearance, admits of a permanent system of surface drainage, requires no mapping, and enables the friends of the deceased to recognise the grave they wish to see without troubling the sexton or any one else. This laying out of the ground in double beds need not be so executed as to have a formal appearance, though it should be sufficiently distinct to give what, in the language of art, is called the expression of purpose, and thus give the lawn of a cemetery a different character from that of the lawn of a pleasure-ground. The double beds may be slightly raised in the middle, so as to slope to the grass paths, and the surface of these paths, if only 3 in. below that of the beds, will be a sufficient distinction, when the whole is near the eye; while, at a short distance, the difference between the beds and the paths will scarcely be perceptible. We mention these things to anticipate objections on account of the supposed formality of this plan. Under every green path there may be a tile drain, which will render it as dry as a gravel walk. The path will answer if only 3 ft. wide, because, in carrying a coffin along it shoulder high, that space is sufficient; but 4 ft. is preferable, as admitting of carrying a coffin by handspokes. Where the hand-bier, to be hereafter described, is used, a 2-feet path would be wide enough.

In making arrangements for the *situations of graves*, regard must be had to the wealth and taste of the persons who will probably use the cemetery, and the proportion of situations for sumptuous tombs and monuments adjusted accordingly. At the same time, we should mark no part of the ground as exclusively devoted to any class of society, of graves, or of monuments*; nor should there be any part in which a monument might not be erected. In general, we would form a broad border, say from 12 ft. to 20 ft. wide, along the main roads; a border immediately within the boundary fence, of the same width as the height of the latter; a border from 8 ft. to 12 ft. wide on each side of the gravel walks; and the interior of the compartments we would lay out in beds or zones, straight or curved, with green alleys of 3 or 4 feet between. These beds ought to be of such a width as to contain two rows of graves, with the headstones of each row placed back to back in the middle of the bed, so as to face the alleys. The necessary width for this purpose is 18 ft.; which will allow 7 ft. for the length of each grave; 1 ft. at the head of each grave, on which to erect a head-stone, or other monument not exceeding 1 ft. in thickness nor the width of the grave; and 1 ft. at the end next the walk, for a foot-stone or number. This head-stone or monument, it may be observed, should in no case be built on the soil, but on two brick piers brought up from the bottom of the soil to the surface of the ground, in the manner to be hereafter described.

The direction of the *roads, walks, and green paths*, is partly a matter of necessity and partly of design and taste. Where the surface of the ground is hilly, undulating, or otherwise irregular, winding roads become necessary; but where the surface is tolerably even, whether a uniform slope or a flat approaching to a level, the choice lies between straight lines and curvilinear

---

* By the cemetery bill brought into parliament in 1842, "both in the consecrated and unconsecrated ground, portions are to be set apart for the poor, a hard-hearted and unchristian proposal, worthy only of barbarous times. Can it be necessary or useful, that now, for the first time, a 'distinctive mark' should be made, after death, between rich and poor, by the express authority of an act of parliament? When even the propriety of distinctions in churches is becoming the subject of controversy, surely the good sense and good feeling of society will never suffer an unfeeling innovation in this respect to be formally legalised in our churchyards. He who has had familiar intercourse with the poor must have observed their sensitiveness with regard to their treatment after death, a subject often of more painful interest than the good or bad in store for them while living. Before the committee, the Bishop of London, much to his honour, expressed the most kindly sympathy with the feelings and prejudices of the poor with regard to interment: will he not set his face against the proposed regulation?" (*Claims of the Clergy*, p. 30.)

ones. The direction of the roads and walks, and consequently the whole of the interior arrangement of the cemetery, are thus in a great measure controlled by the character of its surface. In general, straight roads and walks are greatly to be preferred in a cemetery to winding ones, not only as admitting of a more economical occupation of the ground, every grave being a rectangle, and every rectangle being a multiple or divisor of every other rectangle, but as contributing far more than curved lines to grandeur and solemnity of effect. If all the roads cannot be made straight, there ought, if possible, to be one broad and straight road from the main entrance to the chapel. A winding road from the main entrance, with the chapel concealed by trees, has too much the character of an approach-road through a park to a country residence. The roads may vary from 12 ft. to 20 ft. in width, according to the extent of the cemetery; the walks should not be narrower than 5 or 6 feet, nor the green paths than 3 or 4 feet.

The *chapel or chapels* ought to be placed in a central and conspicuous situation, so as, if possible, to be seen from all the prominent points of view along the roads and walks. The chapels, if there are more than one, ought either to be grouped together in one conspicuous situation, so as to form one pile of building; or placed so far apart, or in situations so different, that they either cannot both be seen from the same point, or that, if seen in the same view, the one shall appear to the eye so much smaller than the other as to appear as a part of the background of the picture. The bad effect, in an artistical point of view, of two chapels placed equally near the eye, that is, in the same plane of the picture, and so far apart as not to group together is strikingly exemplified in those of the Norwood Cemetery. At the main entrance there may be a lodge or lodges, in which the sexton or superintendant of the ground may reside, and in which also there ought to be an office for the cemetery books and plans, or duplicates of them, and for receiving orders for funerals, &c. One lodge will generally be found preferable to two, because, where lodges are of such a size as to be useful, and are widely separated by spacious gates, they attract attention as separate objects, and do not group together so as to satisfy the eye as a whole. If there are two separate lodges with intervening gates, the lodges ought not to be higher than the piers between the gates; and they ought to seem rather as massive terminations to the gates than as lodges, in short as a part of the façade. A striking example of the bad effect of two large lodges is afforded by the Nunhead Cemetery. The Abney Park Cemetery shows a judicious combination of two lodges with gates between; there is a very good single lodge at the west entrance to the Tower Hamlets Cemetery; and the Kensal Green and West London Cemeteries afford examples of the lodge and gateway combined in one edifice, the gateway forming an arch through it. Where it is considered absolutely necessary to have two lodges, either to a cemetery or to the park of a country residence, they ought to be combined with the piers of the gates, as at the Abney Park Cemetery; formed into one pile of building with the gateway, as at the West London Cemetery; or one lodge ought to be much larger and higher than the other, in order to form a central mass or axis of symmetry, or, in Hogarth's language, to form the apex of the triangle.

A *yard and sheds* for the cemetery tools, implements, and other cemetery furniture, including a carpenter's shop, may also be conveniently placed near the lodge; but where the cemetery is large there ought to be two or three sheds for planks, barrows, &c., in different parts of the ground. In most cases a reserve ground for spare earth, produced from time to time as brick graves or vaults are formed, for rubbish of various kinds, and for nursing plants to be placed over the graves when wanted for that purpose, may be requisite. On a large scale, a mason's yard with sheds is essential; unless, which is much the better mode, there should be an establishment of this kind in the immediate neighbourhood, by which all the brick and stone work would be done by contract.

On the introduction of *trees and shrubs* into cemeteries very much of their ornamental effect is dependent ; but too many trees and shrubs impede the free circulation of the air and the drying effect of the sun, and therefore they ought to be introduced in moderation. They ought not, as we think, to be introduced in masses in the interior of the cemetery, nor in strips or belts round its margin, unless under very particular circumstances. Every mode of introducing trees and shrubs which is identical with that practised in planting parks and pleasure-grounds is to be avoided, as tending to confound the character and expression of scenes which are, or ought to be, essentially distinct. Independently of the injury done by masses and belts in impeding the free circulation of the air, they prevent the ground on which they stand from being occupied by graves ; and though there may be no immediate occasion for so occupying that ground, yet an arrangement which seems to be at variance with, or at least to have no reference to, the purpose for which the cemetery was formed is unsatisfactory. There is evidently not the same objection to single trees or single shrubs ; because, in whatever manner they may be placed, still, between and among them, graves may always be formed. There is a specific objection against boundary belts, which is, that they occupy a space that might be advantageously laid out as a broad border for tombs of a superior description, with a gravel walk in front accompanied by another border on the opposite side. For the same reasons that we would not introduce trees and shrubs in masses, we would not, in the case of cemeteries on low or level ground, plant trees which produce bulky heads ; but confine ourselves chiefly to kinds having narrow conical shapes, like the cypress, the form of which not only produces little shelter or shade, but has been associated with places of burial from time immemorial. Almost all the kinds should be evergreen and of dark foliage ; because the variety produced by deciduous and flowering trees is not favourable to the expression either of solemnity or grandeur. Evergreen needle-leaved trees, such as the pines, firs, junipers, yews, &c., we should prefer ; because, when their foliage drops, it produces much less litter than that of broad-leaved trees, such as the holly, common laurel, evergreen oak, &c. On very hilly cemeteries we would introduce round-headed trees along with conical shapes, but still chiefly confining ourselves to evergreens, such as the ilex, Lucombe oak, holly, the dark-foliaged pines, &c.

Supposing all the roads, walks, and green paths laid out, or their situations fixed on, and all the beds and borders also laid out, then we would dispose of the trees and shrubs in the following manner :— Along each side of most or all of the main roads, whether straight or curved, we would plant a row of trees parallel to the road, and at regular distances, so as to form a running foreground to the interior of the compartments, and to whatever there might be of distant scenery. The kinds should be pines and firs of dark foliage. In roads and walks in the direction of east and west, we would either plant the trees farther apart, or plant narrower-growing kinds, such as the common cypress, the Irish yew, the Swedish juniper, the fastigiate arbor vitæ, &c. At many of the intersections of the squares, in those cemeteries where that mode of division is adopted, we would plant provisionary trees, of a kind strikingly different from every other planted in the cemetery, in order to distinguish the angles of the squares at first sight, with the number stone at their base, to be taken up when it became practicable or desirable to substitute obelisks, square pillars, or other monuments, for them. Along the centre of the beds adapted for double rows of graves we would plant trees or shrubs at regular distances, with the intention that, in this and in all other cases whatever, except along the main approach from the entrance to the chapel, the trees should be taken up and replanted, or removed altogether, when necessary, so as to suit the position of graves.

With respect to the kinds of trees, we would, with very few exceptions, plant only those evergreens which have naturally dark foliage and narrow conical heads, or which admit of being pruned with little difficulty into such forms; because such forms not only interfere less with ventilation, sunshine, and the performance of funerals, but, more especially when of a dark colour, are naturally, from their great height in proportion to their breadth, more sublime than spreading forms; as well as artificially so, from their being classically and popularly associated with places of sepulture. For the main avenue we should prefer *Pinus taúrica, P. Pallasiana,* or *P. nígricans*; if the situation were favourable, the evergreen cypress, or the *Juníperus excélsa,* found to be a very hardy conical tree; and, if very unfavourable, the red cedar, or the common spruce. The pines and spruce grow rapidly, and admit of being cut into cones as narrow as may be desirable; but, to render this cutting unnecessary, the red cedar, and some of the rapid-growing conical junipers, might be employed. Along most of the gravel walks, and along the centre of the double beds, we would plant for the most part only fastigiate shrubs, such as the Irish yew, Irish and Swedish juniper, *Juníperus recúrva,* and some other junipers, and the arbor vitæ, box, common yew, &c. We would not plant, as a part of the general plantation of a cemetery or churchyard, weeping willows, weeping ashes, weeping elms, or trees of that kind; because we think that these trees, being of such marked and peculiar forms, are best adapted for being used only occasionally, for particular purposes; and therefore we would leave individuals to select such trees, or trees or shrubs of any other singular shapes that they thought fit, and have them planted over their graves or tombs. Thus, while the general plantations of the cemetery maintained a uniform grandeur and solemnity of expression, the singularly shaped trees and shrubs employed by individuals would confer variety of character.

A cemetery planted in the manner described will have a distinctive character, and one quite different from that of any of the cemeteries that we have seen, either in London or elsewhere. These cemeteries, according to our ideas, bear too great a resemblance to pleasure-grounds. That they are much frequented and admired by the public is no proof that they are in appropriate taste, but only that they are at present the best places of the kind to which the public have access. When our public parks and gardens are extended and improved as they ought to be; when they are ornamented with fountains, statues, immense blocks of different descriptions of rock (named), and with models of celebrated buildings, as covered seats and places of temporary repose or shelter; when they abound in singing and other birds and aquatic fowls, and contain every variety of tree and shrub that will thrive, and many kinds of herbaceous plants; and when they are perambulated, during a certain number of hours every summer's day, by a band of music, as in some of the public gardens in Germany; then will the necessity, as well as the propriety, of having a distinctive character for cemeteries be understood and appreciated.

The planting of *flowers* in cemeteries is very general, not only in the margin of masses and belts, and in beds as in pleasure-grounds, but on graves. For our own particular taste, we would have no flowers at all, nor any portion of ground within a cemetery that had the appearance of being dug or otherwise moved for the purpose of cultivation. A state of quiet and repose is an important ingredient in the passive sublime; and moving the soil for the purpose of culture, even over a grave, is destructive of repose.

Nevertheless, as the custom of planting flowers on graves is common throughout Europe, and of planting them in beds is frequent in the cemeteries about London, arrangements for this purpose must be provided accordingly. We would never plant flowers or flowering shrubs in the margins of masses or belts, or in beds or patches that might be mistaken for those of a lawn or a flower-garden; but, to give them a distinctive character, we would plant them in beds of the shape of graves or coffins, raised above or sunk beneath the general surface, and only in situations and on spots where at some future time a grave would be dug. For example, two graves are seldom dug close

c 3

together, but an intervening piece of firm ground is always left of width
sufficient for forming a grave at a future time ; the object being to have, if
possible, at all times, firm ground for the sides of a grave which is about to be
excavated. Now, on these intervening spots alone would we plant beds
of flowers, or of roses, or of other flowering shrubs. When flowers, shrubs,
or trees are planted on occupied graves, it is done by individuals according
to their own taste. The most highly ornamented cemetery in the neighbourhood of London, as far as respects plants, is that of Abney Park, in which,
as already mentioned, there is a complete arboretum, including all the hardy
kinds of rhododendrons, azaleas, and roses in Messrs. Loddiges's collection ;
and in which also dahlias, geraniums, fuchsias, verbenas, petunias, &c., are
planted out in patches in the summer season.

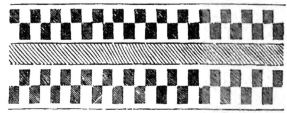

Fig. 3. *A Cemetery Walk with a Double Border on each Side, arranged with Beds for Shrubs or
Flowers, alternating with Spaces for Graves having Tombs.*

Fig. 3. represents a walk with a double border on each side, the shaded
parts of the border representing beds of shrubs or flowers, or of shrubs and
flowers alternately, and the open spaces between being left for graves having

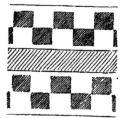

Fig. 4. *A Cemetery Road or Walk with
Double Beds on the Borders, alternating
with Spaces of double the usual Size, intended for Graves having large Monuments.*

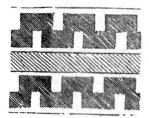

Fig. 5. *Double Borders with Masses of
Shrubs, and Spaces for single Graves at
regular Distances.*

monuments. When these spaces are filled up, those filled with flowers can
be occupied. It is evident that this mode might be varied exceedingly both
in the form of the beds, and in the mode of planting them. (See *figs.* 4. to 10.)

Fig. 6. *Beds of Flowers or Shrubs alternating with Spaces for Graves, for the interior Beds or
Panels of Cemeteries.*

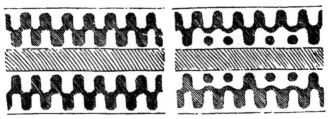

Fig. 7. *Double Borders, with Beds of Flowers or Shrubs alternating with Spaces for Graves.*

Fig. 8. *Beds for Shrubs, and Circles for Flowers.*

A mode of planting and managing which we should like to see tried with all or any of the systems of beds, *figs.* 3. to 6., would be to plant them with common yew, or with juniper, box, *P*ìnus pumílio, or spruce fir, and keep the plants cut or clipped in such a manner as to form low, compact, architectural-looking masses 2 or 3 ft. high.

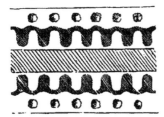

Fig. 9. *Beds for Flowers and Single Shrubs or low Trees, such as Thorns.*

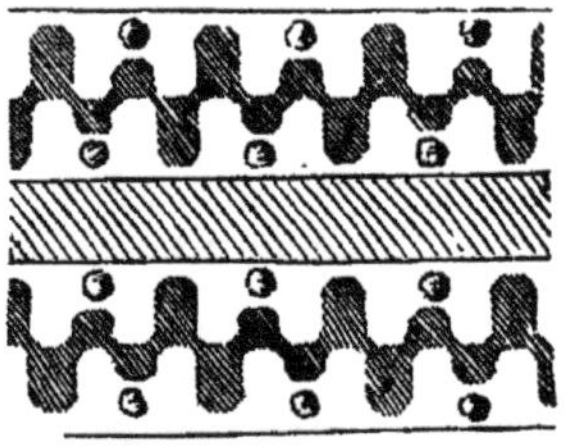

Fig. 10. *Beds for Flowers and fastigiate Trees, such as the Irish Yew, alternating with Graves.*

The *buildings* required in cemeteries may next occupy our attention. A chapel or chapels are generally required, because some persons prefer the burial service read under cover, or this may be rendered necessary by the state of the weather. The size of a chapel, therefore, should be such as to afford seats for the ordinary number of attendants at a funeral, with an open area in the centre, of sufficient diameter to hold two or more coffins on biers ; and, as it is a general custom in Christendom to carry a corpse with the feet before, the body being brought in and set down on the bier in that position is, after the service is over, taken up by men and turned completely round, so as the feet may be in advance before it is taken out of the chapel. In addition, therefore, to the space necessary for holding the bier and the coffin, there must be room for turning the latter completely round, either while on the bier, which has long handles for that purpose, or on men's shoulders. A circle 10 or 12 feet in diameter, or a square that would contain such a circle, will afford ample space for these purposes, and the remainder of the chapel may be occupied with the pulpit, desk, seats, &c.

In the chapels of some of the new London cemeteries, instead of biers for the coffins, there is a table, the top of which has one or two spaces, each of the width of a coffin, filled in with rollers, and the entire top of the table turns on a pivot. The coffin or coffins, when brought in, are put on the table, by sliding them on the rollers ; and, after the service has been performed, the table is turned round on its pivot, when the coffins being thus placed in the right position for going out are carried away by the bearers. The rollers facilitate the sliding on and drawing off of the coffins, and the turning of the table, by means of the pivot, saves the most difficult and awkward portion of the labour performed by the bearers, who, when not much accustomed to it, are apt to stumble, and create alarm in the mourners lest the coffin should fall. When a bier-table of this kind is used, the area left for it need not exceed 8 ft. in diameter, which will thus save 4 ft. in the entire length, and the same in the breadth, of the chapel.

A very convenient apparatus of this kind has been put up at the Kensal Green Cemetery. In the body of the chapel is a bier, in the form of an altar, about 8 ft. long, 4 ft. broad, and 4 ft. high, hung round with black velvet. The upper surface of this altar-like structure consists of a top for holding one or two coffins ; and, to facilitate the putting on and taking off of these, this plate or top is furnished with rollers. After the desk service has been read, the top containing the coffin or coffins can be turned slowly round by machinery, operated on by a small movable winch handle on one side, which is done after the service has been read, when the interment is to take place in the open ground, or in the catacombs at a distance from the chapel ; but, when the coffin is to be removed to the vaults under the chapel, there is machinery below, worked by a man there on a signal being given by ringing a small bell, by which the entire bier, and the coffin or coffins which may be on it, are slowly lowered into a central area in the vault beneath. The mourners having descended by a staircase much too small for a chapel so magnificent in other respects, the coffins are carried from this area to the vaults, which radiate from it in four directions, and occupy nearly an acre of ground. The machinery by which the bier is lowered consists of two vertical male screws, worked by two female screws or nuts, which are moved by means of two beveled wheels set in motion by a man turning a windlass handle. This machine, while it lowers the bier through the floor, moves at the same time two horizontal shutters, which gradually close the opening in the floor as the coffin descends from the view of the spectators in the chapel ; while, by the time they have arrived in the area below, the bier is already at the bottom, with the coffin on it, ready to be removed to the vault. The great advantage of using a screw movement for the descent of the bier is, that the motion can never be otherwise than slow and solemn, and that it cannot run down in case of the handle being set at liberty. This admirable contrivance was invented and executed by Mr. Smith, Engineer, Princes Street, Leicester Square, the patentee of an excellent window shutter, and of several other inventions noticed in our *Encyclop. of Cott. Architecture.* The cost was about 400*l.* In the Norwood Cemetery the same object is effected by means of Bramah's hydraulic press, which raises and lowers the bier with the slightest possible noise, and with a degree of steadiness which cannot be equalled by any other machine. The cost is about 200*l.* There is one drawback, however, to this machine, which is, that during very severe frosts the water is liable to freeze ; but this may be guarded against by shutting all the outside doors of the vaults, and by the use of stoves. In ordinary winters, however, the latter are unnecessary. This machine was put up by Messrs. Bramah, Prestage, and Ball, 124. Piccadilly.

The number of sittings need seldom exceed fifty, at least in the neighbourhood of London, as it rarely happens that more than a fourth of that number attend a funeral. Whatever be the architectural style of the chapel, it ought to contain a bell, the ringing of which, when the hearse is approaching from the entrance gate to the chapel, may be considered as a part of the burial service. The bell ought to be placed in a bell turret, rising from one of the gables, so as to become a conspicuous feature, and distinguish the chapel from a cottage or barn, in the same manner as the chimney tops of a dwelling-house are characteristic of a human habitation.

The *entrance lodge* to a cemetery ought to comprise a room to serve as an office to contain the cemetery books, or, at least, the order book and register, and the map book, where, from the system of squares being employed, such a book is rendered necessary. In small cemeteries, and in common church-yards, where the sexton is also the clerk and registrar, all the books and other documents will be kept in a strong closet in this room; but, in large cemeteries managed by a court of directors, the books are kept by a clerk in the cemetery office in the town or district to which it belongs, and only an order book, and the register and map book, or duplicates of them, are kept in the lodge. *Fig.* 11. is a plan of the lodge and yard at the main entrance of

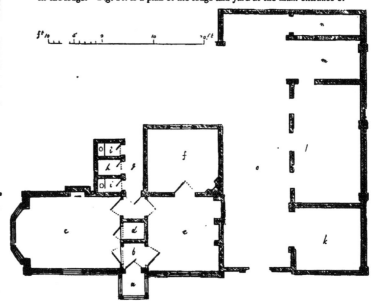

Fig. 11. *Ground Plan of the Entrance Lodge to the Tower Hamlets Cemetery.*

the City of London and Tower Hamlets Cemetery; in which *a* is the porch; *b*, vestibule; *c*, committee room; *d*, strong closet; *e*, gate-keeper's room; *f*, bed-room; *g*, passage; *h*, coals; *i i*, water-closets; *k*, tool-house; *l*, house for planks, tools, carpenter's shop, &c.; *m*, coach-house; *n*, coal-shed; and *o*, yard. The architects of this lodge and cemetery are Messrs. Wyatt and Brandon. The most appropriate cemetery lodge that we know is the one at Newcastle by Mr. Dobson, a figure of which will be hereafter given. Mr. Dobson's lodge can never be mistaken either for an entrance to a public park or to a country residence.

The other buildings or mural structures belonging to cemeteries are, vaults, catacombs, brick graves, tombs or other monuments, head-stones, foot-stones, cenotaphs, walls, and drains.

Vaults are commonly made under churches or chapels, but in the large ceme-teries they are also made in the open ground, in deep excavations descended to by stairs, and ranged on each side of a passage or passages, which are lighted through iron gratings on the surface. One of the best examples, on a small and economical scale, is the public vault in the Abney Park Cemetery. The most classical situation for vaults is in the face of a steep rocky bank, where they require no drainage, and can be entered without descending more than a few steps; such as occurs in the St. James's Cemetery, Liverpool; the Sheffield Cemetery; and the Cathedral, or Necropolis, Cemetery of Glasgow. Catacombs above ground, like those in the London and Westminster Cemetery, like some private tombs in the Kensal Green Cemetery, and like those in the new burying-ground attached to the old church at Brighton, are, in our opinion, in bad taste; since the general idea of burial, no matter by what mode, implies the descent of the body below the surface of the ground. Private vaults for the use of a single family are commonly made of the width of two or three coffins, and of such a depth as to hold several placed one over the other, commonly with iron bars or plates of stone between, so that no coffin may have more to bear than its own weight, and the air may be allowed to surround them, to prevent them from rotting. Sometimes each coffin is placed in a separate cell, and closed up with masonry.

Catacombs. — Sometimes the vault is divided into cells like bins in a wine-cellar, by vertical divisions of brick or stone; and these cells are called catacombs, though the term is frequently applied to a vault or crypt not subdivided into cells. Each cell, when the coffin is inserted, is hermetically sealed by building it up with brickwork, or inserting a tablet of stone or marble, inscribed with the name, age, &c., of the deceased. In the new London cemeteries, the cells or catacombs are frequently only closed with an open iron grating, the end of the coffin being fully exposed to view. In some cases the cells are literally shelves, and the entire side of the coffin is exposed, as in the West London Cemetery. Both of these modes are attended with great danger to the living; whether by the bursting of the lead coffins from the expansion of the gas in the bodies within them, or from its escape through crevices in the lead coffin left accidentally, or through holes made on purpose by the undertaker under the brass plate, as already mentioned (p. 4.). When a private vault is formed on even ground in an open cemetery, steps are made for descending to it; and these steps are commonly covered by a flat stone, level with or slightly above the surface; or in some cases, as where the steps are under a walk or path, the stone is concealed under this. Over the vault is placed a monument of some kind, most commonly what is called a square tomb, as in *fig.* 12.; in which *a* is

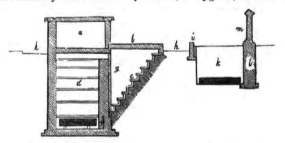

Fig. 12. *Section A B in the Plan fig.* 17., *through a Vault fitted up with Catacombs, and also through a common Grave, k.*

the tomb or superstructure; *b*, the cover to the steps; *c*, the steps; *d*, the catacombs or cells; *e*, a coffin placed in the lower catacomb, and sealed up at *f*; *g*, a door of slate, flag-stone, or iron; and *h*, the grass alleys. In this figure, also, is shown a common grave; in which *i* is the foot-stone; *k*, the grave, containing a coffin at bottom; *l*, the basement wall to the head-stone; and *m*, the head-stone.

A *brick grave* is a substitute for a vault, and differs only from an ordinary grave in having the sides and ends of brickwork or masonry, and in being covered with a large flat stone, technically, a ledger-stone. These graves are generally purchased and built by heads of families. Sometimes they are of the width of two coffins, but generally of one; and they vary in depth from 10 ft. to 20 ft. or upwards. When an interment takes place the stone is loosened by levers, and removed by means of rollers; and, the coffin being let down as in common graves, the ledger-stone is replaced and cemented. The side walls are built concave next the grave, in order that they may act as arches against the exterior soil; and, in some cases, they are furnished with ledges which project 2 or 3 inches from each side, for retaining a flag-stone or slate between each coffin. When this flag-stone is securely cemented, the coffin below may be considered as hermetically sealed, though it is not very likely that this will be done so completely as to prevent the ascent of the mephitic gas. In other brick graves no ledges are projected, but one coffin is prevented from resting on another by inserting two bars of iron in the side walls, so as to support each coffin. When the coffins reach within 3 or 4 feet of the surface, the ledger is put on for the last time; and a putrid mass, of perhaps 15 ft. in depth, is left to generate poisonous air, which will escape, probably for years, through such crevices as may be left, or as may occur from the action of weather or other causes, between the ledger and the side walls on which it rests. The proper mode would be to fill in the uppermost 6 or 8 feet of the grave with earth. The names of the interred are inscribed on the ledger, in the order of their interment; or a monument of some kind is erected on it, of such dimensions, and in such a position, that it can be removed in one piece with the ledger, without being loosened or otherwise disturbed. In the Highgate Cemetery there are ledger-stones weighing with their monuments eight or ten tons, which are removed all in one piece every time an interment takes place. The more common mode, however, is to place a head-stone as a monument, as shown in the section, *fig.* 13. In this section, *a* is the side wall of the grave, here shown with openings to permit the lateral diffusion of moisture and mephitic vapour; *b* is the ledger or covering stone; and *c*, the head-stone. At one end is a common grave (*d*) with its foot-stone (*e*); and one of the two double green alleys, which form boundaries to the raised panel of graves, is shown at *f*.

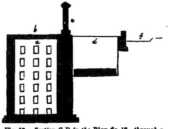

Fig. 13. *Section C D in the Plan fig. 17., through a Brick Grave and a common Grave.*

Brick graves are also used as earth graves, and filled to the surface with soil every time after an interment has taken place. The openings for re-interments should, as we have already mentioned (p. 4.), never be sunk to a greater depth than within 6 ft. of the last deposited coffin; in which case no very great disturbance or danger from putrescence would take place, more especially in clayey or loamy soil, and when it is made a rule to ram the soil hard with a cast-iron rammer, to the height of at least 6 ft. above every coffin as it is deposited.* When the last-deposited coffin is

---

* Family graves, in some of the new cemeteries, are made from 12 ft. to 30 ft. in depth. We lately saw one in the Norwood Cemetery, which had been originally 20 ft. deep, and had one coffin deposited in it, after which it

within 6 ft. of the surface, the grave should be finally closed.   Graves of this kind are not necessarily covered with a ledger-stone; they may be finished with a raised mound of earth, like a common earth grave, or the side and end walls may be finished with kerb-stones a foot above the surface, and the interior left level or planted with flowers.   After the last interment, a cypress or other tree, or a strong-growing herbaceous plant, might be planted in the centre. The walls of graves of this sort should be built with numerous openings, as in *fig.* 13., to permit the lateral diffusion of the products of decomposition, and of the natural moisture of the soil.

Earth graves are of two kinds: *private graves*, in which only one body is deposited, with or without a monument; and *common graves*, in which several bodies are deposited, of poor persons, or paupers, for whom no monument is ever put up, except a mound covered with turf, but which ought always to be marked with a stone number for reference, and to prevent all risk of their being opened again at any future period.

Sepulchral monuments, whether mausoleums (which is a term only applied to the most sumptuous description of tombs), square tombs, ledger-stones with inscriptions, sarcophagi, pedestals, vases, urns, columns, obelisks, pillars, crosses, &c., to have the appearance of security and permanence, ought to exhibit two features; they ought to be perfectly erect or perpendicular, and they ought to rise from an architectural base.   These features it is easy to exhibit when the monument is newly put up, but to continue them, even for a year, it is neces-sary to have a foundation of masonry under ground, as well as a basement above it; and, in order that this foundation may be permanently secure, it must be as deep as the adjoining grave or graves.   In the case of vaults and brick graves, this secure foundation is furnished by the structure itself; but in the case of common earth graves a foundation requires to be built up, and the problem is how to effect this in a manner at once se-cure and economical.   In most cemeteries and church-yards, and even in Père la Chaise and Kensal Green, the greater part of the monuments have no other foundation than the moved soil, and only comparatively few are placed on the firm soil.   The consequence of this is, that, in two or three years after the monuments are put up, they are found leaning to one side; or, if they are composed of several pieces, they are seen with the joints rent, and conveying ideas the very reverse of permanence.   Our remedy for the evil is, two brick or stone piers at the head of each grave, carried up from the bottom, and from 9 in. to 2 ft. square, according to the depth.   The two piers should be brought up at the same time, and tied together by building in pieces of iron hoop; and, when within a short distance of the sur-face, they should be joined by a semicircular arch,

Fig. 14. *Pedestal resting on a 9-inch underground Pier.*

was filled in to the surface with soil. It was, at the time we saw it, being opened to the depth of between 18 ft. and 19 ft., and the smell proceeding from the earth brought up was to us intolerable.   This, and numerous other cases which we have witnessed, or which have come to our knowledge altogether independently of the Parliamentary *Report on the Health of Towns*, for 1842, or Mr. Walker's *Gatherings from Graveyards*, have strongly impressed us with the necessity of a law to limit the proximity of one coffin to another in graves in which more than one interment is made, unless, as before observed, the coffins are put in on the same day. (See p. 4. and p. 43.)

or carried up to the surface and connected by a lintel, which may be the visible base of the head-stone. Where a pedestal ornament of any kind not more than 18 in. on the side was to be put up, one pillar 18 in. square might suffice; or, when there was no danger of the ground being moved, even a 9-inch pier as in *fig.* 14., would keep the pedestal from sinking. Where two graves were built end to end or side by side, three pillars would serve for both graves: and where four graves were to be made side by side and end to end, three pillars would suffice; or, in effect, two pillars, as shown in *fig.* 15., the two half-pillars at *a* and *b* not occupied being charged by the builder to the ceme- tery, which would have a right to sell them to those who made adjoining interments. These pillars may be built in a few hours, by having before- hand portions of them pre- pared with brick and cement

Fig. 15. *Double Foundations for Head-stones to be placed back to back.*

in the manner familiar to every builder; or, in stone or slate countries, under- ground props of these materials might be formed; nor do we see any objec- tion to cast-iron underground props. Where permanent endurance was the main object, we would not use cast-iron monuments; as it is next to impossible to prevent the rust from appearing through the paint, and scaling off so as to destroy, first the inscription, and next the body of the monument. In some of the London cemeteries temporary labels of wood, hav- ing on them the number of the grave or of the interment, and sometimes the name of the party interred, are used; and where economy is an object, and durability to the extent of a generation considered sufficient, we do not see any objection to the use of cast-iron tallies, such as *fig.* 16.; their lower extremities being so fixed to a piece of wood as to prevent them from being pulled out, while a circular disk, resting on two plain tiles or bricks, will prevent them from sinking. The cost of these monumental tablets at the foundery will be under 1*s.* each; and the painting, and lettering, and fixing could scarcely, in any case, exceed 5*s.* each.

Fig. 16. *Monumental Tally of Cast Iron.*

It is in order to supply room for head monuments that we have reserved a space of 2 ft. in width between each double row of graves, as shown in the ground plan *fig.* 17. In this figure *a b* is the space between the two lines of graves, commencing and ending with a number stone; *c c* are common graves with coffins, with piers for head-stones at *d d*, and spaces for foot- stones a foot in width at *e e*; *f* is a brick grave with two coffins inserted, the head-stone to be placed between *g g* and *d*; *h h* are spaces left for common graves, brick graves, or, by occupying four divisions, for vaults; *i*, a vault for two coffins in width, occupying four divisions; *k*, a vault for one coffin in width, occupying one division; *l l*, the green alleys between the double rows of grave beds or panels.

When it is in contemplation to have a double line of brick graves, or to fill up a cemetery regularly, without allowing a choice to the purchasers, as in the cemeteries of the Jews, then a foundation wall 2 ft. in width might be regularly carried up along the middle space, between the lines of graves, from one end of the line to the other.

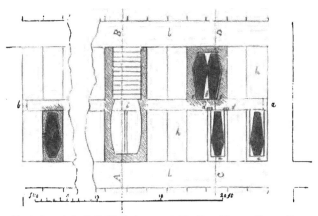

Fig. 17. *Plan of a Double Bed for the Arrangement of two Rows of Graves, with green Alleys between.*

Cenotaphs, as every one knows, are monuments put up to the memory of persons who are interred somewhere else.   They commonly consist of tablets with inscriptions, medallions, busts, basso-relievos, or other sculptural objects, and are very fit ornaments for affixing to walls under cover, or protected by architectural projections, such as those furnished by a chapel, a cemetery veranda, a boundary wall, or a structure erected on purpose, as is not unfrequent in the French and German cemeteries.

Walls, when used as the boundary of a cemetery, and built of brick, may be carried up hollow, which will be a considerable saving of material, and render all piers unnecessary, unless for effect, or, in the case of cemeteries laid out in imaginary squares, the piers which are to contain the stones having the letters and numbers.

The *main conveying-drains* of a cemetery, if built of brick, should be barrel-shaped, in the usual manner ; but, if of stone, the bottom should be laid with flag-stone, and the same description of stone should be used for the covering. *Main collecting-drains* may be formed by semi-cylindrical tiles placed on flat tiles in the bottom, and small stones placed over them to within a foot or less of the surface of the ground.   *Surface collecting-drains* may be 20 in. deep, formed like the last, with tiles at the bottom, and carried up to the surface with small gravel, finishing with coarse sand; and, when these drains are in the green alleys, grass may be sown over them.   When at the sides of the gravel walks or roads, they ought to communicate with surface gratings at regular distances ; and immediately under each grating there ought to be a pit 1 ft. square and 2 ft deep to retain the sand carried in by the water (*fig.* 18.), this sand being taken out once a year. Where the roads and walks are laid with asphalte, gratings of this kind will be more necessary than when they are made of gravel, as a certain proportion of the water always sinks through the latter material, but none through the former.

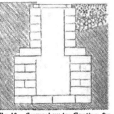

Fig. 18. *Cesspool under Grating, for retaining the Sand brought down by the Water.*

The *furniture*, or tools, implements, and temporary structures, of large and complete cemeteries, consists of picks, spades, shovels, levers, rakes, scrapers, brooms; a rope and pulley, or block and tackle, to be used with a triangle; planks, ladders, grave-boards, dumcrafts, grave-platforms, grave-boxes, grave-moulds, wheelbarrows, buckets for raising soil, a frame for supporting canvass or a tarpaulin over a grave while being dug during rain; and a temporary structure, consisting of a floor of boards or wooden grating, with three sides and a roof of canvass, rendered waterproof by paint, for the protection of the clergyman while reading the service at the grave ; with another structure, of a larger size, for sheltering both the clergyman and the mourners. It is only necessary to notice in detail the grave-boards, the earth-boxes, and the temporary structures, as these are required in all burying-grounds.

The *grave-boards* are required in almost every case where the grave is dug more than 5 or 6 feet in depth, in order to prevent the sides from breaking down; and they are, perhaps, the most important implements connected with the cemetery. The ordinary custom is, to dig the grave 6 in. or a foot longer than is necessary ; to introduce planks, one after another, as the grave advances in depth; and to keep them firmly against the sides by short pieces used as struts at the ends. An improved description of grave-boards has been devised by two superintendants of London cemeteries unknown to each other, viz. Mr. E. Buxton, superintendent of the Nunhead Cemetery, and Mr. Northen, superintendent of the Tower Hamlets Cemetery. In both improvements the side grave-boards are hinged, so as to form a concave side next the grave, by which means, when they are placed against the sides, they resist the lateral pressure in the manner of an arch. According to Mr. Buxton's invention, one board is put in beneath another as the grave is excavated, and each board is kept in its place by the end struts, which are driven outwards at each end of the grave : but, according to the practice in the Tower Hamlets Cemetery, the boards and end pieces are first joined together, and then let down from the top, one above another, as in well-sinking. The difficulty in both cases is to take the boards out, which must always be done by commencing at the bottom and proceeding upwards, the filling in of the earth over the coffin being carried on at the same time. Were the boards taken out from the top, the earth from the sides would be liable to fall in and bury some of the lower boards, or, in the case of graves 15 or 20 feet deep, it might bury the grave-digger. The grave-boards used by Mr. Buxton, the superintendent of the Nunhead Cemetery, are represented in the isometrical view,*fig.* 19. They are in four parts: two sides, each of

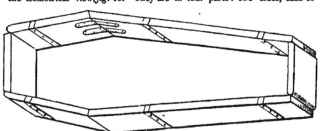

Fig. 19. *The Grave-Boards used in the Nunhead Cemetery.*

which is hinged on a beveled edge, which renders it impossible for them to get out of their places, and two ends which serve as struts to keep the sides apart. These ends are prevented from dropping out, by cutting the grave rather less than the intended width, and driving the ends, which act as struts, home with a large wooden hammer; in consequence of which they cannot be removed without the aid of a flat-ended lever bar. The sides are kept in their places by the pressure of the soil, against which they act as arches. The method of using these boards is as follows. The ground is opened about 1 ft. or 18 in. in depth; then the first pair of boards and ends are fixed, their upper edge being 12 or 18 inches from the surface of the ground. Next, at intervals of their own width, or closer, if the nature of the ground renders it necessary, another pair of boards and ends may be fixed, and so on till the grave is dug to the required depth. When the coffin has been deposited, the lowest pair of boards and ends are first taken out; and the remaining sides and ends are taken out in succession as the grave is filled. Mr. Buxton, to whom we are indebted for a small model from which our engraving was made, and who takes a deep interest in the Nunhead Cemetery, and in the subject of cemeteries generally, states that, by having the head and foot boards of different sizes, graves may be made of different degrees of width, as required for the different-sized coffins. The common length of the head board is 18 in., and of the foot board 16 in.; length of the side 5 ft. 2 in., and of the shorter portion 2 ft. 2 in.; making the total dimensions of the box; inside measure, 7 ft. in length; width at the shoulders, 2 ft. 4 in.: but by the use of different-sized head and foot struts, as before mentioned, any size required may be obtained. A great deal of labour in digging is saved by the use of these boards. It may be added, that a set of side boards are kept about 6 ft. in length, by which graves 5 ft. 9 in. in the clear are produced.

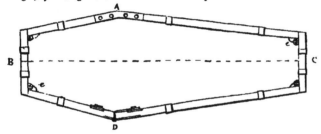

Fig. 20. Plan of the Grave-Boards in use in the Tower Hamlets Cemetery.

Fig. 20. is a plan of the grave-boards invented by Mr. Northen, as they appear when placed together in the grave. One side is hinged at D, and the other retained in its angular position by strong iron plates at the upper and under edge at A. Both boards are fastened to the ends by iron pins, which drop into eyes, as seen at the angles *e e*, and more distinctly in the sections *figs.* 25. and 26.

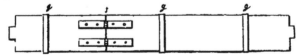

Fig. 21. Elevation of the Side marked D in fig. 20.

Fig. 21. is an elevation of the side D viewed externally, showing the hinges at *f*, and the iron hoops for preventing the boards from splitting at *g g*.

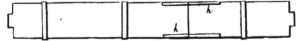

Fig. 22. Elevation of the Side marked A in fig. 20.

Fig. 22. is an elevation of the side marked A seen externally: *h h*, the top and bottom stiffening plates.

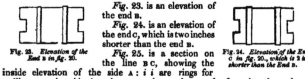

Fig. 23. is an elevation of the end B.

Fig. 24. is an elevation of the end c, which is two inches shorter than the end B.

Fig. 25. is a section on the line B C, showing the

Fig. 23. *Elevation of the End B in fig.* 20.

Fig. 24. *Elevation of the End c in fig.* 20., *which is* 2 *in. shorter than the End B.*

inside elevation of the side A : *i i* are rings for pulling out the side boards ; *e e*, pins and eyes for fastening the ends to the sides ; *h h* are the stiffening plates.

Fig. 25. *Section on the Line B c in fig.* 20., *showing the Side A.*

Fig. 26. is a section on the line B C, showing the inside elevation of the side D ; *k*, an iron hasp which locks the two leaves of the side D, and prevents them from being pressed inwards. A latch of this kind is fixed on every other board on each side of the grave ; and thus, when the board having the latch is loosened, the ends and the opposite board (*fig.* 22. A) readily drop out. The scale shown in this figure applies to it and to the preceding seven figures.

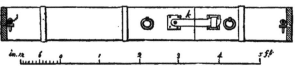

Fig. 26. *Section on the Line B c in fig.* 20., *showing the Elevation of the Side D.*

As the grave is being dug, one tier of boards fastened together, as shown in *fig.* 20., is first let down, like the kerb of a well in well-sinking ; and as the work proceeds, and this frame sinks, another is placed over it, to sink in its turn ; and so on, introducing one frame of boards after another, till the grave is dug to the proper depth. The last 18 or 20 inches at the bottom of the grave are not dug out quite so wide as all above, in consequence of which the boards do not go just so deep as the top of the coffin after it has been lowered. This admits of more readily taking out the boards, which is done by driving out the hasps *h*, and the pins *e*, beginning at the bottom and working upwards as the grave is filled. When the coffin is lowered, settled in its place, and the lowering ropes drawn out, the grave-digger descends to the bottom, and with a hammer drives out one of the hasps, which instantly loosens that board, allows of taking out the two ends, and consequently loosens the opposite one. In this way he proceeds from the bottom to the top, filling in the soil as he goes on.

The manner in which the grave-boards are kept in their position at Musselburgh, near Edinburgh, differs from that employed in most places, and is in some, if not in all, respects superior to it. It is the invention of Mr. Robert Gay, a smith in Musselburgh, and the superintendant of the burying-ground there. It consists in the application of the instrument shown in *fig.* 27., which about Edinburgh is called a dumcraft, and about London a screw lever. Two of these instruments, with the iron plates, spear nails, &c., screwed to the planks, which cost about 6s. 6d. each, are required for every pair of boards, one being applied at each end. A pair of boards, with a pair of dumcrafts fitted up complete, cost at Musselburgh from 20s. to 22s. The iron is made of ¾-inch rod, with a male screw at one end working in a female screw, to which

D

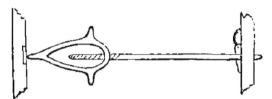

Fig. 27. *Dumcraft, or Screw Lever, in use in the Musselburgh Burying-Ground.*

wings having knobs are attached to facilitate working, and with the other
end pointed and pierced about 3 in. from the point, so as to receive a spear
nail. Every pair of boards requires a pair of dumcrafts; and one end of each
board requires to have a hole about three quarters of an inch in diameter,
guarded by a shield, for one end of the instrument; and, within a few inches of
the other end, a plate of iron fixed on to receive the centre point of the screw,
and allow it to work. By a mere inspection of the instrument, any workman
will understand the manner in which it is to be used. The object of allowing
one end of the rod to go through the boards is to allow the other end to
come freely out when the grave is being filled up; for, although the dumcraft is slackened by unscrewing one end by means of the knobs which
project from the wings, yet, by the pressure of the earth from the sides of the
grave, it would take much longer time to loosen it sufficiently to get it out;
whereas by turning the movable open part of the screw end a little, and
then taking out the spear and allowing the iron rod to go through the boards,
the centre point at the other end is freed at once, and this without any noise,
which is not the case in taking out the strut pieces commonly employed. By
having two or three holes for the spear, and two or three plates with centre
holes for the screw to work in, a difference in length and breadth of grave
may be obtained within certain limits. For an account of this instrument we
are indebted to Mr. William Ballery, the superintendant of the Warriston
Cemetery, Edinburgh.

Fig. 28. is a cemetery plank hook,
for dragging out loose planks used in
the common mode of supporting the
sides of graves, and for moving boards
generally, when they are in a wet and dirty state.

Fig 28. *Cemetery Plank Hook.*

The *grave-box* (*fig.* 29.) is formed of a bottom and sides, the latter readily
separating from the former; and its use is to hold the soil dug out of the
grave, till the grave is ready to have the soil returned to it. From one to four
boxes are required for a grave, according to its dimensions. The use of these
boxes is two-fold : to preserve the soil from mixing with the grass, from which
it is difficult afterwards to separate it so entirely as not to leave a quantity of
it entangled among its leaves; and to return the earth in the most rapid
manner to the grave. The box, before receiving the earth from the grave, is
placed alongside, and raised up in a sloping position; the earth is thrown into
it; and as soon as the coffin is lowered the grave-diggers loosen and take out
the side of the box next the grave, when the soil immediately begins to drop
out, while, by raising the other side of the box, the whole is returned to the
grave, and not a particle of earth is to be seen on the surface of the grass.
This box was first used by Mr. Lamb, an undertaker in Leith, and is now in
general use in the burial-grounds about Edinburgh. There ought to be a
number of such boxes for every cemetery; and it would be an improvement
to place them on low wheels, say those on the side which is to be next the
grave of 6 inches in diameter, and those on the opposite side of double that
height. This, while it would save the trouble of propping up the boxes,

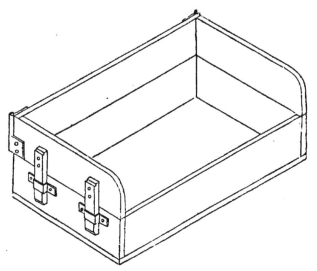

Fig. 29. *Grave-Box in use in the Edinburgh Burying-Grounds.*

would also enable the grave-diggers to wheel them away, one after another, as fast as they were filled, and when the grave was completed, to leave it quite free on every side for the approach of mourners, who would in this case walk on the turf, instead of walking on loose earth or planks. This result is sometimes obtained by throwing all the excavated soil into wheelbarrows, and removing these to a short distance, there to stand till the coffin is deposited. Either of these modes is much better than the common one of throwing up the soil on each side of the grave, and obliging the coffin-bearers to clamber over it. As the grave-boxes are readily taken to pieces, they can be stowed away, in sheds or tool-houses, in little space.

The *grave-platform* is a flooring of boards about 10 ft. long by 5 ft. broad, with an opening in the middle, of the shape and dimensions of an ordinary-sized coffin. It is hinged, so as to fold together lengthwise. Its use is to place over the grave, after the soil has been removed in boxes or barrows, for the double purpose of forming a guide to the lowering of the coffin, and a floor for those who lower it, who in Scotland are commonly the relations or mourners, to stand on. In most cemeteries loose boards, or two or three boards nailed together so as to form a platform, are laid down on each side of the grave, leaving the ground at the end of the grave uncovered ; but this arrangement is far from being so complete and commodious as a hinged platform.

The *grave-cover* is a low roof of light boards, or of a frame and canvass, of dimensions sufficient to cover the opening of a newly made grave, and with handles like those of a hand-barrow, to allow of carrying it readily from place to place. Its use is to exclude rain or snow ; and also, in the case of a very deep grave, to guard against the danger of persons approaching too near its edge. In large cemeteries it is found convenient to have at all times two or three graves prepared, both common graves and brick graves, ready to admit of interments on the shortest notice. The unoccupied brick graves are commonly protected by the ledger which is to constitute their permanent cover and finish, but the common graves are protected from the weather by the portable cover described.

The *grave-mould* is a box without either bottom or top, but with the sides and ends shaped like a coffin, to serve as a guide to the form of the grave-ridge, or mound of earth raised over a grave immediately after interment. When the grave is filled to the brim and properly rammed, the box is placed over the soil, and more is added and firmly rammed till the box is full, when the soil is raised in the middle, and rounded off in the manner seen in all neatly kept churchyards. Afterwards the grave-ridge is covered with turf, or planted with flowers. In some of the London cemeteries the stone-crop is planted on the grave-ridge, and forms a very neat evergreen covering, always within bounds. Some of the evergreen saxifrages might be used for the same purpose; and a friend has suggested that the common thrift would be an excellent plant, as its thick mass of dark green grass-like foliage would contrast with the light green of the grass forming the common covering of the cemetery. Where economy is an object, grass inoculation or grass seeds might be resorted to.

A *clergyman's shelter* is unnecessary where a tarpaulin or a movable shed is used over the grave; but, where this is not the case, it may be formed of five pieces, viz. A flooring of boards, or, to prevent slipping when the boards are wet, as well as to render the floor lighter, of wooden grating, raised one or two steps above the general surface, in order to give the reader of the service a more commanding position. To this floor three sides, each consisting of a frame of canvass, are readily fixed by means of studs in the lower rails of the sides, dropping into holes in the framework of the bottom; and they are as readily connected together by hooks dropping into eyes. The roof-piece, which ought to be raised a little in the middle to throw off the rain, can readily be dropped on four iron bolts, fixed in the upper ends of the styles of the sides. The whole may be painted black; and, when not in use, it should be taken to pieces, and kept in a dry airy situation. A tent or movable structure, to cover not only the clergyman but the mourners assembled, either during rainy weather or hot sunshine, might be formed without difficulty, and at no great expense. The framework might be light iron rods; and the canvass might be so arranged as to be drawn up and let down like the awnings to tulip beds, or the outside gauze shades to hothouses. (See *Sub. Hort.*, fig. 115. p. 175.)

The other articles of cemetery furniture having nothing particular in their construction, and being in use either by mechanics, ground workmen, or cultivators of the soil, do not require farther notice.

Roots and Plants.—In some of the London cemeteries dahlias are planted in the summer season, and these are kept through the winter in the unoccupied catacombs, and, with geraniums and other greenhouse plants, are brought forward in spring in frames in the reserve ground, or in some other concealed part of the cemetery, or perhaps in an adjoining garden or nursery. In the reserve ground of the great cemetery at Rouen, there is a large greenhouse, and the curator lets out plants in pots during summer at so much a pot, undertaking to keep them watered and trimmed, to decorate graves and monuments.

III. The Working and Management of Cemeteries.

By the *working and management of cemeteries* are to be understood the rules and regulations respecting interments, monuments, planting, &c., the fees to be taken, and the books to be kept by the clerk or sexton. We shall only enumerate such rules and regulations as we think ought to be general.

The most important rules respecting a place of burial must necessarily be those which have reference to the sacredness of the place, the security from disturbance of the bodies of the dead, the healthfulness of the living, and their improvement in sentiment and in morals. On these principles we would found the following rules, which should be absolute, even in cemeteries and churchyards as they are at present constituted. Some of these rules have been mentioned before, but we repeat them, in order that they may be strongly impressed on the mind of the reader.

First, We would allow no grave to be dug, except in ground which never had been opened before. When a grave in which an interment has taken place at the usual depth of 6 ft. is opened, one of two things must happen; either the bones at the bottom of the grave must be disturbed, or, to avoid this, the grave must not be dug to a sufficient depth. There may be three exceptions to this case, if the superintendent of the burying-ground could be depended on: first, when the previous interment has taken place to a greater depth than 6 ft., which would be ascertainable if a proper register had been kept; second, where the surface of the burying-ground was to be raised by the addition of a foot or two of earth all over it; or third, when a child was to be interred, 4 or 5 feet, according to the age, &c., of the child, being sufficient in the latter case. Every grave whatever should have a number cut in a number-stone, or on some part of the plinth of the grave-stone or monument, if there be one, for the purpose of registration.

Secondly, We would allow no coffin to be placed nearer the surface of the ground than 6 ft. A German author has shown by calculation the different degrees of depth at which interments may take place, according to the age and other circumstances of the subject. His depth for adults is 6 ft., and for children under a year, 2 ft. The calculation may be useful in Germany, where, in many churchyards, the children are buried in a part of the ground by themselves, and their graves arranged according to the children's ages and lengths; but, in England, the safer mode is to make the rule of having the grave 6 ft. in depth absolute, for it must be recollected that, in the case of children above three years of age, the bones, practically speaking, are almost as indestructible as those of adults. Hence we conclude that a child's grave ought no more to be opened for a second interment than that of a grown up person.

Thirdly, When more interments than one are to take place in a grave of the width calculated for one coffin, we would require a stratum of earth over each coffin of 6 ft. in depth; and supposing one interment made in the bottom of a grave 12 ft., 20 ft., or 30 ft. deep, and 6 ft. of soil placed over the coffin, then on the surface of that soil we would deposit a coffin-shaped slate or flag-stone, as a preventive to the grave-digger from going deeper when he was excavating for a second interment. The protecting stone ought to be taken up when the second interment was made, and used after every interment till the last, when it might either be taken out for use in another deep grave, or, if it were a family grave, it might be left immediately over the coffin for protection of the bones, on the principle mentioned in p. 6. This rule will not prevent the interment of ten or twelve bodies in a grave as at present, but it will require such graves to be an immense deal deeper, viz. at the rate of 6 ft. for every interment; but there is no reason why graves should not be dug as deep as wells. A grave 18 ft. deep, however, will take three interments, which, at the low rate of 10*s.* each, as in the Abney Park Cemetery, will give a return of 5,445*l.* per acre; and in cemeteries where 25*s.* for each interment is charged, of above 13,600*l.* per acre.

Fourthly, When a common or private earth grave was once filled to within 6 ft. of the surface, it should on no account whatever be opened at however distant a period.

Fifthly, Brick graves which are filled with earth after each interment, we would make subject to exactly the same laws as deep earth graves: that is, we would have a stratum of soil 6 ft. in thickness over each coffin. We would allow no interments to take place in brick graves, in which each coffin was not either covered with 6 ft. of soil, or with a flag-stone hermetically sealed. Where the system of hermetically sealing was proposed to be adopted, we would require the walls of the graves to be built with Roman cement, every coffin to be separated by a flag-stone resting on ledges projecting from the walls, the joints of this flag-stone to be made good with cement, and a coating of cement of not less than 3 in. in thickness placed over the entire stone. Or, as a substitute for the use of flag-stones, we would surround and cover every coffin with a mass of Roman cement, so that it should be completely embedded and enveloped in that material. By this hermetically sealing mode of interment, a great many bodies might be got into one grave ; but it is evidently too expensive for general purposes : for large families it may be the cheapest mode, consistent with safety to the living ; but as there is always the possibility of desecration at some future period, for our own feelings we should greatly prefer lateral (side by side) interments in the free soil.

Sixthly, We would allow of few or no catacombs or vaults in buildings, and certainly of none in or under churches, or other places where assemblies of human beings were held ; but, as many catacombs and vaults have been built in the public cemeteries, in the case of all interments, in them, the catacomb or vault should be hermetically sealed the same day on which the interment took place, and should on no account whatever be again opened. Nothing can be more dangerous with reference to the health of the living, than the mode prevalent in the new cemeteries, of merely placing an open grating in front of the coffins deposited in catacombs. Were it not for the current of air established through the vaults, by which the mephitic gas is carried off as fast as it is produced, it would be impossible for a living person to exist for an hour in these cellars for the dead. But even if these catacombs were each, when a coffin is placed in it, hermetically sealed in front, there is scarcely one of them so carefully constructed as to be air-tight, so that the mephitic gas is certain to escape from some part of the catacomb, more especially when we consider the expansive power of air when compressed. And for what is all this disgusting boxing up of dead bodies, as if to bid defiance to the law of nature? We cannot think it in good taste to practise this mode of sepulture, and therefore we would render it expensive by such a heavy tax as should serve for the interment of the poor in a more careful manner, for the general ornament of the cemetery, or for government purposes generally. Nor do we think it could be considered oppressive to pass a law obliging all bodies now in vaults or catacombs under churches, chapels, &c., to be taken out and buried in the free soil.

Seventhly, We would encourage the erection of handsome monuments, and the inscription on them of moral sentiments, the former to improve the taste, and the latter to cultivate the heart and affections. In both we would allow individual taste to be displayed ; but at the same time we would encourage individuals to submit their designs to men of acknowledged skill, and to listen to their hints for improvement.

Eighthly, We would at all times keep every part of the cemetery in the highest order. The grass should be kept short and smooth by frequent mowing ; the gravel free from weeds and smooth by frequent weeding and rolling ; the edges, which we would form of concealed bricks or tiles (*figs.* 30.

 and 31.), low, and constantly clipped ; and the leaves, as they drop from the trees, should be picked up the same day on which they fell ; litter of every

Fig. 30. *Concealed Brick Edging.* kind picked up the Fig. 31. *Concealed Tile Edging.* moment it appeared ; and the walls, chapel, lodge, gates, drains, &c., kept in constant repair.

Ninthly, To insure the high keeping of monuments of every kind, who- ever erected one should, at the time it was put up, pay to the proprietors or directors of the cemetery a sum considered sufficient to preserve it in repair in perpetuity, or for a certain number of years.* Every person having shrubs or flowers planted on a grave, we would require to pay a sum sufficient to keep them trimmed for such a number of years as they might think fit; or to keep them in order themselves, under the penalty of having them rooted up and grass substituted, if neglected for a period varying according to the kind of plants. Flowers and roses require to be attended to weekly during summer, but evergreen shrubs may grow for years with scarcely any attend- ance. As flowers and low shrubs are very apt to get tawdry when neglected, as soon as keeping them in order ceased to be paid for, or otherwise effected, the plants should be taken up and grass substituted. The turf mounds over graves, and the number-stones (of which, as already observed, there ought to be one to every grave, whether it have a monument or not), ought, of course, to be kept in order by the proprietors of the cemetery.

Tenthly, No dogs or improper persons; no smoking, drinking, or even eating; no running or jumping, laughing, whistling, or singing, or other practice that might indicate a want of reverence for the place, should be per- mitted. No person should be allowed to walk on the graves, or to cross from one walk or green path to another in places where the ground was filled with graves.

Eleventhly, Wherever there was the least risk of a grave being reopened for a second interment, or for any other purpose, or even where it was desired to protect the bones in the case of some future unforeseen change taking place, such as making a road through the cemetery or building on it, we would intro- duce a guard or follower of stone over the last-interred coffin, as already described, p. 6. and p. 37.

If the foregoing rules were rigidly attended to, cemeteries, whether in town or country, would be as healthy as gardens or pleasure-grounds, and would form the most interesting of all places for contemplative recreation. As one great object in forming and managing a cemetery, whether small or large, is to render it inviting by being ornamental and highly kept, it is not desirable that all the monuments should be crowded together in one place, and all the graves without monuments placed in another part of the ground. It appears better that the monuments should be seen one after another, with plain spaces intervening; and for this reason it ought to be a rule that any person purchasing a grave may choose the spot where he will have it, pro- vided he makes known whether he intends to erect any monument and what sort. This rule, however, must be taken in connexion with another, viz. that it is desirable to have a considerable display of monuments on the borders laid out on purpose for them along the roads and main walks, and along the boundary wall. The finest ancient monuments in the churchyards of Scotland, and we know nothing to equal them in England out of West- minster Abbey, are the sepulchral structures projected from the walls of Grey Friars churchyard in Edinburgh, and the Cathedral burying-ground at Glasgow. These in general are not vaults, catacombs, or brick graves, but interments in the free soil, where the husband and wife lie side by side, and

---

* The sum per annum, and the number of years during which the party wishes the monument, grave-stone, shrubs, or flowers, kept in order, being agreed on, it is only necessary to find, by the annuity tables (say, *Inwood's,* 12mo, 5s.), the present value of this sum, at the rate of interest obtainable in the public funds. The sum required for keeping a monument in repair, even in perpetuity, is by no means so great as might be expected. The ordinary charge for keeping a common grave and grave-stone in repair is only 1s. a year, and the present value of an annuity of that amount, payable for ever, reckoning the interest of money at 2½ per cent, is 2l. Hence, 5l. paid down would give 2s. 6d. a year for ever, which is quite enough for most monuments.

the space is enclosed by highly wrought iron railings, and superb architectural and sculptural compositions fixed against the wall. Sometimes the whole is covered by an architectural canopy, supported on stone columns. The architecture is of the time of the Jameses, elaborate in composition, rich in decoration, and learned, scriptural, heraldic, or quaint, in inscription; and there is nothing offensive in the mode of inhumation. In our opinion, it is in far better taste for a family to expend money in purchasing as much ground in the open part of a cemetery as will allow the husband and wife, and some of their children, if they have any, making an allowance for a certain number of both sexes to die young, and of the females to die unmarried, to be buried side by side, than to expend it in burying in vaults or catacombs, or even in expensive monuments. In the cemeteries about London we frequently see monuments that have cost upwards of a hundred pounds placed over what are called family brick graves, in which, perhaps, the half dozen bodies constituting the family have been deposited one over the other, without intervening soil or flag-stones hermetically sealed, so as to constitute a mass of putrefaction appalling to contemplate; more especially as contrasted with the chaste marble sarcophagus or other monument placed over it. Such a disgusting mode of interment, to which men have been driven by various causes, which have led to charges so high that they cannot be borne, is not for a moment to be compared to the interment of a family side by side in the free soil. There is nothing at all offensive in the latter mode; nothing to hinder such interments from taking place in a shrubbery or pleasure-ground, or a flower-garden. If the citizens of London were to reflect on this, instead of laying out a large sum on a brick grave or a vault, and afterwards on a monument to be placed over it, they would lay it out in purchasing a greater extent of territorial surface, and in enclosing this surface in such a manner as to mark it for their own. The family name, deeply cut on the stone forming the coping or finish of the enclosing barrier, would say more for the taste of the owner, than a thousand pounds laid out on a monument over a vault or brick grave. The most desirable part of a cemetery for small grave enclosures of this kind is against the boundary wall, as at Grey Friars, Edinburgh, the Glasgow Cathedral, and the old burying-ground at Munich; but it is singular that, in almost all the new London cemeteries, this very desirable situation for graves and monuments is occupied by a belt of trees, as if the cemetery were to be laid out exactly on the same plan as Brown's parks, with their surrounding belts and interspersed clumps.

If men of landed property, however small its extent, were to reflect on this subject, we are persuaded they would greatly prefer laying their bones in a suitable spot in their own grounds, than having them piled up in any family grave, vault, or catacomb whatever.

It ought to be a general rule to place handsome monuments at particular points of view; such as at angles formed by the junction or intersection of roads or walks, terminations to straight walks, points seen from the entrances and from the chapel, &c.

One of the most important rules respecting monuments is, that they be all placed on solid foundations of masonry reaching as deep as the bottom of the grave, by the means already described (p. 29.), or by other equally efficient means. A rectangular tomb over a brick grave will, of course, rest on the side walls of the grave; but over a common earth grave it will require to be supported, either by four pillars brought up from the bottom of the grave, or by two pillars at each end, founded 2 or 3 feet deep in the soil, and 2 or 3 feet distant from the edge of the grave. In this way rectangular tombs, or any description of large monument, may be placed over earth graves of any depth whatever, and in cases where it would be practically impossible to bring up pillars from the bottom of the grave.

It is never desirable to form two graves adjoining each other at the same time, or even after a shorter period than two or three years; because the narrow partition of firm soil between them is apt to give way. At the same time, if there is any particular reason for graves being so formed, such as a wife desiring to be buried by the side of her husband, &c., the weak side of the grave can be supported by grave-boards.

The most economical mode of using the ground in any cemetery would be to begin at one end or side, mark out the graves, and use only every alternate one; then, when the ground was once gone over, to go over it a second time, and occupy all the blank graves. As, however, it has long been customary for persons purchasing graves to have the liberty of choice, the most economical mode cannot often be adopted. When the interments are to commence at one end of the cemetery, and the whole of the ground is to be occupied as they proceed, that end ought always to be the lowest; because, when the interments have commenced at the highest point and been carried down the slope, considerable inconvenience has been found from the fluid putrescent matter following the inclination of the ground. (See Picton in *Arch. Mag.* vol. iv. p. 431.)

No part of a cemetery ought to be exclusively devoted to common graves, because, as a number of coffins are placed in each grave, there would in this part of the cemetery be accumulated such a mass of putrescent matter as would contaminate the air of the whole, and render the locality insalubrious for very many years.

With a view to preventing waste of ground, the proprietors, or director, or curator of the cemetery ought to place common graves either where private graves are least likely to be taken, or where a private grave with a monument might interfere with a grave already existing. Hence it may frequently be desirable to place a common grave, or any private grave to which there is a certainty of no monument being erected, on each side of a grave with a conspicuous monument. Even two or three intervening common graves may sometimes be desirable among monuments, in order that each structure may have its full effect on the spectator while approaching it, as well as while directly opposite to it.

The mound over a common grave, while it is liable to be reopened, should not be finished with turf or flowers; because, to open a grave with the finished character thereby given is more shocking to the feelings than to open an unfinished grave.

Every grave, whether private or common, to which there is to be no monumental stone, should still be finished with a green mound, which itself is a kind of monument, and maintains respect for the spot so long as it remains.

Though levelling the surface of ground filled with graves having no stone monuments, instead of finishing the grave with a raised grass mound, renders the grass much easier mown, yet, as it confounds all distinction between ground filled with graves and ground not so filled, we would not on any account follow this practice. The Society of Friends and the Moravians adopt this mode, and we admit the superior neatness of their grounds on this account; but we disapprove of it, more especially in the case of the Quakers (who forbid even flat stones with inscriptions, which the Moravians admit), because it exhibits nothing characteristic of a place of interment. As it destroys the distinctive feature of a grave-yard, it cannot be considered in just taste, and ought, therefore, as we think, not to be adopted. Technically, the appearance of the turf mound over the grave is the expression of purpose or use, and this expression is essential to every work of art.

In all large cemeteries there ought to be some graves of every kind, ready made and fit for being occupied at the shortest notice. To protect these graves from the rain or snow, the grave-cover described p. 35, should be placed over them.

In order to effect the *registration of graves and interments*, which we have stated to be an important part of the working of a cemetery, it is necessary to recur to the mode of numbering the graves described in a former page. This may either be done by the mode of squares common in large cemeteries as at present laid out, and exhibited in *fig.* 1. in p. 16.; or, in small cemeteries or churchyards, by laying out the ground in broad borders along the walks and walls, and in double beds, calculating the capacity of both beds and borders in single graves, and having a number-stone at each end of the bed or border indicating the number of single graves it will contain, and the direction in which the numbers are counted, as shown in *fig.* 17. in p. 30.; in which the stone at *a* contains Nos. 1. and 50., being the first and last graves on the bed; and the stone *b* contains No. 25., being the last number on one side, and No. 26., being the first number on the other side. The next bed will commence with No. 51., and so on throughout the cemetery. This mode of numbering requires that every grave or piece of ground purchased, which is to be larger than the space allowed for a common grave, must be a multiple of that space: thus, a vault of the smallest size requires the space of one grave for the stair and another for the vault; and hence it would be recorded in the cemetery books under two numbers. A vault of double or treble the size would require the space of four or six single graves, and thus absorb four or six numbers, and so on. This is the mode which we have adopted in the Cambridge Cemetery (in which, in conformity with existing prejudices, we made provision for constructing vaults and cata-combs, if they should be required), because it is of small size; but in one on a large scale we would first lay out every part of the cemetery in beds and borders, and next have one number for each bed and border. The interments in each bed or border should be numbered in the order in which they are made; and in the register the numbers of the bed or border, and the number of the interment, would be found together. We have already (p. 17.) given our reasons for considering this a better mode of laying out a cemetery than the one generally adopted, of throwing it into squares.

This mode of throwing the ground into squares is at present adopted in most cemeteries, more especially where, from the numerous turnings of the winding walks, the ground is laid out in very irregular shapes. In the working of such cemeteries the practice is to number every grave or vault in the order in which it is made, and indicate its place in the cemetery by a reference to the square in which it is situated, and by laying it down in the plan of that square in the cemetery Map Book in the manner hereafter described.

As the interments require to be numbered, to indicate the order in which they are made, as well as to indicate their place in the cemetery, it follows that every grave has two numbers; the one indicating the precise spot in the cemetery in which the grave is to be found, and the other the time or times at which bodies have been deposited in it; because family graves, while they have only one number referring to their locality, have several referring to the interments made in them. By having an index to the interment numbers, and another to the numbers of the graves, and both referring to the Register Book, the particulars may be obtained of every funeral that has taken place in the cemetery from its opening to the time being.

The *cemetery books* which require to be kept are as follows: —

1. An *Order Book*, in which are entered the date, name, description, age, and abode of the deceased, mode and time of the intended burial, size of the coffin, name of the person by whom the order is given, and the charges. These and some other particulars are printed on two columns of a folio page; and, the blanks of both columns being filled up, one column is retained, and the other is cut out and sent to the sexton. A receipt for the money, indi-cating the leading particulars, is at the same time given to the undertaker.

2. A *Register Book*, which is filled up after the funeral has taken place, and contains columns extending across two folio pages, for the following particu-lars: — number of the interment; number of the grave; name and de-scription of the deceased; last residence; disease of which he died; age, date, and hour of burial; in what part of the cemetery; what monumental distinction; purchased by whom and under what date; sum paid for the in-terment; sum paid for keeping the grave-stone, monument, or plants, &c., in

order; time during which they are to be kept in order for the sum paid; name of the undertaker; name of the clergyman who performed the ceremony; name of the sexton. — All these particulars are entered in the order in which they are here enumerated.

3. A *Ledger*, in which an account is opened for each grave in the following manner: two folio pages contain the same number of columns, and the same headings as in the Register, but the body of the pages is divided into spaces, one of which is allotted for each number of a grave, in the same manner as the pages of a ledger are divided into spaces for each name or account, which has been opened; and in this space, which represents the transactions which take place with the grave it represents, are inserted the number of each of the different funerals that have taken place in it. For example, a brick grave, 60 ft. deep, may have ten different interments of as many different numbers, dates, and names, of the deceased; and hence a space at least equal to ten lines will be left for it. A private grave, 36 ft. deep, which will only contain six coffins, requires only six lines; a vault of twenty catacombs a proportionate space; and a single catacomb in a public vault only one line. The utility of such a ledger, in the case of extensive cemeteries, is exemplified in the case of that of Kensal Green, as any one may be convinced of by applying at the office, 95. Great Russell Street, London.

4. *A Map Book.* — In the cemetery office there ought to be one map showing the entire cemetery with all the roads, walks, squares, beds, &c., and even the trees and shrubs correctly laid down. Then there ought to be a book in which every square or bed is laid down on a sufficiently large scale to admit of inserting in it the plan of each particular grave. The scale for these separate squares in the Kensal Green Cemetery book is 2 in. to 6 ft., and in the Tower Hamlets Cemetery 3 in. to 8 ft. In small cemeteries laid out in beds, like the Cambridge Cemetery, such a map book may be dispensed with; but where the imaginary square system of laying out is adopted it is essential.

5. Some subordinate books are convenient for abridging labour, and insuring accuracy, such as printed forms for certificates of registry, for permission within a certain time to place a head-stone or other monument, for receipts for cash or fees, &c. The books for the Kensal Green Cemetery were prepared by Messrs. C. and E. Layton, Stationers, 150. Fleet Street; those of the East London Cemetery by Mr. T. H. Hoppe, 79. Strand; and those of the Tower Hamlets Cemetery, the last London cemetery which has been formed, by Mr. E. Colyer, 17. Fenchurch Street. The common business accounts which require to be kept, of course, do not differ from those in use in general business.

We have omitted to notice some minor details required for the working of a cemetery, but they are such as will readily occur in practice; and they may be foreseen by procuring a printed paper of the rules and regulations of any of the principal London cemeteries, or of the burying-grounds belonging to the Incorporated Trades of Calton, Edinburgh. The latter, which have been kindly forwarded to us by Mr. Hay, the recorder and superintendant, are remarkable for their comprehensiveness and efficiency.

The curator of a cemetery ought to be a man of intelligence, and of cultivated feelings, with a taste for and some knowledge of gardening; for all which reasons we think the situation one well adapted for a middle-aged gardener.

IV. Certain Innovations suggested relative to the Selection of Ground for Cemeteries, Mode of performing Funerals, etc.

Would not a law, enacting as follows, answer every purpose of Mr. Mackinnon's bill? That no graves should be made except on ground that never was opened before; that, when only one coffin was placed in a grave, it should not be less than 6 ft. below the surface; that, when more than one coffin was to be contained in the same grave, each coffin should be separated from the other by a layer of earth not less than 6 ft. in thickness; that all burying in vaults and catacombs be discontinued; and that no new burial-grounds be formed in London within two miles of St. Paul's, nor in country towns within half a mile of their suburbs. Such a law would at once prevent interments from being made in most of the London burial-grounds, while it would admit of all the unoccupied ground, whether in London or out of it, being used; and thus no injustice would be committed towards those who have recently enlarged their burying-ground; it would, at the same time, check the disgusting and dangerous practice of burying ten or twelve bodies close upon one another in one grave, now practised both in the old churchyards and in the new cemeteries.

A law to attain these objects, combined with regulations to prevent graves from being reopened within sixty years if in the country, or not at all if in a town, would, if strictly enforced, probably be found sufficient for every purpose, as far as health is concerned. Under the influence of such a law there seems to be no objection to every sect having its separate cemetery or cemeteries; to individuals forming cemeteries as commercial speculations; or to different trades or professions having their separate cemeteries. The greater the number of present cemeteries, the greater the number of future public gardens.

The law should be modified with reference to Jews and Quakers, since it is a part of the religion of the former that no grave is ever opened a second time; and the latter adopt the same practice, though not, perhaps, from religious principle, but from a general regard to decency and propriety. It would be sufficient to enact that the burying-grounds of these religious bodies, in common with others, when once filled, should be shut up for ever, if in towns, and that the new cemeteries opened by them should always be in the country.

All burial-grounds whatever within the precincts of towns, when once filled, that is, when the whole ground has been buried in, even if with only one body in a grave, should be shut up as burying-grounds, and a few years afterwards opened as public walks or gardens; the grave-stones and all architectural or sculptural ornaments being kept in repair at the expense of the town or village; such trees, shrubs, or plants being planted among the graves as the town council, or, if a village, the parish vestry, may determine.

The distance from a town at which a cemetery ought to be placed will depend a good deal on the elevation of the site, the nature of the soil, and the sources from which the town obtains its water. If there are pervious strata lying on impervious strata, immediately under the surface of the ground intended as a cemetery, and these strata traverse ground without the cemetery in which wells are likely to be dug, and have a descent towards it, the moisture of decomposition will be carried by the rains along the strata to the wells, and to all artificial depositories, or natural outlets for the water. An elevated situation, and a soil of gravel, sand, or chalk, to a great depth, is evidently preferable to all others, because the moisture generated will be carried perpendicularly down by the rains, and the gases evolved will be carried off by the winds. No human dwellings ought to be made within a cemetery, unless we except the entrance lodge, which might, if desirable, always be made outside the gates, or so as not to have all its windows looking directly on the graves. It would frequently be advantageous to have a space outside the cemetery fence, of 50 or 60 feet in width, to be planted with trees, varying in height according to the nature of the situation and soil; the object being to disguise the view of the graves from the nearest houses, without producing too much shelter to impede the action of the sun and winds on the surface of the cemetery.

Such a law as we contemplate should prohibit interment in churches or public buildings; whether in vaults, catacombs, or in the floor of the church or vault, without any exception whatever ; it should prohibit the formation of private vaults, or private or family graves or graveyards, in towns, or any where except in the country, and there they should be placed in spots at least 100 ft. from any other building. The law should also, as we think, enforce the clearing out of all public vaults under churches or chapels, whether in town or country, and not even excepting those of the newly formed public cemeteries. That the vaults and catacombs of these cemeteries are liable, to a considerable extent, to the same objections as those in the old burying-grounds and under churches, is a fact which can be proved by reference to what has taken place both in the vaults of the Kensal Green Cemetery and in those of the London and Westminster Cemetery * ; and, in short, any person walking through them will require no other evidence than that of his own senses.

We may, perhaps, be thought unreasonable in wishing to prevent interments in Westminster Abbey and St. Paul's, or in the royal vault at Windsor, but we consider that the memory of the great men of the nation, including even our sovereigns, would be quite as much honoured by having their bodies buried in the free soil in the country, and appropriate monumental cenotaphs erected to their memory in these and other national buildings, as by having their bodies buried under their monuments, or preserved in wooden or leaden cases in vaults or catacombs. Surely it is pleasanter in idea, when looking on the statue of Dr. Johnson in St. Paul's, to think of his remains being covered by the green turf in the open ground of a cemetery or a churchyard, than to think of them lying in black earth, saturated with putrescent moisture, under the damp paved floor of the crypt of a cathedral. There is no doubt that burying in sepulchres, by which the body is preserved from mixing with the soil, is of great antiquity, and it was doubtless justified by the opinions of mankind in the early ages of history; but it may be fairly asserted that the practice is not in conformity with the opinions and spirit of the present age. Security from desecration was, no doubt, a main object for this mode of burial, and certainly it was a protection from the hyena, the fox, the dog, and other wild carnivorous animals that were common in the early stages of civilisation ; but neither then nor now is it any permanent security against desecration by the human species. On the contrary, it is a certain mode of ending in desecration, sooner or later. Witness the mummies of Egypt, unprotected even by the Pyramids ; or look to what has been taking place for many years past in the vaults of churches in London, as given in evidence in the Parliamentary *Report*, which we have so often quoted; or turn to the volumes of travellers on the Continent since the peace of 1814.† The truth is,

---

* Mr. Jones, undertaker, residing in Devereux Court, Essex Street, Strand, placed a body in a leaden coffin and the other usual cases, and deposited it in the catacombs of Kensal Green Cemetery. It had remained there about three months, when he was informed by the secretary of the cemetery company that " the coffin leaked, and that he must see to it immediately." Mr. Jones, accompanied by his assistants, went to the cemetery, removed the body from the horizontal stone resting-place, which was sealed very carefully at the ends and round the sides. It was necessary to remove the lid of the outer coffin and turn out the body, enclosed, as is usual, in the shell and leaden coffin; these were reversed, when it was found that a small hole existed at the under part of the leaden coffin. This hole was enlarged with a gimlet by one of the assistants, Mr. Thomas Moxley ; the gas which escaped extinguished a lighted candle three distinct times, and he was rendered incapable of following his occupation for several weeks. (*Appendix to Report on the Health of Towns*, p. 208.)

† In the autumn of 1813 we passed two days in and about the small town of Kowna, on the Niemen, celebrated for its lime trees and its honey ; and, looking into the vaults of the church, we observed the floor covered with

that in this matter, as in most others, we follow the practice of those who have gone before us, without enquiring into its reasonableness or suitableness to our present views of nature. A gentleman in the country builds a chapel in his grounds, and his architect tells him that it would not be complete without a family vault, and he therefore has one built, otherwise he would not be like his neighbours. As to public vaults in churches, their origin is security, and they are continued partly owing to the crowded state of the churchyards, but principally on account of the higher fees obtained from those who bury in them by the clergyman and the undertaker. Hence, on account of the expense, burying in vaults becomes a mark of wealth or distinction, and for that reason is adopted by many of the London tradesmen, even in the new cemeteries. How much better for the health and improvement of the living, and the honour of the dead, to expend the money now laid out in vaults and in burial fees, in handsome monuments, or even in increased space round graves in the open ground, so as to admit of interring only one coffin in a grave! How much more natural and agreeable to see the grass graves of a family placed side by side in a small green enclosure, the property of the family, which cannot be disturbed; than to see the cover of a brick grave or a vault, in which we know their bodies have been let down one over the other, and there remain unmixed with soil, a pestilential mass of putridity; or see the coffins which contain them deposited on stone shelves above ground, forming separate portions of preserved corruption!*

The directors of the Kensal Green Cemetery have offered seven acres of their ground for the interment of the paupers of seven London parishes, which exceed in number 1,000 annually. "It has been found," they say, "that seven acres will contain about 133,500 graves ; each grave will receive ten coffins ; thus accommodation may be provided for 1,335,000 deceased paupers, and the seven acres, at an average of 1,000 burials a year, will not be filled for 1,335 years." (*Annual Report of the General Cemetery Company*, dated 9th June, 1842, p. 8.) The idea of accumulating such a mass of corruption in such a limited space is horrible, and we trust will never be listened to for a moment by the public. The directors introduce their proposition by the following passage : " The directors of the General

---

bodies in their shrouds, which had been turned pellmell out of their coffins. On some the flesh and hair were still remaining. We were informed this was done by the French on their retreat from Moscow the winter before, in search for the loaf of bread and bottle of wine, which it was at that time customary for the Poles and Lithuanians to place in the coffin along with the body, previously to its interment.

* The late Sir Francis Chantrey had caused a splendid vault to be built for himself, and, with much kindness, proposed to Allan Cunningham that he also should be buried in it. " No, no," answered Allan ; " I 'll not be built over when I 'm dead ; I 'll lie where the wind shall blow over, and the daisy grow, upon my grave." (*The Builder*, No. 3. p. 40.) In the *Gentleman's Magazine* for December, 1842, a biographical notice of Allan Cunningham, Esq., is given, in which it is stated that he died on Oct. 29., aged 56, and that on the 4th of Nov. his remains were removed to the General Cemetery in the Harrow Road, for interment in the catacombs of that place. Having written to Mr. Peter Cunningham, the son of the deceased, with a copy of the above extract from the *Builder*, to ascertain the facts of the case, his answer is : " My father is buried in the General Cemetery at Kensal Green ; not in a close, damp, pestiferous vault, or in a brick grave (just as bad), but in his native earth, that he may mingle with what he sprung from. The extract you send me is perfectly correct. My father had always an abhorrence of Westminster Abbey vaults and brick-built graves."—*P. C. March* 2, 1843.

Cemetery Company, knowing the difficulty as well as the expense of obtaining ground for burial, (as a cemetery always depreciates the property around,) and contemplating that a Bill may pass to prohibit burials in the crowded metropolis, offer seven acres of their ground at Kensal Green, adjoining the Cemetery, for the burial of the poor, under such regulations as may be thought advisable." (*Report*, &c. p. 8.) Fortunately for the public, the calculation of the directors is altogether erroneous. An acre contains 43,560 square feet, and supposing the pauper graves to be 6 ft. 6 in. by 2 ft. 6 in., this is equal to 16¼ square ft., and hence, dividing 43,560 ft. by that sum, we have 2,680 graves per acre, which multiplied by seven gives 18,760 graves in seven acres ; something more than one seventh of the number which the directors say the seven acres will contain. But let us take even this limited number of 18,760 graves, and multiply it by 10, the number of pauper interments which the directors propose to make in a grave, and we have 187,600 bodies deposited in seven acres. Something less indeed than the 1,335,000 bodies which the directors propose to get into that space, but still enough to put the public on their guard against men who can hazard such statements ; for it must be remembered that this error in the calculation has nothing to do with the intentions of the directors. One million three hundred and thirty-five thousand bodies deposited in seven acres may well depreciate the property around. If it be true, as Mr. Walker, the author of *Gatherings from Graveyards*, observes (*Report on the Health of Towns*, p. 412.), that " layers of earth, of several feet in depth, can no more intercept the transmission of gas into the atmosphere, than they can by their density prevent the infiltration of water," then indeed these seven acres, if occupied even with the smaller number of 197,600 bodies, might be considered as the crater of a volcano, vomiting forth poison in the form of a column of gaseous matter, which, changing in direction with every change of the wind, would poison the atmosphere for many miles round ; while the water of decomposition would poison the springs of the subsoil.

It is lamentable to witness in the proprietors of cemeteries, and in some members of the Committee for enquiring into the Effect of Interments in Towns, the manner in which the subject of the interment of paupers, and of the poor generally, is discussed. We do not limit the remark to the proprietors of cemeteries, the committee referred to, or to the rich or influential classes in this country, but extend it also to every other class which considers itself above the poor ; for example, to parish vestries. One would think that the poor were considered as animals of a different species, or as totally without the feelings which belong to the rest of mankind. While the bodies of the dead rich in every capital in Europe are to be placed singly in catacombs or graves, those of the poor are to be trenched in in layers as in France, thrown into a common pit as in Naples and Leghorn, or buried ten or fifteen in a grave as in London.* Some of the committee who examined witnesses seem particularly anxious to abridge the process of taking care of the poor, by placing quicklime in their coffins. The questions put by some of these persons evinced, in our opinion, great want of humane feeling generally, and an utter disregard of the feelings of the poor.

" Should you have any objection, if there was a law made that there

---

* The price of land, within ten miles of London, is much too high to admit of burying paupers singly in the London cemeteries ; but one thousand, or even two thousand, acres of poor waste land, admirably adapted for burying-ground, might be purchased in the parishes of Woking, Chobham, Horsall, Perbright, Pyrford, &c., at from 4*l.* to 8*l.* per acre. The land alluded to is too poor to admit of cultivation for arable purposes; but it would grow yews, junipers, pines, firs, and other cemetery plants, with which it might be planted in rows, in such a manner that the graves could be made between the rows.

*D 8

should be so much lime put in with the body, so as to destroy it in a certain
time ? "

" Do you think there would be any objection to burying bodies with a
certain quantity of quicklime, sufficient to destroy the coffin and the whole
thing in a given time ? "

are questions continually recurring. One honourable member put the quicklime question so often, that we took the trouble of counting the number of
times, which we found to be twenty. It would no doubt be very desirable in
the eyes of those who find themselves above the poor, to get rid of "the
whole thing" at the expense of a little quicklime; but, unfortunately for this
desire, and fortunately for the poor, and sometimes for the cause of justice,
there are the bones, which, as we have before seen (p. 3.), are not to be
got rid of so easily. Very different indeed were the feelings expressed
by the Bishop of London, and some other clergymen who were examined.
It is very natural for the rich to hate the poor, and wish to dispose of
them, and of "the whole thing," with as little trouble as possible; but this
is the feeling of wild nature, exactly the same which leads a herd of deer to
forsake a wounded individual. Cultivated nature, whether that cultivation be
the effect of religion or philosophy, ought to lead to a very different mode of
feeling. Sympathy with the whole of human nature must surely be productive of more happiness to the individual who feels and exercises that sympathy, than when it is limited only to a part; to those in the same circumstances as ourselves, or who are connected with us by the ties of relationship
or friendship. It is certain that many of the rich have very little sympathy
for the poor, and equally certain that there are others among the rich who
evince much sympathy for them. Which of these parties comprises the most
useful members of society, and by which is the most happiness enjoyed ?

It should never be forgotten, that what are called the poor and paupers are
fellow creatures, and that the difference between the former and the latter is
very frequently matter of accident. Every poor man, however honest, in-
dustrious, and even talented, is liable to become a pauper. The common idea
is, that a pauper is a person that has brought himself into destitution by im-
providence or misconduct; but, admitting this to be sometimes the case, it
cannot generally be so. Most paupers, in the ordinary state of the country;
are aged persons, no longer able to work from infirmity or disease; many in-
dustrious persons are brought to the state of paupers by unforeseen accidents;
from fire, water, storms, robberies, the death of persons on whom they chiefly
depended, and from a variety of other causes over which they had little or no
control. Admitting that a number of pauper children have become so by
the recklessness of their parents, is not that the fault of the government in not
having provided for the education of the poor, by which they would have
acquired habits of self-control, and been taught the advantage of foregoing a
present enjoyment for a future good ? Admitting even that a number of persons have brought pauperism on themselves, is that a sufficient reason for
interring them in a different manner from the other poor ? We think not;
and therefore we contemplate the provision of no particular part of a cemetery for paupers, but would bury them indiscriminately in those parts of the
ground destined for graves without monuments; and also among those parts
having monuments, in order that by surrounding the latter with plain spaces,
they may, as already observed, have more effect.

The following suggestions are made with a view to the interment of the
poor, of paupers, and of such persons as desire no monuments to their graves,
belonging to London; and they may apply also to some other very populous
towns, such as Manchester or Liverpool. — Suppose London divided into
four or more districts; then let each district, besides its permanent cemetery,
have a temporary one for the use of all persons whatever who did not wish to
have monuments to their graves, and of course including paupers without
friends sufficiently wealthy to bury them in a monumental cemetery. This
temporary cemetery may be merely a field rented on a 21 years' lease, of such

an extent as to be filled with graves in 14 years. At the end of seven years more it may revert to the landlord, and be cultivated, planted, or laid down in grass, in any manner that may be thought proper; the landlord binding himself and his successors by such a deed as should be inseparable from the transfer of the property, that the field should never again be let for the same purpose, or for building on. To render this the more certain, the transaction ought to be recorded in some public register, and also on monumental stones placed at the angles of the field, or one stone in its centre. Landed property held by public companies, as being least likely to change proprietors, is peculiarly suitable for this kind of occupation. There is, for example, along the Uxbridge Road, near Acton, an estate belonging to the Goldsmiths' Company, which would make an admirable cemetery of this description.

We see no objection to taking land for temporary cemeteries at a considerable distance from a town, provided it were on the line of a railway, as, for example, at Bagshot Heath; and we can see no difficulty in the different districts of such a city as London having a place of temporary deposit for their dead, whether paupers who paid nothing, or poor persons who paid moderately. There are depositories of this kind in Frankfort and Munich*; and they are found to add greatly to the convenience, economy, and salubrity of persons having only small dwelling-houses, and moderate incomes. Were depositories of this kind established in the metropolis, it might be so arranged that a number of bodies should be conveyed to the place of interment at the same time, and this might be done with appropriate decency and respect in a railway or a steam-boat hearse. There are thousands of acres of the poorest gravelly soil, which the Southampton railway passes through, that at present do not rent for more than 3s. or 4s. an acre, which would afford a cemetery sufficient for all the poor of London, and the rich also, for ages to come; and the same may be said of some thousands of acres not far from the Thames, in the neighbourhood of Chertsey. In proportion as the land was filled with graves, it might be planted with trees, or laid down in grass.

We can see no sufficient reason against having permanent monumental cemeteries, as well as temporary ones which are to have no monuments, laid out on poor soils at great distances from London, along the railroads,

---

* The cemetery of Frankfort on the Main is entered through an open propylæum between two wings. In one of these wings is the residence of the overseer and assistants; while the other contains ten cells, in which bodies in coffins are deposited for some days previously to interment. As a precaution against premature inhumation, cords are fixed to the fingers of the deceased, communicating with a bell, so that the least motion, in case of a person's revival, would be instantly made known to an attendant stationed in the apartment adjoining these cells. There is also a spacious waiting-hall on each side of the entrance, for the accommodation of those who accompany the funerals. It is strictly prohibited to inter any corpse till infallible signs of decomposition shall have become obvious; and, though this might occasion considerable inconvenience in a private house, no evil results from it here, because interment takes place immediately afterwards. There is also a receiving house (Leichenhaus) to the large cemetery at Munich. (Arch. Mag., vol. ii. p. 136.)

The general cemetery at Munich is surrounded by a border of trees and shrubs, with the exception of one end, in which is placed a semicircular building, composed of an open colonnade in front, with vaults underneath. In the centre of this semicircular building is a projection behind, called the Leichenhaus, containing three large rooms, in two of which (one for males and the other for females) the dead, as shrouded and deposited in their coffins by their relations, are exposed to view for forty-eight hours before they are committed to the earth. The other room is for suicides and unowned bodies.

E

with cooperative railroad hearses, and other arrangements to lessen expense; which would admit of more ground being spared in the suburbs for public gardens and breathing-places. Nor does there appear to us any objection to union workhouses having a portion of their garden ground used as a cemetery, to be restored to cultivation after a sufficient time had elapsed. The bones in this and in every case where the ground was planted or cultivated would be at least 6 ft. below the surface, and, where it was thought necessary, they might be protected by covering-plates, as already described. Proprietors of land, we think, ought to be encouraged to bury on their own grounds in the free soil; a proper officer, who might be the local registrar, or one of the churchwardens, taking cognizance that the grave was of the proper depth, and that all the other conditions necessary for insuring decency and salubrity were fulfilled.

The expense of funerals has last year been considerably lessened about the metropolis by the introduction of one-horse hearses, which convey the coffin and six mourners to the place of interment. These appear to have been first suggested in 1837, by Mr. J. R. Croft, in an article in the *Mechanic's Magazine*, vol. xxvii. p. 146., and the idea has subsequently, in 1842, been improved on and carried into execution by Mr. Shillibeer, to whom the British public are indebted for the first introduction of the omnibus. Mr. Shillibeer's funeral carriage embraces in itself a hearse and a mourning coach, is very neat, and takes little from the pomp, and nothing from the decency of the ordinary funeral obsequies, while it greatly reduces the expense; the hire of a hearse with a single horse costing only 1*l.* 1*s.*, and with two horses, 1*l.* 11*s.* 6*d.* These carriages have one division for the coffin, and another for six mourners; and when the coffin has been taken out for interment, before the mourners reenter to return home, the front part of the carriage and the fore wheels are contracted and drawn close up to the hinder or coach part of the carriage by means of a screw, so that the part for containing the coffin disappears, and the whole, when returning from the place of interment, has the appearance of a mourning coach. The invention is ingenious and most useful.

Perhaps the expense to the poor might be still farther lessened by the use of light low four-wheeled vehicles for conveying the corpse, which might be moved by a man, or by two men. We see no reason why the attendants at the funeral of a poor man should not move this carriage by turns; as in various country places, more especially in Scotland, where the bodies even of respectable farmers are, or were forty years ago, carried to the churchyard on handspokes by the relations of the deceased. The same idea has occurred to Mr. H. W. Jukes, whose carriage for walking funerals is shown in *fig.* 32. In

Fig. 32. *Mr. Jukes's Truck-Hearse.*

this figure, besides the cross handle in front for two persons to draw by, there are two handles behind for assisting to push it up steep hills, or by pressure or drawing back to retard it when going down hill. These last handles should be made with a hinge to let down when the coffin is being taken out; and in a level country they may be altogether omitted. The pall, or mortcloth, lies over the coffin. The dimensions of the body of the carriage should be about 7 ft. by 2 ft. 6 in. inside measure; the height from the bottom to the roof may be 4 ft., and from the roof to the ground 6 ft. In a funeral with this machine, no hired men are necessary; the man who precedes the procession should be one of the mourners, or the joiner who made the coffin, and the labour of drawing should be shared by the whole in turns. Persons who have not attended a walking funeral are not likely to be aware, not only of the fatigue to the bearers and attendants, but of the very disagreeable effects, more especially to the man at the head, whose head and shoulders are under the pall, of the smell, and sometimes the moisture, proceeding from the coffin. Could Mr. Jukes's truck-hearse, therefore, be generally introduced, not only in towns, but in country parishes, it would be a great blessing to the poor. The expense of funerals to the poor might be still farther diminished by the use of the hand-bier, a figure of which will hereafter be given, as practised formerly in Scotland, and as it still is in various parts of the Continent, more par-ticularly in Poland. In the latter country the body is put in a coffin of coarse boards, in which it is carried to the church, placed on a bier, and a bottomless coffin of a superior description placed over it. The service being read, two of the mourners carry the bier to the side of the grave, when, two cords being introduced under the coffin, the whole is lowered to the bottom of the grave, while the case is drawn up by two back cords which are at-tached to its top.* These innovations will probably be resisted at first, because, among other things, they would render unnecessary some of the under-taker's men†; but, as mankind cease to become slaves of custom, various

---

* We saw a funeral performed in this way in the neighbourhood of War-saw, in June, 1813. The body was not buried in the churchyard, but in the margin of a wheat field, the son of the deceased not being able, as we were informed, to pay the churchyard fees. In Rome, and some other cities of Italy, the body is placed in a stone sarcophagus, while the funeral ceremonies are performed; after which it is deposited, sometimes only for a day or two, and in the cases of people of greater rank for some weeks, in a vault or cata-comb: it is then taken out and buried in the free soil.

† People are not generally aware that the origin and type of the array of funerals commonly made by undertakers is strictly the heraldic array of a baronial funeral, or the funeral of persons entitled to coat armour, all of which were attended by heralds; the two men who stand at the doors being supposed to be the two porters of the castle, with their staves in black; the man who heads the procession, wearing a scarf, being a representative of a herald at arms; the man who carries a plume of feathers on his head being an esquire, who bears the tabard of arms, including the shield, sword, helmet, gauntlet, and casque, with its plume of feathers; the pall-bearers, with batons, being representatives of knights-companions at arms; the men walking with wands being supposed to represent gentlemen ushers, with their wands. The cost of the men who bear staves covered with black, and who re-present the two porters of the castle, varies from 18s. to 30s.; and the man who heads the procession, representing the herald at arms, costs from 2l. 11s. 6d. to 5l. 5s., and so on. In general the poorest person does not fool away less than 3l. 3s. for attendants of this kind. (E.C.S.) In the case of truck-hearses and hand-biers, all these expenses might be spared, by the mourners acting in succession as the leader or herald; or dispensing with the leader altogether, as is generally the case in Scotland. At the funerals of persons of rank, heralds and hired mourners have in every age attended, and formed an array of pomp and simulated grief; but the practice seems inconsistent with real sorrow, and should therefore be rejected by people of common sense. " If, says a correspondent, " the poor were wise, their funerals would be as simple as possible: a plain coffin, borne by near male relations, and followed by the family and friends of the deceased in decent mourning, but without any of the undertaker's trappings on their persons, would be sufficient. The poor like funeral pomp because the rich like it; forgetting that during life the con-

innovations of this kind will be adopted, which at present will be rejected as absurd; but which it is nevertheless desirable to suggest, with a view to induce men to examine into the possibility of departing from the beaten track. The thick crust of prejudice must be broken up before it can be dispersed; and the debacle must precede the clearing of the river.

V. Design for a Cemetery of moderate Extent, on level Ground, exemplified in one now being formed at Cambridge.

We shall here copy the Report which we made to the Directors, having obtained their permission for that purpose, omitting some details which have

---

dition of the dead was entirely different, and that there ought to be a consistency in every thing belonging to the various orders of society. The cause of the mistake which the poor make is this: that, by so uncalled for an expense, they think they show their greater respect for the dead, as if a dead father or mother (unless he or she were wrapt up in selfishness) would deprive their children of necessaries or comforts to gratify an imaginary and false pride."— S. H. N.

The following case shows that where there is a genuine respect for the feelings and wishes of the dead, it soars high over all the ordinary pomp of funerals. It also shows how very careful persons ought to be on their death-bed, not to utter wishes that may give much pain and inconvenience to their relations. What considerate person would have expressed the wish which led to the following instance of

Extraordinary Resolution and Perseverance. — We have now to record a feat of extraordinary perseverance, so rare indeed, that we much doubt whether its parallel can be found. On the 19th of November last, a person of the name of Thomas Wrassel, aged sixty-three, died at Wisbeach, in the county of Cambridge, and previously to his demise he expressed a wish to his only sister, who resided with him, that his remains should be interred in the churchyard at Clarborough, near Retford, at which place he had formerly lived, and where his mother and some of his family had been interred. With astonishing resolution the sister resolved on fulfilling his last injunctions, and set forth with the remains of her brother in a donkey cart. The distance between Wisbeach and Clarborough is ninety-seven miles. During the journey the coffin, which projected from behind the cart, was covered with a ragged coverlet, upon which the wretched sister sat. At length, after being eleven days on the road, she and the coffin reached Clarborough on the 2d of December, and the body lay as it had travelled in the cart, in an outhouse of one of the village inns until Sunday December 4., when the last rites of the church were performed over it by the Rev. W. R. Sharpe, curate: and, after its long transit, it was committed to its last earthly resting-place. The woman herself was not attired in decent mourning, but readily paid the funeral expenses, and expressed her determination to return to Wisbeach by the conveyance in which she had come, in order to dispose of some little property there, preparatory to residing at Clarborough; so that she may be sure of laying her bones beside his bones, and that the kindred dust of the family may commingle together, until the trump of the archangel shall summon them to meet the Lord in the air. The woman is sixty years of age, and the remains of her brother were only placed in a single coffin, although he had been dead for the long period of fifteen days ere the earth received back its own. (*Nottingham Journal*, as quoted in the *Times*, Dec. 24. 1842.)

already been given in Divisions II. and III. as belonging to the subject of cemeteries generally.

Report on the Design for a Cemetery proposed to be formed at Cambridge: made, by Order of the Directors, by J. C. Loudon.

[Referring to Plans and Sections, Nos. 1. to 15.]

The *Ground* purchased by the Cambridge Cemetery Company was, by the desire of the directors, inspected by us on Nov. 8. 1842. It lies in an open airy situation, in the neighbourhood of the town. The extent is 3¼ acres, and the tenure freehold. The surface is flat, with a gentle inclination to one end, from which there is a tolerably good drainage, by means of a public drain along the margin of the New Huntingdon Road, to the river. The soil is a compact blue clay; its present state is in broad high ridges, which have recently borne corn crops, and the soil is therefore favourable for vegetation to the depth of 8 or 9 inches. The ground is enclosed on three sides by a recently planted thorn hedge, and the fourth, or north, side is open to a field of similar surface and soil.

The *Object* of the Cemetery Company is to form a cemetery chiefly for the middle class of society, the total expense of which, including the purchase of the land, shall not exceed 2000*l.*; that being the sum raised by the Company in 200 shares of 10*l.* each. The sum paid for the land being 400*l.*, there remain 1600*l.* for building and arranging the ground.

The duties of the reporter, therefore, are to show the directors, by plans, specifications, and estimates, how the ground may be arranged, and the necessary buildings erected, for the sum of 1600*l.*; to suggest rules and regulations for the use and management of the cemetery; to point out the duties of the curator; and to offer any other suggestions to the directors that may occur to him.

The *Principles* which have been borne in mind by the reporter, in complying with the desire of the directors, are as follows:

That, to prevent all risk of desecration or indecency, the arrangements be such as that no part of a coffin, or of its contents, can ever be again exposed after interment, and, in particular, that no human bone can ever be disturbed. That, the cemetery being intended for all sects and parties indiscriminately, consecration by any one party would be improper. That a lodge for the curator, and a shed and yard adjoining and connected with it, for his implements, planks, barrows, &c., are essential. That a chapel, for all who may choose to make use of it, is also essential. That the frontage, and a portion of the ground along the Histon Road, be not included in the plan in the first instance, in case the cemetery should not succeed; but that the general plan be so contrived that the frontage may be added afterwards, without deranging the cemetery part of the original design. That, the general outline of the ground being rectilinear, and the surface nearly level, the interior walks, borders, and beds, should be chiefly rectilinear and level also, as well for the sake of harmony of forms and lines, as for economy of space. That, in order to throw the whole into an agreeable shape, and form a reserve ground [R, in the plan *fig.* 33. p. 56.] for soil, bricks, and other materials produced or required in digging graves, building vaults, &c., the walk and hedge at one end should be formed within the outer fence. That, as moisture in a moderate degree contributes to the decomposition of animal matter, while in excess, in a strong clayey soil, it changes muscular fibre into adipocere, and also because there is a prejudice against burying in a very wet soil, it is desirable that the ground be drained; but that, as there is not a sufficient outlet for deep drainage so as to carry off the water from the bottom of brick graves or vaults, it is desirable that the surface of the ground should be so arranged as to carry off as much as possible of the rain water falling on it. That, to contribute to the dryness of the surface, and also because it has been ascertained that the gases from decaying bodies will rise to the surface from

E 3

a very great depth, no trees (except such as may be hereafter introduced for ornamenting particular graves) should be planted in the interior of the cemetery, but only along the borders of the main walks and of the terrace walk, in order to allow the full effect of the sun and wind to dry the ground, and renew the air.   That the trees proposed to be planted should occupy as little space as possible ; and, hence, should consist of kinds which have narrow conical shapes like the cypress, a form connected with places of interment by classical and even popular association.   That these trees should be all evergreens, as being from their unchangeable aspect more solemn than deciduous trees ; and that they should be of dark shades of green, as being more solemn than light shades of that colour.   That no flowers, flowering shrubs, or deciduous trees, be planted in the cemetery by the Company, but only in the reserve gardens, for sale to such persons as may wish to plant them over graves.   That, in order to combine security and a solemn effect with economy, the surrounding fence be a *holly hedge* rather than a stone or brick wall ; but that, for immediate privacy and security, the whole be surrounded with a park paling outside the holly hedge, to be retained there till the hedge has overtopped the paling.   That the graves should be so arranged that funerals may be commodiously performed, or any grave visited, without treading on graves already occupied.   That no catacombs be constructed above the surface of the ground, because the reporter considers every mode of burial, except in the free soil, as unpleasant in idea ; and as more or less dangerous to the living from the effluvia which unavoidably proceeds from the coffins, even when bricked up, as that operation is ordinarily performed ; and, finally, because this mode of burial is no security against the disturbance of the coffins at some future time.

Nevertheless, to meet the opinions and wishes of those who still prefer burying in vaults and underground catacombs, ample space should be provided for them, and also for brick graves ; while those who desire to plant flowers or flowering shrubs on the graves of their friends should have full permission to do so ; or, if the directors should desire to plant flowers and shrubs for the general ornament of the cemetery, some may be planted in beds in the situation where graves are to be made, and of the shape of these graves (see *figs.* 3. to 10., in p. 22. and p. 23.) ; on the principle that the taste of individuals, and even, to a certain extent, of public bodies, ought to be free.

The *general Arrangement* of the plan, as founded on these principles, is as follows.

The Buildings. — The design, estimate, and working plans of the curator's lodge, the chapel, and the responsibility that the cost of execution shall not exceed the estimate, are committed to E. B. Lamb, Esq., architect, whose estimate amounts to 1000*l.*, leaving 600*l.* for the arrangement of the grounds.

The Grounds. — The proposed general arrangement of the grounds is shown in the plan No. 1. [*fig.* 33.], with the signature of the reporter, and is as follows.

The entire area of 3¼ acres is shown enclosed by a holly hedge, planted on the top of a broad bank of soil.   The main entrance is proposed to be made at the west end, opening into the Histon Road ; and a secondary entrance will be required from the New Huntingdon Road, at the south-east corner, partly for hearses, but chiefly for carting in and carting out materials.

On each side of the main entrance, a piece of ground, G G, is reserved, with a view to the following objects.   As the curator of the cemetery cannot be supposed to have full employment for two or three years after the cemetery is opened, he may rent these two pieces of ground, and cultivate them as gardens, which, if partly devoted to flowers for sale, might, it is thought, prove an attraction to the cemetery ; while the cemetery in its turn would form a motive to walk from town to the gardens, and ultimately lead to an attachment to the cemetery as a place of interment.   Or, should the cemetery not be so generally adopted by the public as it is hoped it will be, these pieces of ground, being valuable on account of their frontage, may be let off for building on; or, should the cemetery be prosperous, and more room required, the spaces alluded to may be added to it.

The chapel is proposed to be placed in the centre of the ground, as most convenient. The entrance being at the end c, a sufficient area is formed in front of that end to admit of turning a hearse and four horses, which may either return by the main entrance A, or go out by the secondary entrance at D.

A piece of ground is reserved at E for laying down any superfluous earth which may occur in the course of digging the graves, and more especially in forming brick graves, vaults, or catacombs. Here also bricks and other materials used in forming graves, vaults, or catacombs, may be deposited; and, some years hence, when the cemetery is in full demand, either in this piece of ground or near the Huntingdon Road Lodge at w, a shed may be formed, in order that the earth-box (described in p. 34.), with wheelbarrows, planks, casks of cement, lime, sand, &c., may be kept under cover, and also as a place for a mason or bricklayer to work in. This shed is placed close to the side of the approach road, in order that materials may be the more readily laid down or taken up without the necessity of leading the cart off the road. F is a piece of ground, which may be let as a garden to the cottage or lodge at D; and, indeed, till the cemetery is in full operation, the reserve ground E may also, in great part, be let for cultivation for a year or two. It is thought that the cottage at D, and the ground F attached to it, and also the shed w, after the cemetery is once established, might be advantageously let to a statuary mason. The shed w is shown with a chimney in each gable, in case it should afterwards be thought advisable to turn it into a labourer's cottage.

In laying out the interior of the cemetery, the first object was to obtain a carriage-road down the centre; not only for general purposes, such as cartage for materials for building tombs, brick graves, &c., but to allow of the hearse approaching the graves as near as possible.

The next object was to form borders, u u, &c., to the main road from west to east, and to the cross roads from south to north. These borders are 18 ft. wide, planted with trees at regular distances; and they admit of being divided into spaces for letting, as permanent places of interment for families who are willing to pay more than for permanent graves in the interior. Between every two trees there may be one burial-place, rendered ornamental by some description of tomb, monument, or enclosure.

The interior is divided into beds 18 ft. in width, with paths between them 4 ft. in width; and a space 2 ft. in width, and raised about 3 in., is shown in the middle of each bed, on which space all the head-stones are proposed to be placed on a foundation of brickwork or masonry carried up from the bottom of the grave, in order that these head-stones, or whatever description of monument or memorial may be placed at the head of a grave, shall always stand firm and independent of that grave. (See p. 28.) The paths between the beds are connected with a common path of 5 ft. in width, which surrounds the beds, and communicates at intervals with the main or central road; so that a funeral may be performed in any part of the grounds, or a grave in any part of the grounds visited, without once deviating from these paths, or treading on any graves.

The surface of the ground being naturally flat, and very nearly on a level, there will be no difficulty in carrying off the surface water to the point D, though there is no outlet for deep drains. It therefore becomes necessary to render the surface drainage as perfect as possible, and for this purpose the interior of the compartments is raised in the middle as shown in the cross section No. 6. [not given], in which a is a level line, and b the line of the ground; in consequence of which the water will drain to each side to the green paths under which tile drains will be formed, as indicated by the dotted blue lines R R, &c. The bottom of these drains will not be more than 18 in. under the surface, and they will be covered entirely with small stones or

E 4

gravel, for the purpose of more immediately and effectually absorbing the water which falls on the surface of the beds. In order
to carry off the water from
the main road, and also from
the walk on the terrace,
small branch drains are to
be formed, as indicated in
the blue dotted lines in the
plan.

Trees are shown planted
along the walks at regular
distances. Those along the
central road are supposed
to be chiefly Taurian pines
(*Pìnus taúrica*), because
that species has a dark and
solemn air, readily clothes
itself with branches from
the ground upwards, and
its branches admit of "cutting in" to any extent, so
as to form the tree into as
narrow a cone as may be
desirable.   Add to these
advantages, that this is one
of the most rapid-growing
of pines. The trees marked
s s, &c., are supposed to
be cedars of Lebanon; and
the four marked T T, &c ,
deodar cedars. The trees
v v, &c., bordering the
terrace walk, are proposed
to be Irish yews.   The
trees round the reserve
ground, E and F, are to be
either Taurian or black Austrian pines (*P*. austrìaca);
the latter a tree that has
most of the properties of
the Taurian pine, with the
advantage of being some-
what cheaper to purchase.

At any future period,
should there be a demand
for catacombs, a range of
these can be substituted for
the curvilinear walk at the
eastern extremity, by re-
moving the holly hedge, and
by forming a handsome
arcade there, with vaults
behind and underneath, as
in the Munich and Kensal
Green Cemeteries.

Details. — The following
is a summary of the details
of the ground plan, No. 1.
[*fig.* 33. : owing to the

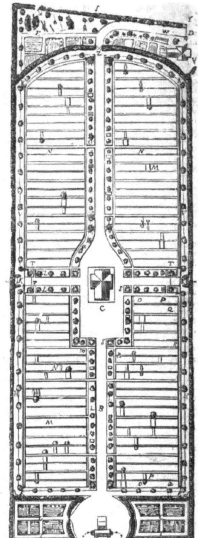

Fig. 33.   *Ground Plan of the Cambridge Cemetery.*

reduced scale of this plan, several of the letters of reference have been of necessity omitted.]

A, Principal entrance lodge and gates, opening into the Histon Road.

B, Carriage road.

C, Chapel, standing on a platform, and ascended by a flight of steps.

D, Entrance from the New Huntingdon Road.

E, Reserve ground for spare earth, for bricks, stones, mortar, and various articles required in digging graves, building brick graves, vaults, &c.

F, Garden to the New Huntingdon Road Lodge. This lodge not being essential, no plan or estimate of it is given. It is thought that it might let sufficiently well as a cottage, to render it worth building on that account.

G G, Reserve ground fronting the Histon Road, which may be used as garden ground, added to the cemetery, or let for building on, as may ultimately be found most desirable.

H H, &c., Terrace walk surrounding the cemetery, and 3 ft. above the general level.

I I, &c., Holly hedges, forming the outer boundary, and also the separation fences between the cemetery and the reserve grounds.

K K, &c., Seats or benches, for the use of persons walking round the cemetery.

L L, &c., Borders for graves with monuments, or otherwise rendered ornamental.

M M, &c., Beds where the graves may either be plain or turf graves, graves with head-stones, or be rendered otherwise ornamental at pleasure.

N N, &c., Space along the centre of these beds, on which alone head-stones are to be placed on foundations of brickwork or masonry. Brick graves or catacombs may have the monuments, ledger-stones, or whatever is used as a covering or finish, resting on their side and end walls.

O O, &c., Single grass graves.

P P, &c., Brick graves occupying exactly the space of two single ones.

Q Q, &c., Vaults descended to by stairs occupying exactly the space of four single graves.

R R, &c., Tile drains for carrying off surface water, all terminating in the public drain in the New Huntingdon Road.

S S, &c., Cedars of Lebanon.

T T, &c., Deodar cedars.

U U, &c., Lines of Taurian pines.

V V, &c., Lines of Irish yews.

W, Workshed for masons, and repository for planks, wheelbarrows, earth-box, &c., not to be built till after the cemetery is in full operation.

X X, Histon Road.

Y, Y, Public drain along the New Huntingdon Road.

Z, Archway to be formed in the holly hedge as it grows ; or, if the funds permit, an architectural archway may be here formed at the time the hedge is planted.

No. 2. [omitted] is an elevation of that side of the cemetery which lies along the Histon Road.

No. 3. [omitted] is a cross section on the line CC DD, showing a rise of one foot in the centre of the compartment at a, in order to throw the water to the sides at b b.

No. 4. [omitted] is a longitudinal section on the line AA BB.

No. 5. [omitted]. Elevation of the south side of the cemetery fence, including the entrance from the New Huntingdon Road.

No. 6. [omitted] is a section across the lodge and the chapel in the direction of A B O Z.

No. 7. [omitted] is a section along the middle road, to show the fall of the ground from west to east, and the consequent power of surface drainage.

No. 8. [omitted]. A similar section to No. 6., but on a scale four times larger.

No. 9. Section across the terrace on the line II KK, to the same scale as Nos. 7. and 8.

No. 10. [*fig.* 34.] Section across the terrace on the line E E FF, in which *a* is the gravel walk; *b*, the grass walk, 5 ft. wide; *c*, the raised space for the head-stones between the two rows of graves; and *d*, the grass walks between the double beds of graves.

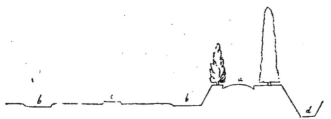

Fig. 34. *Section across the Terrace, and one of the Double Beds for Graves.*

No. 11. [*fig.* 35.] Section across the hedge and bank forming the boundary along the Histon Road, on the line G G H H.

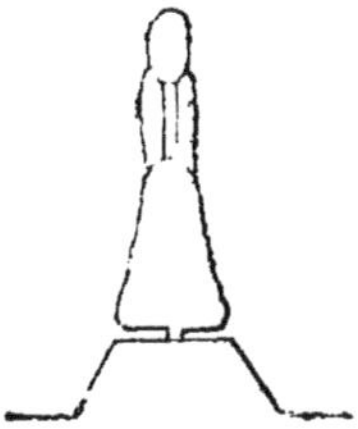

No. 12. [*fig.* 17. in p. 30.] A plan showing a vault, a brick grave, a common grave, and the mode of numbering the graves.

No. 13. [*fig.* 12. in p. 26.] Section through a brick or stone vault and a common grave.

No. 14. [See *fig.* 13. in p. 27.] Section through a brick or stone grave and a common grave.

No. 15. [*fig.* 40. in p. 60.] Isometrical view of the whole. [Though this view is on a very small scale, it is sufficient to indicate the style of the buildings, and the character of the trees: the two gardens in front are also shown, the reserve ground partly turned into a garden, the Huntingdon entrance lodge, and the mason's shed.]

Fig. 35. *Section across the Hedge and Bank forming the Boundary along the Histon Road.*

Designs for the main entrance lodge and chapel were given in by Mr. Lamb, both in the Gothic and Italian styles. The directors chose those in the former style, as will appear from a glance at the isometrical view; but, as the designs in the Italian style have great merit, we have had them engraved, partly on this account, and partly because the elevations suit the same plans as those which have been adopted.

Fig. 36. is a ground plan of the chapel, in which *a* is the porch; *b*, four sittings; *c*, four sittings; *d*, coffin; *e*, twenty-four sittings; *f*, twenty-four sittings; *g*, pulpit; *h*, registry; *i*, terrace.

Fig. 37. Elevation of the main entrance lodge and gates. The ground plan contains a porch, a room to be used as an office, living-room, kitchen, and back-kitchen, open court, and shed for implements, &c. The floor above contains three bed-rooms and closets.

Fig. 38. is a perspective view of the elevation, and *fig.* 39. a longitudinal section. [As stone is remarkably abundant at Cambridge, and very easily worked, Mr. Lamb has designed all the buildings with a view to

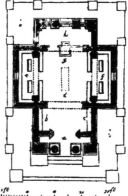

Fig. 36. *Ground Plan of the Chapel.*

Fig. 37. *Entrance Lodge in the Italian Style, designed for the Cambridge Cemetery.*

their being executed in that material. The coins are of hewn stone; the columns of stone hewn and rubbed; and the body of the walls of rubble, as indicated in *fig.* 38. The roof, in the Gothic designs, is steep, and will be covered by a peculiar description of ornamental flat tile, of which a figure

Fig. 38. *Chapel in the Italian Style, designed for the Cambridge Cemetery.*

will be hereafter given. In the Italian design, the roof is flat, to admit of being covered with tiles, bedded either in Roman cement, or in the new cement of Mr. Austin; or covered with asphalte. The platform on which the building stands will be surrounded by a kerb-stone, and the interior laid with asphalte.]

Fig. 39. *Longitudinal Section of the Chapel designed for the Cambridge Cemetery.*

Capacity of the Cemetery and the probable annual Expenses and Returns. — The number of spaces for graves in the double beds, each grave occupying a space of 8 ft. by 3 ft., exceeds 900; and the number of border graves exceeds 200. Under the surrounding terrace 200 more graves may be obtained, and from 800 to 1000 under the front reserved gardens, and the roads, walks, and paths; but, as it is not proposed to open the ground under the terrace, or in the reserved gardens, till the beds and borders are nearly full, nor to bury in the paths and roads, till the cemetery is about to be closed as such for ever, we shall take the number of spaces for graves immediately available as 1200. In order that these may return a suitable interest for the money expended, it is evident that more than one interment must be made in each grave, whether the grave be a private or family grave, or a common grave. Every common grave we shall suppose to be 24 ft. deep, which will give four interments, allowing 6 ft of soil over each. The family graves may either be made in the free soil, or they may be brick graves or vaults, and they may be made of any depth the proprietors may choose. The family graves made in the free soil we shall suppose to be of the same depth and capacity as the common graves; and the brick graves may either be of the same depth and capacity, or, by embedding the coffins in cement, or hermetically sealing each with a flag-stone, the capacity of each grave may be at least doubled.

Hence the 1200 graves may give at least 4800, or say 5000, interments; but, as the space allowed for each grave along the borders is more than double that allowed in the interior beds, 1000 interments at least may be added. Whether or not 5000 or 6000 interments will afford a sufficient return for the capital expended, and the necessary annual expense, will depend on the sum charged for each interment, and the number of interments made in a year.

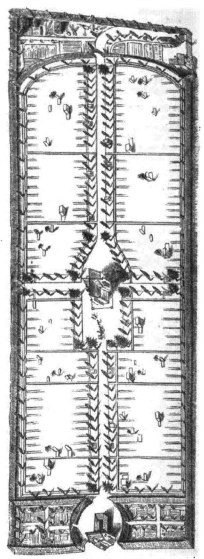

Fig. 40. *Isometrical View of the Cambridge Cemetery.*

	£	s.	d.
The Interest of the Money expended, allowing 1 per cent as a sinking fund to return the principal, we shall estimate at -	120	0	0
Salary of the Curator, and Annual Expenses chargeable to the Cemetery - - - - - -	180	0	0
Sum which the Cemetery ought to produce annually £300	0	0	

In order to show how this sum may be produced, we shall suppose that there are 200 interments made in a year, and that the sum charged for a single interment in a common grave is 1l. 10s. which is only 5s. per interment more than is charged in the Tower Hamlets Cemetery, where from twelve to fifteen bodies are placed in one grave; and this will give the sum required.

Taking the number of interments which will be afforded by the 1200 available graves at 6000, that number, at the rate of 200 interments in a year, will be exhausted in thirty years. The remainder of the ground will afford at least an equal number of interments, which might extend the use of the cemetery to sixty years.

To supply 200 deaths per annum, reckoning the deaths at 2 per cent of the living, a population of 20,000 is required, or about four fifths of the entire population of Cambridge.

As therefore it would be unreasonable to suppose that so large a proportion of the people of Cambridge would bury in one cemetery, we are forced to the conclusion, either that the price for each interment must be increased, or that the shareholders must be content with less interest than 6 per cent. Suppose we make the calculation at 3 per cent, that will reduce the annual charges to 240l., which will require only 160 interments at 30s. or 120 at 40s.

Whatever sum is fixed on as the regular price of an interment in a common grave will give the amount of the fee-simple of that grave; and thus, according to the calculation which we have made of six interments to a grave, the price of a family grave ought to be at least 6l.; except in the borders, where, from being a place of distinction, it ought to be higher. This price is exclusive of every other expense, and also of a fee which will require to be paid every time an interment takes place.

The price to be charged for a single interment in a common grave should be fixed on partly from the market price for such interments in the best part of the churchyards of Cambridge, but chiefly from the great superiority of the principle on which the cemetery is founded, viz. that no coffin, nor any part of its contents, when once interred, can ever by any possibility, humanly speaking, be again exposed to view.

If, on calculating on the capacity of this cemetery, we were to proceed on the supposition that the common graves might be opened for reinterments at the end of fourteen years, the result would be very different. But on opening at the end of fourteen years, or at any period whatever, it would be impossible to avoid exposing an immense number of human bones, which constitute one of the great nuisances in our present crowded churchyards.

The *Mode of conducting the Cemetery* is supposed to be as follows.

The choice of a situation for a grave may be made in any part of the beds in the interior, or of the borders along the main walks; but, till the cemetery is nearly full, it is not desirable that graves or vaults should be made under the surrounding terrace walk. When they are made there, the 5-feet grass path which separates the terrace from the beds may have one foot in width added to it from the terrace, and may be laid with gravel from the terrace walk, which may be covered with grass taken from the 5-feet walk referred to. The use of the terrace being thus changed from a walk to a platform for graves, it will of course no longer be walked upon.

As none of the coffins will ever be disturbed by the reopening of the graves, as in common burying-grounds, there is no objection to the use of leaden, zinc, or iron coffins.

The interments may be classed as those made in common or public earth graves, in private earth graves, in brick graves, in vaults having catacombs, and in border graves.

Every grave in the cemetery is supposed to be numbered, and this may be effected in the following manner.

1. *The Borders* may be considered as divided into spaces by the trees, and these spaces may be numbered in regular series, beginning with the right-hand border on entering the cemetery from the main lodge, and terminating with the last space on the left-hand border. A number-stone may be put in in every tenth or twentieth bed or space.

2. *The Beds in the Interior.* Beginning at one end (say with the first bed on the right hand on entering by the principal lodge), a stone with a smooth end, 6 or 8 inches by 2 ft., and at least 2 ft. in depth, is to be inserted in the ground at each end of the middle space of the beds, as at *a* and *b* in the plan No. 13. [*fig.* 17. in p. 30.]. On the stone *a* is to be cut the first number of the bed, I. ; and the last number, viz. L.: and on the stone *b* the last number of the one side, xxv., or one half of the graves in the bed; and the commencing number of the second side, xxvi. Thus, in every double bed throughout the cemetery, the stone at the north end will exhibit the number of the first and the last grave on that bed, and the stone at the opposite end the number of the last grave on one side, and of the first grave on the other. Should any two adjoining spaces adapted for earth graves be occupied as a brick grave, or any four spaces be required as a vault, in these cases the brick grave would be entered in the cemetery books under the head of two numbers, and the vault under the head of four numbers.

It is not necessary to begin by putting number-stones to all the beds; but when choice is made of a bed at a distance from one that has already been numbered, a calculation must be made of the numbers that would occupy the intervening beds, and the two number-stones placed accordingly at the ends of the bed in which the interment is to be made.

Every brick grave or vault must, therefore, necessarily be a multiple of a common grave, otherwise the numeration will be deranged.

When a bed is to be spoken of as a whole, it can be designated by the first or lowest number in the bed. Thus, supposing the beds to contain fifty graves each, we should have beds No. 1, 51, 101, 151, 201, and so on: or, in addition to the numbers, a letter may be placed on each stone, and we should, therefore, have beds A, B, C, &c.; and, after a single alphabet was exhausted, AA, BB, &c.

3. The *Graves or Vaults under the Terrace* will require to be similarly recorded to the border graves, a number being allowed for every space between the trees; or two numbers, if that should be thought necessary.

4. When the *Reserve Spaces*, a G [in *fig.* 33.], are added to the cemetery, the separation hedge will be removed; and the border, terrace, and beds extended; and, hence, the graves there will be recorded according to the modes already mentioned.

The *Earth Graves*, or graves of the simplest kind, are to be made within a space 8 ft. by 3 ft.; which, allowing a margin of 3 in. at the sides, and 1 ft. at the end next the 4-feet path, will give 7 ft. by 2 ft. 6 in., which is 6 in. longer than is allowed in the Kensal Green Cemetery, besides allowing a space of 1 ft. by 3 ft. for a foot-stone or number, if the purchaser of the grave should think either of these necessary. For a single interment it must be dug at least 6 ft. in depth; but, if it is intended to make two or more interments in it, it must be dug 6 ft. deeper for each additional interment; and, as the limit to depth need not be settled, any number of interments may be made in a common grave that the proprietors of the cemetery may fix on, or in a family grave that its owner may determine.

In order that the sides of the earth graves may remain firm, and not be pressed in by the loose earth of an adjoining grave, they should chiefly be formed alternately with firm ground which has not been buried in, or moved within six or seven years, or next to brick graves or vaults; but, should it become necessary to open one grave adjoining another which has been recently made or opened, recourse can always be had to planks or grave-boards [*figs.* 19. and 20.]; which, indeed, may be considered absolutely necessary as safeguards in the case of all graves dug above 6 ft. deep adjoining ground which has been moved.

Every reopening of a family grave for another interment should be charged according to the depth when it is an earth grave; say for a depth of 6 ft. 3s., 12 ft. 6s., and so on; and, when it is a brick grave or vault, according to the expense of removing the ledger or covering stone, &c.

In order to keep gravestones, monuments, and flowers planted over graves in order, the fee-simple of the estimated annual expense of doing so should be paid down by the proprietor of the grave, at the time of putting up the monument, or planting the plants [on the principle laid down in p. 39.].

Brick Graves. These require to have side walls of from 9 in. to 18 in. in width, according to their depth; and these walls should be curved, so as to resist the lateral pressure of the soil, as shown in plan No. 11. [*fig.* 17. in p. 30.] Brick graves, when of great depth, require to occupy the space of two earth graves, and hence the charges for them ought to be double that for earth graves, exclusive of the expense of building; but when two brick graves are built close together, each need not occupy more than an earth grave, because the party wall will save 14 in. in width, thus:—

	ft.	in.
Width of space allowed for two graves - - - -	8	0
Deduct three walls, each 14 in. thick - - - -	3	6
Leaving a clear space of 2 ft. 3 in. in width for each grave	4	6
Length of the ground, including half the width of the space on which the gravestones are to be placed - - - -	9	0
Deduct two 14-inch walls - - - - -	2	4
Leaving the clear length of the grave - - -	6	8

The ordinary dimensions of the coffins which are always kept ready made by undertakers are 6 ft. long by 20 in. wide, and 16 in. deep; the largest size is 7 ft. by 2 ft. 4 in., but coffins of this size are very seldom required.

If the walls were built in cement, then 9 in. in thickness would in many cases be sufficient; and this would add 10 in. to the length and 10 in. to the width of the clear space, leaving it 7 ft. 6 in. by 3 ft. 1 in.; which would afford ample room for any coffin whatever.

The ordinary mode of burying in brick graves is to let down the coffins one over another, without covering them with earth, but merely laying a flat stone or ledger over the mouth of the grave a few inches above the level of the ground's surface. In some cases a flag-stone, resting on ledges projecting from the side walls of the grave, is placed over each coffin as it is deposited; and when each flag-stone is securely cemented, so as effectually to prevent the escape of gas [see p. 37.], a greater number of interments may be made in one grave by this mode than by any other, and at the same time with perfect safety to the living.

The *Vaults* may be constructed in the usual manner, as shown in the general plan, No. 1. [*fig.* 33. in p. 56.] at q q, and in the enlarged plan No. 12. [*fig.* 17. in p. 30.], and section No. 13. [*fig.* 12. in p. 26.]. A vault of 12 ft. in depth, and 2 coffins in width, will contain 12 coffins.

The Books required for conducting this Cemetery are chiefly: 1. An order book; 2. A register or record of interments; and 3. A ledger of graves, an account being opened for each grave, as in the Kensal Green Cemetery. The other books required do not differ from those in common use. Forms of the order-book, register, and ledger will readily be obtained by applying to any of the London Cemetery Companies, or their stationers. [The essential forms, and the names of the stationers, have been given in p. 43.]

Specification of Work to be done on the Ground, including the Formation of the Roads, Walks, Drains, &c.

Form the surrounding terrace and hedge banks, agreeably to sections Nos. 8, 9, 10, and 11, of the best of the surface soil in the interior of the enclosure; the slopes to be built with a grassy surface, which will be obtained from the most grassy parts of the surface soil; and the whole to be rendered solid and compact, by ramming with cast-iron rammers as the soil is laid down. Form the walk on the surface agreeably to the sections.

Level and smooth the ground on each side of the terrace walk, in order to be sown afterwards with grass seeds, with the exception of a space 2 ft. in width, on which the holly hedge is to be planted. Plant the hollies in April at 1 ft. apart, and mulch them with littery stable dung.

Form the hedge banks as shown in the section No. 11., the sides to be of grassy sods, and the whole firmly rammed; the upper surface being left quite level, smooth, and clear of grass and weeds, for the space of 2 ft. in width along the centre, on which is to be planted the holly hedge. Insert the plants at a foot apart, as above directed.

In depositing the soil both in the terrace banks and the hedge banks, the greatest care must be taken to place nothing but good soil under the line on which the holly hedges are to be planted, in order by that good soil to promote their growth as much as possible.

Surround the whole of the outer holly hedge with a park paling 6 ft. high.

The terrace and banks being completed, level the whole of the interior surface, so as to have one general slope from the point A in section No 7. to the point D in plan No. 1., the fall being supposed to be about 2 ft., as shown in the section.

Form, at the same time, that part of the surface which is laid out in beds, as shown in plan No. 1. [*fig.* 33. in p. 56.], raised in the middle, and sloping towards the sides, as shown in the enlarged section No. 8.

Form the carriage-road of broken stones below, and gravel above, raised 3 in. higher at the centre than at the sides, as shown in the section.

Form the borders to the main roads with a concealed brick-edging next the walk, as shown in section at No. 8. *b b* [see *figs.* 30. and 31. in p. 38.], and place a mass of good soil where each tree is to be planted, raised in the centre 1 ft. above the general level, and forming a flattened cone 6 ft. in diameter. As temporary plants, and for immediate effect, introduce one spruce fir 6 or 8 feet high, if such plants can be got, between every two pines, and between every two Irish yews; the intention being that these spruce firs shall be removed as soon as the pines and yews attain the height of 6 ft.

Form the interior into beds 18 ft. wide, with a space 2 ft. wide, and 3 in. higher than the rest of the surface, along the centre of each bed; and form alleys between them 4 ft. in width, and a surrounding path 5 ft. wide, as shown in sections Nos. 8, 9, and 10.

Form the tile drains and the branch drains, as shown by the blue dotted lines in plan No. 1., and also in the sections Nos. 8. and 9., at *c c*.

Plant the pines, cedars, and yews, as shown in the plan No. 1., taking the greatest care to place nothing but good soil under and over the roots, and to unwind and stretch out the roots of all those that have grown in pots. Protect the cedars with circular constructions of wickerwork, and mulch the surface round all the trees, and along both sides of the hedge, with littery stable dung.

Sow the whole of the surface shown green in the plan No. 1. with perennial rye-grass and white clover, at the rate of 1 bushel of rye-grass, and 1 lb. of white clover to the acre.

Estimate of Expense.

		£	s.	d.
2400 cubic yards of Terrace-bank, at 6d.		60	0	0
300 cubic yards of Hedge-bank, at 6d.		7	10	0
480 lineal yards of Terrace-walk, 6 ft. wide, at 1s.		24	0	0
1761 square yards of Road, at 6d.		44	0	6
1813 feet of Park Paling, at 2s.		181	6	0
16,300 square yards of Surface, to be levelled and formed into Beds and Borders, at 2d.		135	16	8
2900 feet of Tile-drain, at 6d. per foot, including sink-stones or gratings, where necessary		72	10	0
2120 Hollies, at 10s. per hundred		10	12	0
94 *Pinus* taúrica, in pots, at 1s. each		4	14	0
20 *Pinus* austriaca, in pots, 1s. each		1	0	0
14 Cedars of Lebanon, in pots, 2s. 6d. each		1	15	0
4 Deodar cedars, in pots, 5s. each		1	0	0
76 Irish yews, at 1s. 6d. each		5	14	0
200 Spruce firs at 6d.		5	0	0
Rye-grass and Clover seeds		2	0	0
Planting the hollies and the above trees with the greatest possible care, including mulching with littery stable-dung		6	0	0
Allow for a temporary Gate to the entrance from the New Huntingdon Road, for unforeseen expenses, and for superintendence		37	1	10
		£600	0	0

Should it be desired to reduce the above estimate, the means are as follows : —

	£	s.	d.
Omit altogether the gravel walk on the terrace, and let it be a grass walk	24	0	0
Form only one half of the surface into beds, leaving the other half to be formed by the curator at convenience; deduct, say	60	0	0
Drain only one half instead of the whole ; deduct, say	50	0	0
Instead of pines, cedars, and yews, plant Scotch pines instead of the Taurian pines, and spruce firs instead of the Irish yews, to be clipped into cones and pyramids, by which a saving will be made of	12	0	0
	£146	0	0

Rules and Regulations for the Management of the Cemetery. — The general management being invested by the company in the directors, they have appointed a secretary and a curator, and the latter shall appoint graves-men and body-bearers.

Duty of the Secretary. — To keep the cemetery books, and communicate between the directors and the curator. To concoct with the directors a scale of prices for interments, as well as a set of rules and regulations, to be varied from time to time, as trial and convenience may justify.

Duties of the Curator. — To take his instructions from the secretary. To receive the burial fees, but no perquisites. To devote the whole of his time, or only a certain portion of it, to the cemetery, as may be agreed on ; the remainder of the time, if any, to be employed in the plots of ground which he is supposed to rent from the company for a few years at first, &c., as before explained.

F

To superintend the opening of every grave, and take special care that no coffin is placed nearer the surface than 6 ft.; and that, when more than one coffin is placed in a grave which is filled in with earth, there shall be at least 6 ft. between the coffins, unless the two coffins are deposited at the same time, in which case the one may be placed on the other.

To take special care that a protecting stone [before described, p. 37.] be placed in every grave filled in with earth, that is to be reopened, at the proper distance (6 ft.) above the last-deposited coffin; and to take care that, when a grave with a protecting stone is reopened, the protecting stone shall be taken out, and again replaced at the proper distance, or taken away altogether if the grave is to be finally closed.

To attend in like manner to the interments made by hermetically sealing up the separate coffins, whether by intervening flag-stones, or by embedding them in cement as before described.

To keep the whole of the grounds in the neatest possible manner; to watch the progress of the trees and hedge plants, and stake them when loosened by the wind, or water them when dry. To see that all the implements, planks, &c., are kept in order, and laid up in their proper places.

To pay the graves-men and body-bearers according to some scale, either of fees, or by the day, as may be arranged after ascertaining the rates of payment in the Cambridge churchyards.

[The remainder is omitted, as being either too local to be generally useful, or so general as to be included in Divisions II., III., and VII.]

VI. Design for a Cemetery on Hilly Ground.

The engraving *fig.* 41. is an isometrical view of a cemetery, supposed to be situated on hilly ground, the use of which is to show that an uneven surface may be thrown into beds and borders for graves on the same general principles as in a cemetery having a flat surface. In this design, there are supposed to be two chapels included in one building, and entered through porticoes on opposite sides. The surface of the ground is supposed to rise considerably from the entrance lodge to the chapel, and to fall from the chapel to the north-east on one side, and the south-west on the other. If the reader will trace with his eye the direction of the main road from the lodge at *a*, till it returns to *b*, he will find that a view of the entire cemetery may be obtained from it, without going over any part twice; but, as it might be desirable, on account of the view, to descend along the road which leads to the chapel, as well as ascend, the branch road *c* is laid out, in order that after having entered at *a*, and returned by *b*, *c* might be entered; and, after proceeding as far as *d*, the visitor might return by the chapel, and come out where he first entered at *a*.

It will be observed that there is a border for graves immediately within the boundary wall, which a walk separates from another border. There are also broad borders to all the carriage roads; and the interior of the compartments formed by these borders is laid out in beds 18 ft. wide, separated by grass paths 3 ft. in width, as in the design for the Cambridge Cemetery.

At the four principal angles of the boundary wall are enclosed yards, in each of which there is a shed for tools, planks, grave-boards, and other necessary implements and articles.

On the outside of the entrance gates are shown one of Shillibeer's two-horse hearses arriving, and one of his one-horse hearses screwed up, so as to resemble a common mourning-coach, returning. At *e*, in the interior, is shown a funeral with a truck-hearse; and, at *f*, one with a hand-bier.

The great extent of the borders in this cemetery renders it particularly eligible for being planted as an arboretum.

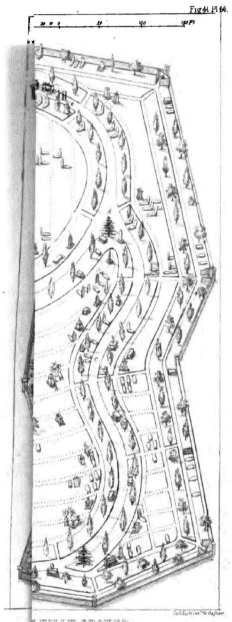

Fig 41 Pl 66.

HILLY GROUND.

VII. THE PRESENT STATE OF THE LONDON CEMETERIES, CONSIDERED
CHIEFLY AS CEMETERY GARDENS.

FROM the discussions in the preceding pages, the reader will have anti-
cipated much of what is contained in the present article, in which, indeed, we
shall chiefly recapitulate what has been stated before more in detail. Of the
eight cemeteries which have been formed within the last ten or twelve years
we shall not single out any one by name, but notice chiefly objections which
apply more or less to all of them.

We object to interments made in catacombs above ground, and to all interments in catacombs, however situated, in which the cell is not hermetically
sealed (instead of placing an open grating before it), the joints within being
previously covered with a thick coating of cement. In the last-formed
cemetery the catacombs are not yet built; but, in all the others, so great an
expense has been incurred in the catacomb department, that it must operate
as a serious drawback to the profits of the shareholders. As far as we have
been able to ascertain, interment in catacombs is on the decline, as well in the
London cemeteries as throughout the country; and in our opinion it would
be well to tax it in such a manner as to do away with it altogether.

The interments made in a single grave, whether common graves or family
graves, are too numerous in proportion to their depth. The distance at
which coffins are placed apart is seldom more than a foot, sometimes even
the coffin is laid bare, the evils resulting from which are: 1st, that when
an interval of two or three weeks or months elapses between the interments, the earth to be removed is so offensive as to reduce the grave-
digger to drinking, and shock the bystander by the smell of the earth
brought up to the surface; and 2d, that by placing so many bodies in one
grave the gases of decomposition must, when the grave is filled, unavoidably reach the surface and escape into the atmosphere. The remedy for
both evils is to place and retain a layer of earth of 6 ft. in thickness over each
coffin; because we consider it as proved by the general experience of grave-
diggers throughout Europe, that no evil results from the decomposition of a
body with this thickness of soil over it. The manner in which the soil
operates is this: having been recently moved and the parts separated, the in-
terstices are necessarily filled with atmospheric air; and as the gases are
generated in the coffin they expand, rise into the soil, and displace the atmospheric air, or mix with it. In this way this poisonous gas, instead of
rising into the air itself, only forces out of the soil a portion of atmospheric
air equal in bulk to what was generated in the coffin. When the layer of 6 ft.
of soil over the coffin is not next the surface, but perhaps many feet beneath
it, the mephitic air may still be assumed as driven into the soil immediately
above the coffin, so that in whatever position the layer of 6 ft. may be relatively
to the ground's surface, it may always be assumed, for all practical purposes,
to contain the greater part of the mephitic gases which escape from the
coffin. A certain proportion of these gases will also escape laterally, at least
in all soils through which water will filtrate freely, such as gravels and sands;
but scarcely any will pass laterally through clays, and none through the sides
of a brick grave, unless these are built chequered with openings, as has been
recommended in p. 27.

If the principle of having 6 ft. of soil over every coffin were adopted, the mode
suggested in p. 6. and p. 37., of having movable covering stones to be inserted
after every interment, as soon as 6 ft. of soil had been filled in and well
rammed, would be found a useful guide to the grave-digger, who would stop
whenever he came to the stone, and take it out and reserve it till after the interment was effected.

All the inconvenience that would result to cemetery companies by com-
pelling them to have 6 ft. of soil over every body would be merely that of
excavating to a greater depth; and, as we have said before (p. 37.), there can
be no reason why graves should not be as deep as wells.

F 2

In some of the London cemeteries the coffins in brick graves are placed one over another, and separated only by two iron bars, the ends of which are inserted in the side walls, the space between the last-inserted coffin and the ledger or covering stone at the surface of the ground being left open, and consequently the whole of the coffins in the grave communicating with its atmosphere. It is evident in this case that all the gases of decomposition will escape into the open space, and, by their expansive power, force out part of the mortar or cement under the covering stone; but, even if it should not do this, there must be great danger every time the covering stone is taken off, and more especially as it is necessary for a man to descend to the last-deposited coffin, in order to insert two bars over it to bear the coffin about to be deposited. The remedy for this evil is to cover every coffin with a flag-stone or slate, resting on ledges projecting from the side walls, and rendered perfectly airtight, by covering the joints with a coat of cement of several inches in thickness; or, in default of this mode, embedding and covering the coffin with cement in the manner already described in p. 38. By no other mode can so many coffins be got into one grave, and with perfect safety (if the operation of sealing up is effectually performed) to the grave-digger and the public.

We object to the system of laying out a cemetery in imaginary squares, for various reasons: it does not allow of an obvious order and arrangement of the graves; it does not admit of walking among them on a continuous path; it affords a very unsatisfactory mode of registration, since it depends on the accuracy of the mapping of the graves in the map book; it renders it next to impossible for the relations of the deceased to find out the grave without the aid of some person connected with the cemetery, unless the grave has a monument; it prevents an efficient system of grass paths from being formed; and it totally prevents the establishment of a permanent system of surface drainage by having the drains under the paths. It will not be denied, we think, that in all the London cemeteries there is an appearance of confusion in the placing of the graves and monuments; there is no obvious principle of order or arrangement; no apparent reason, except in the case of graves placed along the margins of the walks, why monuments should be situated where they are, rather than any where else; the greater part of them seem to be put down at random; and, in the crowded parts of the cemeteries, the time is fast advancing, when, as in the Père la Chaise Cemetery, no monument will be approachable, but by scrambling through between a number of other monuments. In our opinion all the cemeteries require reformation in this particular without a day's delay.

As the greater number of the London cemeteries are on a retentive clayey soil, a system of surface drainage is absolutely necessary to allow the grass to be walked on with comfort during the greater number of days in the year: but we pronounce it to be impossible to execute a system of surface drainage which shall be permanent, where the imaginary square system is adopted; because, in the carrying out of that system, every drain is liable to be interrupted by a grave either made or to be made.

The system of laying out the roads is objectionable in some of the cemeteries; because it is not continuous, but interrupted by branches claiming to be equally important with the main road. The purposes for which a road is made are, to allow of using, and also of displaying, the country, estate, or scenery, which it passes through; and hence in every country residence, garden, and cemetery, there ought to be one master road, by going along which the whole residence, garden, or cemetery, might be surveyed, without the attention being drawn off by side or branch roads of equal breadth and importance with the main road. The whole of some of the London cemeteries could not be seen without going over a considerable part of the roads twice, a circumstance which, with reference to use, is attended with loss of time, and, in regard to effect, with diminished force of expression. In some the main road, even when conducted near a straight wall, is made to serpentine in a manner which, being unaccounted for either by natural or artificial obstacles, such as inequalities of surface or trees, is quite ridiculous.

Day's Knightcliff "to the Quarm

There ought not to be a road or a walk in any cemetery, the direction of which is not accounted for, by the boundary fence, the inequalities of the surface of the ground, by cemetery buildings or tombs, or by the disposition of trees and shrubs.

In all the cemeteries there is a great want of gravel walks, which always afford fine opportunities for borders of graves, with intervening trees or shrubs. (See the plan *fig.* 41.)

The planting of all the cemeteries is, in our opinion, highly objectionable, for various reasons already given. It is too much in the style of a common pleasure-ground, both in regard to the disposition of the trees and shrubs, and the kinds planted. Belts and clumps can never be required in a cemetery either for shelter or shade; because nothing is so desirable as to have a free current of air, and admit the drying influence of the sun; and because it is impracticable to form graves in clumps and belts. By scattering the trees and shrubs singly, graves may be everywhere formed among them; and, by placing trees continuously along the roads and walks, shade is afforded to those who are on them, and a foreground is established to the scenery beyond. But the plantations in most of the London cemeteries appear to have been made without the guidance of any leading principle. In one we have a thick belt round the margin, occupying one of the finest situations which any cemetery affords for border graves; in another we have scarcely any trees along the walks, while we have a number grouped together along the centre of the compartments, where they lose much of their effect; in another we have clumps scattered throughout the grounds without any connexion among themselves, or with any thing around, destroying all breadth of effect, and producing neither character nor expression. In one cemetery there are so few trees that the whole of the ground and the buildings are seen at one glance as soon as we enter the cemetery gates; in another trees have been planted which it might have been foreseen would never thrive.

The kinds of trees we object to, because they are chiefly deciduous, and such as produce light-foliaged bulky heads, while fastigiate conical dark needle-leaved evergreens shade much less ground, produce much less litter when the leaves drop, and, by associations both ancient and modern, are peculiarly adapted for cemeteries.

The Norwood Cemetery Company has published an engraved view of its grounds, of which *fig.* 42. is a fac-simile; and, to show the different effect which dark-foliaged fastigiate and conical trees would have had, we have prepared *fig.* 43., in which it will be observed that the foreground and distance are the same as in *fig.* 42., and that we have confined our alteration to the middle of the picture. We do not say that every one who compares the two pictures will prefer ours to the other, because we do not allow every one to be a judge in this matter; but we do expect that all will acknowledge that there is a distinctive character in our view, and this is what we chiefly contend for. Every one knows that this character is aimed at in the new cemeteries formed on the Continent, and that the cemeteries of the ancients were characterised by the cypress. To show that this is also the case with the cemeteries of the East, we have given some views of Oriental cemeteries. See *figs.* 44, 45, and 46.

In several of the cemeteries pines and firs have been planted without properly preparing the soil, in consequence of which they have become stunted and diseased, so as to disfigure rather than to adorn. On the whole it appears to us, that almost all the cemeteries have not only been badly planted, as far as respects design and taste, but even in regard to execution, and in particular in the preparation of the soil.

The next point on which we would remark is the tombstones, many of which, we are happy to say, exhibit progressive improvement in taste. Many, at the same time, appear to have been placed on insufficient foundations, and are in consequence already leaning on one side. Every head-stone, monument, or tomb, to be secure and stand permanently upright, ought either to

be founded on ground which has not been moved, or built on piers or walls of
brick or stone brought up from the bottom of the grave.

The keeping of the new London Cemeteries is in general good, though it
is very far from what it might be. In some it is highly discreditable, sheep
being admitted to eat the grass, to save the expense of mowing, and the
young trees being in consequence cropped by the sheep, and poisoned by their
wool. In general a sufficient number of hands are not allowed for high keeping, and day-work is had recourse to, where letting by the job would be more
economical to the company, and satisfactory to the labourers. The mowing
of the grass, and the keeping of the roads, might be let by contract, and
the grass kept much shorter than it is at present; because the contractor
would soon discover that the shorter he kept the grass, the less mowing would
be requisite; whereas at present, by way of being economical, the grass is
allowed to attain several inches in length between each growing; or its roots
are nourished by the dung of the sheep that graze on it.

In conclusion, we have to observe that, in our visits to the different London
cemeteries, we have received the greatest civility and attention from the superintendants; and, at the respective offices in London, every information has
been afforded us by the secretaries with the greatest readiness and politeness.

As examples of the Eastern mode of planting cemeteries with cypress-like
trees, we shall give from the *Encyclopædia of Gardening*, by the permission
of the proprietors, engravings of the Turkish cemeteries at Pera and at Eyub,
both near Constantinople, and of the Cemetery of Hafiz in Persia. We
shall add two examples of Chinese cemeteries, in which are planted trees of
various forms and characters.

The *Turkish burying-grounds* " are generally favourite places of public resort.
The principal promenade in the evening, for the inhabitants of Pera, is a very
extensive cemetery, which slopes to the harbour, is planted with noble cypresses, and is thickly set in many places with Turkish monuments. The
opulent Turks have their graves railed in, and often a building over them, in
some of which lights are kept constantly burning. The inscription on the
head-stones is usually a sentence from the Koran, written in letters of gold.
The Turks, like the Welsh, adorn the graves of their friends by planting
flowers upon them, often the myrtle, but sometimes the amaryllis. (*fig.* 44.)

Fig. 44. *The Turkish Cemetery of Pera.*

Fig. 45. *Cemetery of Eyub, near Constantinople.*

(*Williams's Travels*, &c., p. 201.) The vicinity of a cemetery is not in the capital of Turkey judged by any means disagreeable, and no spot is so lively and well frequented as the Armenian and Frank burying-ground, at the outskirts of Pera, called Mnemata, or the tombs. It is shaded by a grove of mulberry trees, and is on the edge of some high ground, whence there is a magnificent view of the suburb of Scutari and a great portion of the Bosphorus. (*Hobhouse's Travels in Albania*, vol. ii. p. 837.) The cemetery of the Turks at Constantinople is the fashionable quarter of the Franks, and the pleasure-ground of the Levantines. ·It is the only place of recreation in Pera. (*Madden's Turkey*, p. 204.) The Turkish cemeteries are generally out of the city, on rising ground, planted with cedars, cypresses, and odoriferous shrubs, whose deep verdure and graceful forms bending in every breeze give a melancholy beauty to the place, and excite sentiments very congenial to its destination. (*Eustace's Travels*, &c., p. 45.) The Cemetery of Eyub, near Constantinople, is crowded with graves ; those which contain males have generally a turban at the head of the flat tombstone, and nearly all have plants growing from the centre of the stones. (*fig.* 45.) The magnificent burial-ground of Scutari extends for miles in length, and among high and turbaned tombstones, with gold-lettered inscriptions, mournful cypresses are thickly planted. (*Alexander's Travels from India*, p. 240.) There is a very large burying-ground, shaded by an extensive forest of cypresses at Bournabat, a village of elegant country houses built in the European fashion, belonging to the merchants of Smyrna. (*Hobhouse's Travels in Albania*, vol. i. p. 640.)" (*Encyc. of Gard.* ed. 1834, p. 300.)

Persian Cemeteries.—" There are said to be 1001 mausoleums at Shiraz; those of Chodsja Hafiz and Saadi Sjeraft (both celebrated poets) are the most beautiful. The burial-place of the first (*fig.* 46.) is situated at Muselli, an estate pos-

Fig. 46.   *The Cemetery of Hafiz.*

sessed by Hafiz, who, it is remarked, was not buried by the nation, but had the expenses of his funeral defrayed out of his own private fortune. His cemetery is square and spacious, shaded by poplars (a rare tree in Persia), and having a lion carved in stone on each side of the entrance. The wall is built of brick, and coincides in direction with the cypress trees of the surrounding garden. The ground is strewed with tombstones, and divers sepulchral memorials of those who had desired to be buried under the guardian influence of the poet. Entering from the neighbouring garden, which was bequeathed to the cemetery, the keeper conducts a stranger into the place of the sepulchre. This is surrounded by lattice-work, and contains three tumuli besides the grave of the poet ; one encloses the remains of a secular prince, and the other two illus-

Fig. 47. *The Cemetery of he Vale of Tombs, in China.*

trious individuals, who, when living, were disciples of Hafiz. In the place of the sepulchre sits a priest, who repeats verses from the Koran in praise of the illustrious dead, and enumerates their virtues; when he has finished, another, and afterwards a third, in the open burying-place, take up the same theme; so that the lamentations are incessant. The tombs are placed in a row; and the form of all of them is the same. They are about the size of a sarcophagus, and have each a large stone, about a man's height, at both ends. The stone of which they are made is of a common kind, and unpolished. On each side are sculptured verses from the Koran, and on the stones placed at the feet are elegant epitaphs. Hafiz died A. D. 1340. (*Kæmpfer's Amœn. Exot.*, &c. fas. ii. rel. vi. p. 367.) " (*Encyc. of Gard.*, ed. 1834, p. 371.)

In the *Chinese cemeteries*, trees of various descriptions are introduced, and the tombs are of very remarkable forms. "About Canton and Macao the high lands are very little cultivated, being generally set apart for burying the dead; those about Canton are entirely occupied as cemeteries, the low grounds, which can be covered with water, being the only ones which will produce rice. (*Dobell's Travels*, &c., vol. ii. p. 191.) Sometimes, however, the Chinese choose a valley for a cemetery, as that of the Vale of Tombs near the lake See Hoo. (*fig.* 47.) The Chinese burying-place near the Yellow River (*fig.* 48.) is a specimen of a cemetery on high ground." (*Encyc. of Gard.*, ed. 1834, p. 338.)

VIII. COUNTRY CHURCHYARDS; THEIR PRESENT STATE, AND MEANS OF IMPROVEMENT.

WHAT traveller or tourist is there that does not make the churchyard of the village one of the first scenes which he visits; and does not receive from it his first impressions of the clergyman, the people, and consequently of the general character of the inhabitants? If such be the effect of a glance at the churchyard on the passing stranger, what must it be on those to whom its image is constantly present, and by whom it is associated with all that is reverential in feeling? To the local resident poor, uncultivated by reading, the churchyard is their book of history, their biography, their instructor in architecture and sculpture, their model of taste, and an important source of moral improvement. Much, therefore, must depend on the manner in which churchyards are laid out, and the state in which they are kept. A country labourer may not have the habits of attention and observation sufficiently developed to derive improvement from the style or taste displayed in the architecture of the church; but there is not one countryman that does not understand the difference between slovenliness and neatness, between taste and no taste, when applied to walks, grass ground, and gardens. All of them, therefore, may have their taste for neatness and order improved, or their habits of slovenliness confirmed, by the weekly impressions made on them while passing through the churchyard to the church; and, while their habits of life are thus improved or deteriorated, their hearts are softened and ameliorated, or hardened and diseased, by viewing the graves or monuments of their friends and relations neatly kept or utterly neglected, and reflecting that they also must soon take their place among them and be neglected in their turn. The intellectual and moral influence which churchyards are calculated to have on the rural population will not, we think, be disputed. Every person, indeed, who has been brought up in the country must feel this. How far then does the appearance of our churchyards answer the important educational ends which they are calculated to effect? It will not be denied, we think, that very few of them are kept in a manner to answer the end proposed, and that a very great many are in a state of deplorable neglect. In many cases we find the lawn and pleasure-ground of the clergyman displaying the greatest order and neatness, while his churchyard has no care bestowed on it; or is perhaps disfigured by the state of the surface, or the want of repair of the surrounding

Fig. 48. *Chinese Cemetery, near the Yellow River.*

fence. But the wretched state of the churchyards has been, perhaps, sufficiently dwelt on both in this and in other publications, and we shall therefore
confine ourselves to pointing out the causes of their present state separately,
and suggesting the modes by which these causes may be removed.

Want of Order. — The cause of this evil in churchyards is, that they have
not been originally laid out on any regular or systematic plan. Not only is
there no gravel or paved walk round the churchyard in many cases, but in
some there is nothing more than a footpath from the yard-gate to the door of
the church. In many churchyards it is too late to remedy this evil in an
effectual manner, but we have never seen one in which the evil might not be
removed to a considerable extent, without that which at first sight seems
absolutely necessary, levelling the turf mounds over the graves. This is to
be avoided by bringing in soil sufficient to raise the space between the grave
mounds to a level or even surface, varying the direction of the walk, and
expanding, contracting, branching, divaricating, and inosculating it, so as never
to disturb a gravestone or any description of stone monument. The idea of
such a walk is given in the sketch, *fig.* 49., in which it is indicated by the
lines *a a ;* and the effect, after the trees have been planted, is shown in
fig. 50., p. 79. In this figure is also exhibited an addition made to the
old ground, laid out in a regular manner. In the interior of the ground,
grass paths ought to be formed to the graves to which there is not
direct access from the gravel walks to enable spectators to view the
tombs without the appearance of treading on graves. The walk would
seldom require to be raised more than 18 in., and it ought to have a
grass margin on each side of the same height as the gravel, of at least 2 ft.
in width. Where a flat gravestone was to be crossed over, it might be raised
up to the proper level ; some other descriptions of stone might be sunk ; and,
in cases of great difficulty, a gravestone might be crossed by a bridge
composed of a flag-stone of the width of the walk, supported on two piers ;
but such would be of rare occurrence. When they did happen, advantage
might be taken of the circumstance to make a raised seat, which would give a
bird's-eye view of part of the churchyard ; or a handsome open structure
might be erected in harmony with the scene, and suitable for taking shelter in,
or for strangers to witness the performance of a funeral. We never saw a
case where a bridge would be necessary ; but we suppose one, in order to
show the resources of this mode of improvement, and, if possible, to convince
our readers that there is not a churchyard in the country that might not
be surrounded with a gravel walk, leaving a border between it and the wall ;
provided the clergyman and the other parties whose duty it is were to set
earnestly about it. Cross green paths might be formed 2 or 3 feet in width,
and they may be even more irregular than the surrounding gravel paths.

Another source of disorder and also of waste ground in churchyards is, that
no systematic plan has been laid down and followed in allotting the graves.
The graves are put down at random, leaving spaces between them either too
narrow for graves, or of shapes so irregular that they cannot be filled up, so
that in many churchyards a large proportion of the ground is thus rendered
useless. It most frequently happens that the places are chosen by the deceased during his lifetime, or by his friends afterwards ; and, some persons
having partialities for particular parts of the ground, especially high and dry
parts, the graves are crowded together in such parts, while in others there are
comparatively few. Many persons have an objection to being buried on the
north side of a church, probably from the comparative dampness and gloom-
iness of that side as compared with the south side. Hence we often see the
south side of a churchyard crowded, while the north side is comparatively
without graves. The radical cause of this evil is the placing of the church in
the direction of east and west, in consequence of which a considerable portion
of the churchyard is in shade during the whole of the winter, and the greater
portion of every day throughout the year, whereas, had the church been placed
in the direction of S. W. and N. E., or of N. W. and S. E., the sun would

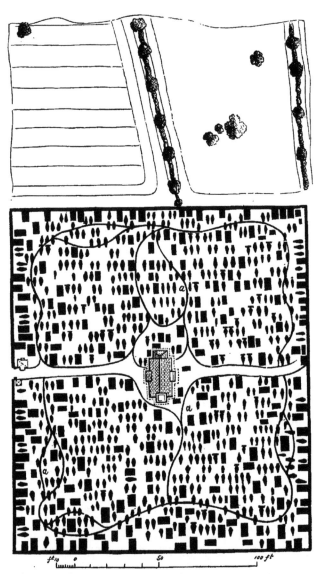

Fig. 49·*A Churchyard no longer used for burying in, with Lines showing the Direction in which Walks may be made, without removing any Head-stones or other Monuments.*

have shone on every side wall of the church, and consequently on the ground on every side of it, every day in the year on which he appeared, and hence the churchyard would have been every where equally dry and inviting.

Every grave is a parallelogram in plan, and for practical purposes these parallelograms may be considered as all of the same length and breadth. It is obvious, therefore, that, to get as many of these parallelograms as possible into a limited space, they ought to be placed in rows side by side. Supposing the walks to be bordered with spaces sufficient for a single or a double row of graves, as we have recommended for adoption in laying out cemeteries, then the interior should be laid out in double beds, in the manner which we have already described as calculated to make the most of any given space (see *fig.* 17. in p. 30.). The beds need not in every case be regularly formed like the beds of a garden; but, whether this is done or not, they should be marked off with sunk stones at the angles and at each end of the central space on which the gravestones are to be placed, in order that the true position and dimensions of the beds may never be doubtful, and may never undergo any change through the carelessness of the grave-digger. An arrangement of this kind would not hinder parties from choosing graves in any part of the ground as at present; while it would prevent the great waste of surface that now takes place, and obviate the necessity of ever walking over graves, either to look at gravestones, or for the performance of funerals. In whatever manner a churchyard is arranged, leaving the choice of ground free is decidedly advantageous, both in point of utility and appearance. In point of utility, it is better that the whole of the churchyard should be open to the choice of the parishioners, and thus the graves scattered over it, and consequently the water and the gases of decomposition diffused over a large underground space, and thus diluted and weakened, than that they should be concentrated in one spot, and their bad effects aggravated; and it is more picturesque to have the graves and tombstones scattered here and there over the whole ground, than to have one part closely filled with graves and tombstones, and all the remainder without any.

Want of Perpendicularity in the Monuments and Gravestones. — From not placing the head-stones and other monuments on secure foundations, they are, in almost every churchyard, seen leaning in all directions; and, when composed of more than one stone, the joints are cracked, and the whole threatens to fall in pieces. This is an evil which admits of a remedy both with a view to the past and the future, without the slightest degree of desecration, though the expense of resetting monuments in a churchyard crowded with them might be found inconvenient. With respect to monuments to be erected in future, it will be sufficient for the manager of the burying-ground to insist on the monuments being placed on solid ground, or on a sure foundation of masonry or brickwork, as deep as the grave, as already indicated with reference to cemeteries in p. 28.

The slovenly State of the Grass and Herbage is the next evil which we shall notice. The surface of most graveyards is covered with long grass and rank weeds; and, though this is apparently a less evil than those which have been mentioned, it is in reality a greater one, because its removal requires little or no outlay. Hence it bears on the face of it the most unequivocal marks of negligence and slovenliness, instead of setting an example of neatness, care, and respect. In crowded churchyards the soil, from the water of decomposition, is necessarily rendered much damper than in ordinary ground, and it is proportionately richer. Hence the extraordinary vigour of the grass, docks, nettles, thistles, brambles, &c., and other large plants, which it produces; and the annual decay of this vegetation, saturated with the gases which emanate from the masses of putrefaction below, must be productive of malaria, more or less according to circumstances. The unoccupied corners and those parts of churchyards most distant from the eye, or from their dampness or other causes least frequented, are particularly obnoxious in these respects; and hence one of the great advantages that would result from having every churchyard surrounded by a

Fig. 50. *A Churchyard no longer used for burying in, planted as a Cemetery Garden, and a new Piece of Ground added and laid out.*

gravel walk, with a border between that walk and the boundary fence. The next remedy for the evil of rank grass and weeds is, to carry off as much as possible of the surface water. This may be effected by forming the surface in such a manner as to favour the descent of the water which falls on it to gratings connected with drains, or to surface gutters, which shall carry the water out of the churchyard. The tile-draining system may in many cases be applied under the green paths and gravel walks; and, where there are springs, it is almost needless to state that deep underground drains should be made under the main walk. By thus effectually drying the surface, the grass will grow much less luxuriantly and be easier kept under by mowing, clipping, or shearing, than when left in the moist state now so general in churchyards.

The grass should be kept constantly very closely cropped, by the scythe, the hedge-shears, the sheep-shears, or the hook. In some churchyards the grave mounds are so clumsily made, and laid up in such rough lumps, that it is difficult to mow the grass which grows on them, and in this case the reaping-hook or shears ought to be used. In most parishes there are aged persons, male or female, who would gladly undertake this work; and a very good mode of getting it executed would be to divide the ground into portions, and let out the keeping of each portion to persons whose pride it would be to keep their charge in as high order as possible. By this means some interest would be given to what is now a heartless kind of labour, and the competition would insure efficiency. The mowers or clippers would soon discover that the shorter they kept the grass the less it would grow, and the less would be their labour. Clipping, however, would only be necessary occasionally; for, wherever the grave mounds are neatly formed and smooth on the surface, they may always be mown with the scythe, which is much better than cropping with the reaping-hook, the mouth of the operator in the former case being so much farther from the soil and its exhalations.

In some churchyards sheep are admitted with a view to crop the grass, which they do effectually when in sufficient numbers, and when aided by the spud to eradicate broad-leaved coarse-looking plants which sheep will not eat; but, as in the case of sheep being admitted into churchyards, it is impossible for any person to ornament a grave with shrubs or flowers, and, as the poor have frequently no other means of showing their respect for the dead, we would prohibit the introduction of sheep into churchyards except where a portion of the ground had not been buried in, and that portion we would separate from the rest by a fence of wire hurdles, and keep it short by sheep to save the expense of mowing.

Desecration. — Not only sheep, but cows, horses, and swine, are admitted to graze the churchyards in some places; and, in the intellectual town of Haddington, the minister of the cathedral burial-ground not only allowed his sheep to graze in the churchyard, but carted in turnips to them there, and fattened them for the butcher. In many parts of the country, particularly in Scotland, the boundary fences of churchyards are in such a state that swine and dogs have free access to them, and the former are allowed to tear up the grave mounds, and even to burrow into the graves. Where houses are built on the margins of churchyards, as they frequently are in small country towns*, the waste water and other refuse from the house are thrown from the windows among the graves; and, shocking as it may be to relate, in some parts of

---

* The churchyard of Carlow is in the centre of the town, and so closely surrounded by tenements, that in some places the wall of the dwelling-house, often loosely built, alone divides the bed of the occupant from the (perhaps newly tenanted) grave; this, although rendering the air sufficiently insalubrious, is not the only cause of impurity, as the annual decay of noxious plants, luxuriant in a place so rank and untrodden as our graveyards, universally neglected, are, where vegetable decomposition above ground is as much a consequence as animal decay beneath, injures most seriously the surrounding atmosphere. (*Health of Towns*, p. 197.)

Scotland, as there are no privies, either public or private, for the common people, the churchyard is the place of common resort. That we may not be accused of exaggeration, we shall refer to the burying-ground of the established church in Stranraer, as it was in 1841. A more hideous spectacle of the kind we never saw; but it is doubtless in a better state now, because the Earl of Stair, with his accustomed liberality and public spirit, has since presented the town with a piece of ground for a general cemetery; and is about to erect another structure for public convenience equally necessary. Bad as the churchyards are in England, they are much worse in Scotland; for there the extra-professional pursuits of the clergy are more frequently directed to farming than to matters of taste.

The charnel-house, or bone-house, needs only to be mentioned to excite disapprobation; for, if churchyards were properly managed, no fragment of a coffin or human bone would ever be disinterred or seen by the living. There are two modes of effectually attaining this object: the first is by never placing more than one coffin in a grave; or, if more are placed in it, either interring them at the same time, or placing the first coffin so deep as to admit of a stratum of 6 ft. in thickness between it and the second coffin; the last-deposited coffin, in either case, being not less than 6 ft. under the surface of the ground: and the second mode is by placing on the last-deposited coffin a guard, or following stone, as already suggested in p. 6.

Allowing public passages to be made through churchyards is a common source of desecration; but, as these passages are generally conducive to the convenience of the living, they cannot be dispensed with; therefore, to prevent desecration, they ought to be fenced off on each side.

No kind of games ought ever to be allowed in churchyards, nor dogs admitted if possible, nor smoking, nor in short any thing that would indicate a want of reverence for the dead.

By far the greatest desecration which takes place in churchyards results from their crowded state, in consequence of which a grave cannot be dug without disinterring coffins and bones. There is no remedy for this evil but the enlargement of churchyards, which is required in every part of the country, and should be effected from time to time, according to some principle or rule derived from the population returns, and the average annual burials.

Want of Trees and Shrubs.— We have often stated it as our opinion, that country churchyards might be greatly increased in interest, by being carefully and systematically laid out, and moderately planted with proper kinds of trees and shrubs. These being named would create a great interest in them, and the whole of the ground being very neatly kept would diffuse a taste for order and neatness among the parishioners. This improvement is beginning to take place in various parts of England, though but rarely in Scotland, where flowers are considered light and gaudy, and where the great object to be attained is to subject the mind to the bondage of fear, by continually reminding the spectator that " he also must die*, and that death is only the

---

*   " From whence you come, or whosoe'er you be,
          Remember, mortal man, that thou must dee."
                    Lines on the Sundial in the Garden at Brougham Castle.

          " Alas! the little day of life
            Is shorter than a span,
          Yet black with many hidden ills
            To miserable man."
                    *Lines on a common Tombstone in Kirkmichael
                              Churchyard, Wigtonshire,*

one of the most gloomy scenes of the kind in the West of Scotland: it contains "the corpse of Gilbert McAdam, who was shot by the Laird of Cullean and Ballochmill, for his adherence to the word of the Lord, and the work of Reformation, in July, 1682."

G

door to everlasting life." (*Gard. Mag.*, 1842, p. 617.) Far be it from us to dispute the justness of this taste, relative to those who hold particular opinions ; for our own part we prefer the decorated churchyard, but we would no more decorate it in the manner of a flower-garden, than we would dress a mourner in the same manner as a bride or a bridegroom.

We shall show at the end of this article the mode in which we think trees and shrubs ought to be introduced in new churchyards, and for those already long occupied we shall give a few general directions.

Suppose a walk to be formed immediately within the boundary, leaving a border, regular or irregular in width, as the state of the graves and gravestones may admit, then a few trees may be scattered along each side of it, singly, so as to form a running foreground to the interior of the churchyard, and to break the formality of the boundary fence. As the walk may be supposed to be very irregular in direction and in width, the distance between the trees should be irregular also ; and occasionally two trees, or a tree and a shrub, or a tree and a honeysuckle or other climber, may be planted in one hole. In the interior of the compartments, where the ground is already so completely filled up that there is no chance of any other graves being formed, a few trees and shrubs may be so placed as to group with some of the more conspicuous of the gravestones, and along the cross green paths one or two trees may be planted at the angles or turns of the walk, by way of accounting for these turns. But, whether in planting in the interior or along the green paths, care must be taken to preserve lengthened glades or vistas to be seen from the main gravel walks. These vistas should not extend from one boundary wall to the other, so as to show everywhere the length and breadth of the ground, but should rather terminate in an apparent mass of trees or bushes, or in a view of the church, so as to leave abundant exercise for the imagination. Along the boundary fence, if a wall, which is generally the case, we would plant creepers, evergreen and deciduous, but chiefly the different kinds of ivy, as being evergreen, and Virginian creeper, *Rhús radícans*, &c., which, like the ivy, adhere to the wall, and consequently require little care. Where the expense of training was not an object, we would introduce roses, magnolias, laurustinus, *Cydònia japónica*, Chimonánthus frágrans, and various other shrubs, deciduous and evergreen, adapted for walls. Where the fence was a thorn hedge, we would measure it into regular spaces, so as to train up shoots from the top of the hedge at regular distances, in order to form artificial heads, round or square, at such places; or we would train up a single stem, and graft on each a different kind of thorn, or other rosaceous tree or shrub. On a holly hedge we would graft variegated hollies, and on a yew hedge the golden yew, which makes such a splendid appearance grafted on the common yew at Elvaston Castle. If we had to plant a holly hedge or a yew hedge round a churchyard, we would form piers or pilasters at regular distances in both, which should be carried up higher than the hedge, and terminate in balls. The piers, in the one case, should be variegated hollies, and in the other variegated yews. If we had to plant a hawthorn hedge, we would form the piers of green holly.

Where a churchyard, though long in use, was not yet filled up, we should take care to plant no trees and shrubs, the permanent effect of which was essential, in situations where they would have to be removed when a grave was dug. We should place them chiefly along the walks, at such distances as to leave room for one or two graves between every two trees.

In few or no cases would we plant large-growing deciduous timber trees in churchyards, such as the oak, ash, elm, beech, white or black Italian poplar, Huntingdon willow, alder, sycamore, &c.; because, from the size they attain, they would interfere with the effect of the church and of the monuments. We should confine ourselves to low-growing trees, and, where only a few could be planted, to evergreens of fastigiate forms.

Want of Monuments.—Monuments form a great source of beauty and interest in churchyards, and it is gratifying to observe, in the neighbourhood of the metropolis and of other large towns, that as they increase in number they are improving in taste. Every encouragement, we think, ought to be given to their introduction in village churchyards, on account of the effect which they cannot fail to have on the taste of the inhabitants, and more particularly on all those connected with the building arts, such as carpenters, masons, brick-layers, &c. It seems unfortunate that the revenues of the clergy are made to depend partly on the permission granted to put up monuments, and thus a man is taxed for his reverential feeling, and for erecting an instructive and beautiful object, which he would, probably, have rendered more beautiful still by the amount of fees paid to the clergyman.* A better mode would be to encourage the erection of monuments, by giving the ground as a present on condition of the monument being proportionately handsome. We would en-courage every kind of monument, from the most frail to the most permanent, as tending to cultivate reverential feelings and improve the taste ; and we would encourage the naming of all the trees and shrubs, as tending to excite curiosity and intellectual exercise.

The churchyard at St. Michael's, at Dumfries, is perhaps the most remark-able in Britain, on account of the number and good taste of its tombstones. The appearance of these at a distance is singularly grand and picturesque.

Erecting tombstones at Dumfries is quite a mania among the middle classes, which has been brought about chiefly by the cheap and easily wrought red freestone, and the talents of the late mason and sculptor, Mr. Alexander Crombie. The cheapness of these tombstones, compared with the price of similar erections about London, is so great, that we are per-suaded they might form a profitable article of commerce for the metropolitan cemeteries. To enable those concerned to judge how far this may be the case, we give, through the kind-ness of Walter Newall, Esq., architect, Dum-fries, figures from the designs of two monu-ments, not long since erected at the heads of the graves of two nurserymen, Messrs. Hood, father and son ; that of the father (*fig.* 51.) cost 38*l.*, and that of the son, William (*fig.*52.), 25*l.* The carriage to London, by Whitehaven, we are informed, would not amount to 5*l.* for each of these monuments. (*Gard. Mag.* for 1831, p. 529.)

Fig. 51. *Monument to Mr. Hood, sen., in Dumfries Churchyard.*

The improvement of the church is chiefly the business of the architect ; but the gardener may in various cases cooperate with him, or even supersede his exertions. It is desirable in all cases that a church, like every other large building, should stand on a level terrace or platform ; but, as most old churches are buried or earthed up by graves in such a manner as that the ground is higher without than it is within the church, this platform

---

* The fees for permission to erect the simplest and cheapest of all stone memorials placed by graves, a head and foot stone, vary in the London church-yards from 2*l.* 2*s.* to 6*l.* 6*s.* ; for permission to place a flat stone over a grave, from 4*l.* 4*s.* to 12*l.* 12*s.* ; and the price for more ambitious monuments varies from 5*l.* 5*s.* to 105*l.* For the right to erect " stones and vaults" in the Hackney churchyard, though it was greatly enlarged some years ago, from three to forty guineas have been paid. (*Claims of the Clergy*, p. 25.)— See *An Examination of Mr. Mackinnon's Bill*, p. 117. ; *Cauch's Funeral Guide* ; and *Health of Towns*, &c.

or terrace can seldom or never be formed, without incurring a degree of de-
sceration that would be unjustifiable. Still, in a m jority of cases, a space
round the walls of the church might be
cleared away to the width of 2 or 3 feet,
and of such a depth as to be at least 6 in.
below the level of the floor of the church.
This space ought to be carried completely round the church on a perfect
level, or with merely a very gentle inclination from the middle of the building
to each end, for the purpose of carrying
off surface water. Under this space
there should be a tile-drain within a few
inches of the surface to carry off rain
water, or a deep drain if the subsoil requires it. The ground round this narrow
level platform should either be supported
by brickwork or sloped down with turf,
according as the graves are nearer or
more distant; and both the width of the
platform and the angle of the slope may
be irregular, if circumstances should
require it. The grand essential object is
to get a level base for the walls to rise
from, the surface of which shall be 6 in.
lower than the surface of the floor of
the church. The walk to the church
door will require to descend to this platform by an inclined plane, and there will
of course be one step of ascent to the
porch of the church.

Fig. 52. *Monument to Mr. Hood, jun., in Dumfries Churchyard.*

It is unnecessary to state that the walls and roof of the church should be
kept in good repair, and that in many cases ivy and the Virginian creeper
might be planted against it ; but we cannot recommend roses and other plants
requiring dug soil at the roots, on account of the injury they would do to the
platform, and the expense that would be incurred in training. It is always
much better not to attempt to do more than can be done well.

Perhaps it would greatly facilitate the improvement of churchyards, the
erection of handsome monuments, and the economy of burial to the poor, if
the fees of the clergymen from the church and churchyard were commuted
for a fixed sum to be raised annually by a general rate on the parish ; but this
is a part of the subject not within our province.

Laying out and planting a new Churchyard. — Churchyards, like every other
description of yard or garden, ought to be laid out, planted, and managed,
with reference to their use; and the scenery produced should, in its expression and general effect, indicate what that use is, or, at all events, be in
accordance with it. A churchyard ought not to be laid out so as to be mistaken for a pleasure-ground, a shrubbery, or a flower-garden ; neither, on the
other hand, ought it to be left in a state of utter neglect, without regular
walks, and overgrown with weeds and rank grass. The uses of the churchyard
are, as a place of burial, as an enclosure and protection to the church, as a
place sacred to the memory of the dead, as a place of weekly meeting for
solemn purposes, and as an approach to the church. All its uses are of a
serious and important nature, and it is therefore to be considered as a grave
and solemn scene. Now, the question to be solved in laying out a churchyard is, what trees, what treatment of the surface of the ground, the grass,
walks, graves, gravestones, and tombs, will be most conducive to solemnity of
effect. The expression of the exterior of the church is grave and solemn, by
its long-established association with our religious feelings ; and it therefore

may be considered as having a similar influence on the scenery around. The feeling of solemnity is one more of a passive, than of an active, nature: it neither needs much cultivation, nor much exercise of the imagination. Strong contrasts are not required to excite this feeling, nor varied and intricate scenery to prolong it. On the contrary, this will be more decidedly the effect of sameness of form and colour, and their repetition. The solemnity of a churchyard has its origin in the uses of the place, and will only be interfered with or weakened by the introduction of such objects as interfere with these uses. Simplicity, therefore, ought to be a governing principle in every thing relating to churchyards; and, as the appearance of neglect or slovenliness always implies want of respect, order and neatness are next in importance. By order, we mean the avoiding of every thing like confusion in the placing of the graves, tombs, and gravestones, and the disposition of the trees: and by neatness, we allude more particularly to keeping the turf short and smooth; the walks firm, even, and free from weeds; the gravestones upright; and the tombs in a state of repair.

The character of a churchyard, as a place of burial, will always be more or less influenced by the character and manners of the people to whom it belongs. In Britain, churchyards have much less care bestowed upon them than in Central Germany, and in some parts of France, Belgium, and Holland. The sentiment of respect to the memory of deceased persons in these countries is shown by planting flowers over the graves, and frequently cultivating them there for some years afterwards. Among the Moravians, on the Continent, the churchyard is sometimes laid out in compartments, with walks between, like a garden; and the compartments are kept dug, and planted with flowers and ornamental plants. Two powerful arguments are advanced in favour of this practice: the first is, that a churchyard so managed costs less than if it were in turf, and kept short by mowing; the second, that the surface of the ground has always the same appearance, there being no gravestones or tombs, and the ground being left level, and replanted with the plants which stood on it before, after every interment; these having been carefully taken up, and placed on one side, before the grave was dug. It is evident that this mode of treating a churchyard, however consonant it may be to the ideas of those who adopt it, is not in accordance with our desiderata. It does not indicate its use, as it has neither raised graves, tombs, gravestones, nor any other appearance of its being a place of burial; and it is not calculated to excite solemn emotions, as it has all the gaiety of a flower-garden.

In Britain, respect for the dead is not generally shown by the introduction of flowers over their graves; but the practice prevails in some places throughout the country, more especially in Wales, and is not unfrequent in the metropolitan and other cemeteries. Perhaps it ought to be commended and encouraged, as rendering burial-grounds inviting as places to walk in, and as the frequent recollection of deceased friends has a tendency to sober the mind and cultivate the affections of the living. In every part of Germany where the inhabitants are in the habit of cultivating flowers on the graves of their friends, or even of visiting these graves annually on a certain day and decorating them, the inhabitants are a reflective, and very humane and amiable, people; for example, at Munich. The introduction of flowers in churchyards, therefore, where they are planted over the graves by the relations of the deceased, is a very different thing from their introduction in the margins of plantations of trees and shrubs, in imitation of shrubberies, as is done in some of our public cemeteries; to the utter neglect, as we think, of appropriate character and expression.* Bearing in mind, therefore, the three

---

* Hanover Chapel, Brighton, has a burying-ground which is quite unique. A straight avenue of elm trees leads from the entrance gate to the door of the chapel; and on each side of the gravel walk, which runs down the centre of the avenue, is a narrow margin of smooth highly kept grass. Next, there is

principles of simplicity, order, and neatness, as guides in laying out churchyards, we shall next proceed with the details.

Situation and Soil.—It is almost unnecessary to observe that a country
church ought either to be built adjoining the village for which it is intended,
or, if it is to serve two or three villages, in a situation central to them. The
surface of the ground ought to be an elevated knoll, in order that the church
and the spire may be seen on every side, and, if possible, throughout the
whole extent of the parish. The knoll should be sufficiently large to admit
of its summit being reduced to a level, or, at all events, to a nearly level,
platform, or piece of table land, about the size of the churchyard; a level
surface being more convenient for the purpose of interment than a sloping
one, for a reason that will be given hereafter. Besides which, the ground
plan of a church being a parallelogram, to see it rising out of a round knoll
would be contrary to every idea of a suitable and secure foundation. Where
there is no want of room, or not many burials likely to take place, the surface
of a churchyard, instead of being level, may be quite irregular; but, in this
case, the places for graves, and the walks of communication to these places,
must be rendered easily accessible, and, to a certain extent, level. This can
always be effected by laying the ground out in terraces; a mode of disposition
which may be as advantageously adopted in churchyard gardening, as it is in
gardening as an art of culture. The soil should, if possible, be sandy or
gravelly, as being most suitable for promoting animal decomposition; and
also because there is a general prejudice in favour of being buried in dry soil.
The worst of all soils for a churchyard is a stiff wet clay; which, by its com-
pactness and retention of water, prevents the natural decomposition of the
body, and changes it into an adipose substance.

The Size of the Church, and the Extent of the Churchyard, will depend on the
population for whose service they are intended; and on the probable slowness
or rapidity of its increase. The form of the church may be considered as
fixed, by precedent and immemorial usage, in that of a parallelogram, with or
without projections at the sides, so as to give it the form of a Latin cross;
and having a tower, steeple, or cupola, at one end, for the church bells and a
clock. There are some examples, however, of churches having been made
semicircular, circular, or polygonal, in the plan, so as to suit them to particular situations.

The form of the churchyard is not fixed, like that of the church, but will

---

on each side a neat low wire fence, and beyond this is the burying-ground, the
greater part of which is dug and planted with herbaceous plants, interspersed
with low trees and flowering shrubs, and divided by walks, in some places
straight, and in others winding. The whole is interspersed with graves and
gravestones; and, as the gates in the wire fence are all kept locked, no person
is allowed to walk among the graves who is not admitted by the gardener.
Every recent grave is covered with a mound of green turf, kept smooth by
clipping or mowing, and all the rest of the ground is kept dug and planted;
so that no flowers can be said to be grown on the recent graves, but only
beside them. The recent graves are those in which interments have taken
place within two or three years; and are always known by being covered
with green turf, which is kept fresh by watering, and short and thick by frequent mowing. Nothing that we ever saw in a cemetery or churchyard comes
up to the high keeping displayed in this one. The walks and their edges
were perfect; the grass every where like velvet; the dug ground as fresh and
garden-like as if it had been recently dug and raked; the flowers neatly staked
and tied up, where tying was required; and not a single decayed flower or
leaf could we observe any where. The boundary walls were covered with
ivy and other climbers, and we observed trained on them one or two fig trees
and some other plants of the tree kind; but as, in consequence of the wire
fence, we could not get into the interior walks, we speak only of what we saw
from the avenue. (*Gard. Mag.*, 1842, p. 349.)

naturally be determined jointly by the form and position of the church, and the form of the ground which surrounds it. If the ground be level, or nearly so, then the outline of the churchyard may coincide with that of the church, so as also to form a large parallelogram, in the direction of east and west, that being the prescribed bearing of all Christian churches. There is, however, as we have already seen (p. 76.), a great disadvantage in placing the church so as to bear east and west, which is, that the north side, both of the church walls and the part of the churchyard next them, is kept great part of the year in the shade, and the ground is consequently rendered damp, and uninviting to bury in. We are happy to find that in some parts of the country the advantage of a diagonal bearing is beginning to be understood and acted on, both in dwellings and churches. Indeed, no single building or row of houses, or street, should be set down in the direction of east and west, unless there is some very decided reason for doing so.

If the church be situated on the summit of a conspicuous conical hill, or dome-like knoll, then the outline of the churchyard will be determined solely by the ground, and may be circular, oval, or roundish ; and we may here observe, that, when cases of this kind occur, as they are not very common, we think the ground plan of the church ought to be round, or roundish, also. In general, the position and form of the churchyard ought to be such as will have a good effect from all the different parts of the surrounding parish from which it is seen ; while, at the same time, it should look well from its immediate vicinity, and also from the different doors and sides of the church.

The Site of the Church should be central to the natural shape of the ground which is to constitute the churchyard, when that shape is in any way remarkable ; but, where the surface of the ground is level, the church may be placed nearer one end of the parallelogram, or other-shaped piece of ground, which forms the churchyard, than another ; or even nearer to one side, provided this is not attended with injustice to the parishioners. In general, the exact position of the church within the churchyard, when not determined by natural circumstances, ought to be regulated by the number of sides on which it is approached. If the parish lie equally round the church on every side, there will be at least four gates to the churchyard, corresponding with the four cardinal points ; and in that case the church ought to be in the centre of the churchyard ; but, if there be only a gate at one end, or if there should be several gates all nearer one end than the other, the church ought to be placed accordingly.

The Ground Plan of the Church, its exact position in the churchyard, the boundary lines of the latter, and the different churchyard doors or gates being fixed on, before any thing farther is done, the church ought to be built ; and we shall suppose that its elevation is so designed as to appear to rise from a platform of gravel or pavement, of from 10 ft. to 20 ft. wide, according to the size of the church ; this platform, or terrace, being supported by a sloping bank of turf, at an angle of 45°, and furnished with flights of steps opposite each of the churchyard gates. Underneath the surrounding platform there ought to be a deep barrel-drain or box-drain, for receiving the rain-water from the roof of the church, and thus keeping the foundations dry; and from this drain there ought to proceed others of the same kind, under each of the walks which lead from the church platform to the boundary wall. These last, besides carrying away the water collected in the drain which surrounds the church, will dry the subsoil of the churchyard generally, and enable it the better to absorb the water of decomposition; and receive the surface water from the walks, through gratings placed at regular distances.

The Boundary Fence of the churchyard should be such as to exclude every kind of domestic quadruped ; but it is not, in general, necessary that it should be so high as to prove a barrier to man; because it may fairly be supposed that most persons will reverence the interior more or less, and that those who are without this reverence will have, in general, nothing to gain by breaking into such a scene. We here exclude altogether the consideration of body-

G 4

stealing, which a recent judicious law has rendered no longer a profitable business, more especially in country places As swine and rabbits are particularly
offensive in churchyards, especially where the soil is sandy, the boundary fence
should either be a low wall of 3 ft., surmounted by a holly or thorn hedge; or
a wall of 6 or 7 feet in height, without any hedge. In the latter case, the
inner face of the wall may be planted with common ivy.   Where the churchyard is to be united with the adjoining lawn, garden, or pleasure-ground of the
parsonage, the boundary fence on the side next the residence may be an open
iron railing; and, where it is to be united with a pleasure-ground on a large
scale, or a park, it may either be surrounded by an open iron railing, or by a
deep and wide sunk fence. If a hedge is in any case determined on as the
boundary to a churchyard, it ought to be kept much broader at bottom than
at top, in order that it may grow quite thick and close there; and the only
plants fit for such a hedge are the common white thorn and the holly.

The Walks of a Churchyard are of two kinds : those for proceeding from the
different gates in the boundary fence to the church doors, for persons going
to, or returning from, the church; and those which make the circuit of the
churchyard, for the more conveniently viewing the tombs and graves, and for
conducting funerals. The walks proceeding from the entrance gates in the
boundary fence to the church doors should be always in straight lines, and of
a width proportionate to the size of the church and churchyard, but never
narrower than 6 ft.; because this is the least width which will allow two persons abreast, carrying a coffin between them on handspokes, to pass solemnly
along ; the width, indeed, should be greater rather than less, because nothing
can be more indecorous than to see a funeral procession crowded and huddled
together for want of room. In every case, we would, if possible, place the
entrance gates so that the walk from them to the church, whether to its sides
or its ends, might always meet the building at a right angle.

With respect to the walk round the churchyard, it should in every case, and
whether the churchyard were small or large, be at a distance of at least 10 ft.
from the boundary wall, in order to leave a border sufficiently broad for a
range of graves to be placed at right angles to the wall.   This walk should be
of the same breadth as the others ; and, like them, in no case less than 6 ft.,
for the reasons already mentioned. In most churchyards this boundary walk,
and the cross walks necessary as approaches to the church, will be sufficient ;
but, where this is not the case, cross walks from the boundary walk to the
terrace round the church may be added ; or a second surrounding walk may
be formed, half-way between the terrace or walk round the church, and the
circumferential walk.

The grassy Surface of a Churchyard, when it is newly laid out, should, of
course, be even; and the nearer it is to level, the more convenient will it be
for all the purposes of interment. Whether even or uneven, it should always
have a descent from the church, rather than towards it, for the sake of throwing off the surface water; and in strong clayey soils, in moist climates, provision ought to be made by surface gutters, even in the turf, for conveying the
water to underground drains, or directly along the surface to the boundary of
the churchyard.

Trees in Churchyards.—The number of trees which may be introduced into
a churchyard depends on its situation and soil ; the great object, next to that
of leaving abundance of room for the graves, being to preserve dryness, in
order to permit the escape of the mephitic effluvia that may rise to the
surface, which can only be effected by the admission of abundance of light and
air. Where the soil is clayey, and the situation low, very few trees are
admissible; and these few should be small fastigiate-growing kinds, that neither
cover a large space with their branches, nor give too much shade when the
sun shines. In an elevated open situation, where the soil is sandy or gravelly,
the trees in a churchyard may be comparatively numerous ; because the shelter
which they will afford in winter will produce warmth to persons crossing the
churchyard to church ; and, from the airiness of the situation, and dryness of

the soil, they will not produce damp when their leaves are on in summer, but will freely admit of evaporation from the surface.

Supposing a new churchyard to be planted, we should place the trees chiefly at regular distances, in rows parallel to the walks. There are very few churchyards that would bear more trees than a row on each side of the circumferential walk, and also on each side of the walks leading from the entrance gates to the church doors; while, in cases of limited extent, and a clayey soil, a row of trees, planted at regular distances along the boundary fence, will, perhaps, be as many as can be introduced without producing damp; and, in others, a few trees along each side of the principal walk from the entrance-gate of the churchyard to the church will, perhaps, be enough. It must not be forgotten, that the principal part of the area of a churchyard, in general, lies from east to west; and, consequently, that all trees planted in that direction will throw a shade upon the ground the greater part of every day that the sun shines, throughout the year. For this reason, where the soil is so damp, or the situation so confined, as to render it advisable to introduce but very few trees, these ought either to be in lines along such of the approaches to the church terrace as lie in the direction of north and south; or to be introduced as single trees, at the intersections of the cross walks with the boundary walk.

The kinds of trees to be planted in a churchyard form a subject of as great importance as their number; because a single tree of some species will produce more bulk of head, and consequently more shelter, shade, and damp, than half a dozen trees of some other kinds. As a guide in the choice of the kinds of trees, it may be adopted as a principle, that none ought to be planted which will grow higher than the side walls of the church; because to conceal the church by its appendages or ornaments is inconsistent, not only with good taste, but with common sense. By good taste, in this instance, we mean allowing the church to have its proper expression, as the principal and most dignified object in the landscape. Thorns, hollies, maples, sycamores, yews, mountain ash, wild service, &c., are suitable trees for the churchyards of very small churches; and the common maple, some species of oaks, such as the evergreen oak, the Italian oak, and some of the American oaks, with a host of other middle-sized trees, are suitable for the churchyards of churches of the ordinary size. There are very few country churches, indeed, which have even their towers or spires sufficiently high to admit of the stronger-growing elms or poplars being planted in their churchyards. The Oriental plane (not the Occidental) may be especially recommended, on account of the stone-like hue of its bark and foliage, its finely cut leaves, and agreeable shade, for churches of both the largest and the middle size. The purple beech would harmonise well in churchyards with the dark yew; and the flowering ash is, also, a very suitable tree.

As all trees in churchyards must be liable to have their roots injured by the digging of graves, this is one grand argument for planting the trees alongside the walks; because in that case there will be always one side of the tree the roots of which will remain untouched, viz. those which spread under the walk. For the same reason, trees with roots that spread near the surface, such as the pine and fir tribe, should seldom be made choice of. Were it not on this account, the cedar of Lebanon would be one of the most fitting of all trees for a churchyard, from the sombre hue of its foliage, and its grand and yet picturesque form; from the horizontal lines of its spreading branches contrasting strongly with the perpendicular lines of a Gothic church; and, above all, from the associations connected with it, on account of its frequent mention in Holy Writ. For all these reasons, it were much to be wished that, in all new churchyards, two or three spots (each of about 30 ft. in diameter) were set apart, not to be broken up for interments, and each planted with a cedar of Lebanon. In many old churchyards in the country, a spot sufficiently large for at least one cedar might easily be spared; and the clergyman or the churchwardens who should plant a cedar on such a spot, and

fence it sufficiently while young, would confer a grand and appropriate ornament on the church, and would deserve the gratitude of the parishioners.

No trees should be planted in a churchyard the natural habit of which is
to grow near water, such as willows, alders, &c.; because the expression
conveyed by such trees, being that of a moist situation, is altogether unsuitable for a churchyard; nevertheless, as the public in general do not partici-
pate in these associations, one of the most popular trees in churchyards every
where is the weeping willow. On the whole, the cypress, the yew, the Irish
yew, the red cedar, the Swedish and Irish junipers, the Juníperus recúrva,
the Oriental arbor vitæ, the different species of thorns, the common Montpelier, mountain, and other maples, the wild service, the whitebeam tree and
its hybrids, the holly, and a few others, are the most suitable low trees for
churchyards; next, those which grow about the height of the Norway maple;
and, lastly, those which rank in point of size with the Oriental plane.

The System of Interments in Churchyards is, in general, very imperfect; and,
indeed, in many cases no system whatever is adopted. The obvious principle is, to place the tombs near the eye, and consequently near the walks;
and to place the graves without gravestones in the interior of the compartments. For this reason, we would reserve a strip of ground, 10 or 12 feet
in width, along both sides of the walks (which would include the whole of the
space between the boundary walk and the boundary wall); these strips
should be devoted exclusively to family burial-places, whether merely indicated by corner stones, or railed in, or containing gravestones or tombs.
The whole of the compartments being thus bordered by strips for family
burial-places or purchased graves, the interior of each compartment might
either be laid out in strips parallel to the borders, with gravel walks between;
or devoted to graves without marks, laid out in the manner of a garden, with
regular alleys of turf between. The manner of arranging these graves, and all
the regulations respecting them, should be much the same as those recommended for cemeteries, p. 30.

In Germany, it is customary, in some churchyards, to bury all the children
under a certain age, who are not to have grave-marks, in a compartment by
themselves; not only because the waste of ground occasioned by placing
large and small graves together is thus avoided, but because it is found that,
in the case of children, the ground may be used again much sooner than the
ground in which adults have been buried. But we do not think it necessary
to recommend such a practice for Britain, where churchyards are, or may be,
increased in size with the increase of population; and where it is desirable
that no grave should be opened after it has once been filled.

On the Continent, as well as in many parts of Britain, the extent of the
churchyard in country parishes remains the same as it was several centuries
ago; the consequence of which is, that, in districts where the population has
increased, the graves are crowded together so as to obliterate one another,
and the ground raised considerably above the surrounding surface, as well as
above the floor of the church. Every time a grave is dug in such churchyards a great number of bones are thrown up; which are deposited in the first
instance in the charnel-house, and, in many cases at least, sold afterwards to
bone collectors, who ship them to Britain, along with the bones of quadru-
peds, to be crushed for manure. (See *Gard. Mag.* for 1842, p. 546.)

Fig. 54. is the ground plan of a churchyard laid out agreeably to the
foregoing principles; and *fig.* 53. is an isometrical view, supposing the trees to
have been ten or twelve years planted, and some of the gravestones and tombs
to have been erected. The churchyard is of small size, and is adapted for an
agricultural parish, where the majority of the inhabitants are in moderately
good circumstances, and whence it is supposed the superfluous population
will migrate to the towns, and leave the number of permanent inhabitants
comparatively stationary. There is only one entrance to the churchyard, at *a*
(*fig.* 54.), over which there is an archway for the protection of persons waiting
during rain or snow. The walk is 8 ft. broad, and proceeds direct to the steps

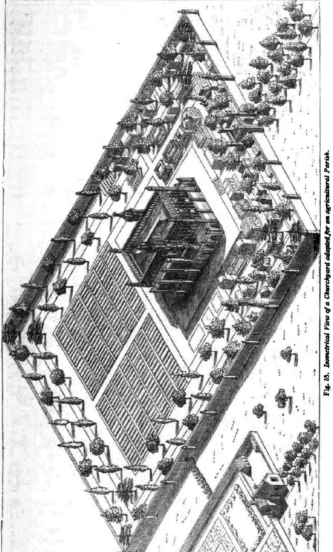

Fig. 53. *Isometrical View of a Churchyard adapted for an agricultural Parish.*

(*b*), which ascend to the platform on which the church stands. The circumferential walk (*c*) is 6 ft. wide, with a border for tombs and gravestones on each side, 12 ft. wide. There is also an inner walk (*d*) of the same width, between which and the platform on which the church stands there is another 12 ft. broad for tombs. The space for graves without marks lies on each side of the walk *e*, and is in 14 divisions, with room in each for 24 graves. Each of these divisions is separated by a grass path 2 ft. wide. The two surrounding borders, intended for tombs, are planted with trees 20 ft. apart. At the angles (*ff*), these trees are cedars of Lebanon ; at the main entrance (*g g*), they are yew trees ; and the remainder of the trees are different species of thorns (*Cratæ'gus*) (*h*), and evergreen cypresses (*i*), alternately ; except opposite to the side entrances to the platform, and at the angles adjoining the cedars, where there are yew trees marked *k k k k*. Whatever tree is‸ introduced on one side of the walk, the same sort is also planted on the other ; for the sake of preserving uniformity in the perspective. The number of trees wanted for this churchyard will be 8 cedars of Lebanon, 20 yews, 28 cypresses, and 32 plants of *Cratæ'gus*. The latter may be of the following 16 species or varieties : —

C. coccínea.	*C. Arònia.*
C. c. corállina.	*C. Oxyacántha ròsea.*
C. punctàta.	*C. O.* múltiplex (flòre plèno).
C. Crús-gálli.	*C. O.* melanocárpa.
C. C. salicifòlia.	*C. O.* præ'cox.
C. orientàlis (odoratíssima).	*C.* glandulòsa.
C. tanacetifòlia.	*C.* heterophýlla.
C. t. Cels*iàna.*	*C.* flàva.

Half the yews may be of the upright Irish variety ; but the cypresses should be all of the common upright-growing kind. In many parts of England, and generally in Scotland, the climate is too severe for the cypress ; but in all such places the Irish yew, Irish juniper, Swedish juniper, weeping Nepal juniper (*Juníperus recúrva*), the upright-growing variety of the Oriental arbor vitæ, or the *Pìnus Cémbra*, may be substituted. The common holly is also not a bad substitute; and, if deciduous cypress-like trees were required, we know of none more suitable than the *Quércus pedunculàta fastigiàta* and the *Cratæ'gus Oxyacántha strícta*.

The parties wishing to bury in the borders are not to be considered as obliged to erect tombs of any sort, or even to enclose the spot which they have purchased with an iron railing ; all that they will be held under obligation to do will be, to confine their operations within the limits of the parallelogram which they may purchase (and which may be either single, as shown in the plan at *t*, or double, as at *u*), and the four corners of which will be indicated by four stones let into the soil at the expense of the parish. The party purchasing the ground may erect any description of gravestone, tomb, statue, or monument, he chooses within it ; or he may leave it in naked turf, which will be mown or clipped at the expense of the parish ; or he may plant it with shrubs and flowers, in which case he must keep it in repair himself. We have suggested the idea of not rendering it compulsory to erect tombs or iron railings, in order that we may not seem to exclude those who cannot afford the expense of such memorials, from purchasing a grave to hold in perpetuity. A poor man may be willing to afford the price of a grave, in order to preserve the remains of his family from being disturbed ; though he might not be able to afford the farther expense of decorating it, by setting up a gravestone or erecting a tomb.

The Church shown in the figures is on what is supposed to be an improved design, suggested by an architect in the *Architectural Magazine* ; and it differs from the ordinary plan of churches in the manner of the entrances, and also in the general form being nearer that of a square than is usual. The author of this plan adopts it as a principle, " that the point in the outer walls from which each pew, and each class of pews, can be gained by the shortest pos-

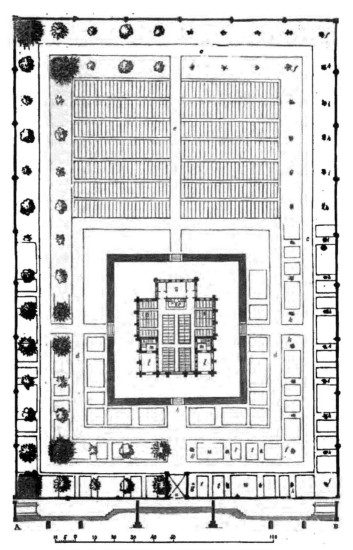

Fig. 54. *Ground Plan of a Churchyard adapted for an agricultural Parish.*

sible distance, is the best situation for an entrance; and for the following
reason: that a person entering a church after the congregation has partly
assembled, or, as frequently happens, after service is commenced, may gain
his sitting as soon as possible, and avoid at least one half the disturbance
otherwise created, by having only half the length of an aisle to traverse."
With respect to the general form, this architect considers " that plan the best
which concentrates the greatest number of benches or pews within a given
distance of the preacher; and hence he prefers a square to a parallelogram."
He adds : " Never let the inner entrance door of a church open under a
gallery, or the effect of the interior of the church will be irrecoverably lost.
If you will have western entrances and western galleries, contrive to have
porches or cloisters, so as to take you to the gallery front before you enter the
body of the church." (*Arch. Mag.*, iv. p. 568.) The ground plan in *fig.* 54.
is made in accordance with these principles : *l l* are the entrance porches;
m m, staircases, from which the body of the church is entered through lobbies
at *n*. The inner lobbies are formed by two pairs of folding doors, with a
space between, equal to the thickness of the walls of the towers which contain the stairs. The inner doors of the lobbies may be glazed with stained
or painted glass. If the body of the church be fitted up with benches, the
effect would harmonise better with this style of architecture; and, in the
opinion of several clergymen with whom we are acquainted, this arrangement
would be more suitable to the spirit of Christianity, according to which all
are equal in the sight of God. It is worthy of remark, that in the Russian
churches there are no benches or seats of any kind whatever, and nothing to
prevent the meanest slave from standing by the side of the highest noble,
or even of the emperor himself. The portion of the sittings marked *o o*, to
the right and left of the pulpit, our architect considers should be free. The
communion table is to be placed at *p*, the pulpit at *q*, and the reading-desk at
r. " The vestry and singers' seats (*s*) should be divided from the body of
the church by a pierced screen, finished upon the same level with the gallery
fronts; and above this screen should be a niche and canopy to the pulpit, designed as much as possible to improve the sound." (*Ib.*, p. 571.) Whoever
wishes to enter into farther detail on the subject of churches, and to see
plans and elevations on a large scale of the one shown in *fig.* 53., may con-
sult the *Architectural Magazine*, vol. ii. p. 393., vol. iv. p. 237. and p. 566.,
and vol. v. p. 223.

The *Parsonage House and Grounds* will, in general, be most conveniently
situated adjoining the church and churchyard; and the church will always
form a most appropriate object in the principal view from the parsonage. The
churchyard, also, may sometimes be seen as a part of the view.; and at other
times it may be so united with the grounds of the parsonage as almost to
seem a continuation of them. In the greater number of situations, however,
we believe the clergyman will prefer having his residence at a short distance
from the churchyard; not only from the idea that there may be mephitic exhalations from it (especially in churchyards where the graves are crowded
pell-mell together, and opened without any regular system), but also because
familiarity with the interments taking place in it may lessen the sentiment of
solemnity excited by them in his children and domestics, and may obtrude
that expression more powerfully than is desirable upon the minds of strangers
who may be his guests. Another and a decisive reason why the church and
churchyard should generally stand alone is, that the expression of solemnity
is heightened by this circumstance. Solitariness is unquestionably a powerful
ingredient in all feelings which are the opposite to those of gaiety; and, on
this account, the church and churchyard should stand completely isolated,
and, as we have said before, they should, if possible, be so elevated as to be
seen from all the surrounding country. (See the subject of Parsonage Houses
treated of in the *Suburban Gardener*, p. 607. to p. 615.; in which the plan of
Dunchurch Vicarage, laid out from our designs in 1837, is given as an example
of the pleasure-grounds of a parsonage united with the scenery of an adjoining churchyard.)

IX. LISTS OF TREES, SHRUBS, AND PERENNIAL HERBACEOUS PLANTS, ADAPTED FOR CEMETERIES AND CHURCHYARDS.

IN the following selections we have chiefly included plants that are quite hardy, and that, when once properly planted and established, will grow in turf or other firm soil without having the surface annually dug, or kept clear of weeds or grass. We have avoided most of the species of such genera as C*y*tisus, Genísta, Colùtea, Ribes, Ròsa, &c., which not only require dug soil, but are short-lived, or are very apt to die off. To those who do not require such lists for cemeteries or churchyards, they will be useful as indicating the principal permanent trees and shrubs adapted for pleasure-grounds, which are sold in British nurseries. The number might have been increased, but we have judged it best to be comparatively select.

Our classification of the trees and shrubs is founded on their different degrees of suitableness for burial-grounds ; and we have given references to our *Arboretum Britannicum*, where portraits of the entire tree, and copious details, botanical, descriptive, historical, geographical, &c., will be found ; and to the *Encyclopædia of Trees and Shrubs*, which is an abridgement of that work, in which engravings will be found of every species, and such details as are necessary as guides to their culture, management, and uses in plantations. We have added after each species the height which it generally attains in the climate of London, and the price of good plants in the London nurseries when one plant only is ordered; when several are wanted, of course the price will be lower, according to the number. We can vouch for their being obtained correct to the names, and at the prices mentioned, at the Fulham Nursery.

EVERGREEN TREES.

Evergreen Trees with Needle Leaves, and the Branches fastigiate and vertical.

Cupréssus sempervìrens *Encyc. of Trees and Shrubs* p. 1073. *Arb. Brit.* p. 2464., the Italian Cypress. Height 30—40 ft. 1*s.* 6*d.* The best of all trees for a cemetery, but not suited for exposed situations.

Táxus baccàta fastigiàta *E. of T.* p. 939. *A. B.* p. 2066., the Irish Yew. Height 20—30 ft. 2*s.* 6*d.* The second best cemetery tree, and quite hardy.

Táxus baccàta erécta *E. of T.* p. 940. *A. B.* p. 2066., the upright Yew. 2*s.* 6*d.* Third best.

Juníperus commùnis suécica *E. of T.* p. 1081. *A. B.* p. 2489., the Swedish Juniper. Height 10—12 ft. 1*s.* 6*d.* Equally good with the Irish yew, except that it is of a lighter colour.

Juníperus commùnis hibérnica *E. of T.* p. 1082., the Irish Juniper. Height 6—8 ft. 1*s.* 6*d.* Equal to the Swedish juniper.

Juníperus excélsa *E. of T.* p. 1088. *A. B.* p. 2503., the tall Juniper. Height 20—30 ft. 10*s.* 6*d.* This promises to be an excellent cemetery tree, in climates suitable for the Cupréssus sempervìrens.

Evergreen Trees with Needle Leaves, of narrow conical Forms, the Branches horizontal.

Cupréssus sempervìrens horizontàlis *E. of T.* p. 1073. *A. B.* p. 2465., the spreading Cypress. Height 30—40 ft. 1*s.* 6*d.*

Juníperus virginiàna *E. of T.* p. 1084. *A. B.* p. 2495., the red Cedar. Height 30—40 ft. 1*s.* 6*d.* Suitable, and very hardy.

Juníperus phœnícea *E. of T.* p. 1087. *A. B.* p. 2501., the Phœnician Juniper. Height 10—20 ft. 2*s.* 6*d.*

Juníperus chinénsis *E. of T.* p. 1809. *A. B.* p. 2505., the Chinese Juniper. Height 15—20 ft. 2*s.* 6*d.*

Thùja occidentàlis *E. of T.* p. 1068. *A. B.* p. 2454., the American Arbor Vitæ. Height 40—50 ft. 1*s.* 6*d.*

Thùja orientàlis *E. of T.* p. 1070. *A. B.* p. 2459., the Chinese Arbor Vitæ. Height 18—20 ft. 2*s.* 6*d.* More suitable, and also hardier, than the preceding species.

Evergreen Trees with Needle Leaves, conical in Shape, the Branches horizontal, but somewhat taller than those before enumerated.

A'bies álba *E. of T.* p. 1030. *A. B.* p. 2310., the white Spruce Fir. Height 40—50 ft. 2*s.* 6*d.*

A'bies nìgra *E. of T.* p. 1031. *A. B.* p. 2311., the black Spruce Fir. Height 60—70 ft. 2*s.* 6*d.*

Pícea balsàmea *E. of T.* p. 1044. *A. B.* p. 2339., the Balm of Gilead, or American Silver Fir. Height 20—30 ft. 1*s.* 6*d.*

Pícea pectinàta stricta (*Rivers*) *Gard. Mag.* 1843, p. 61., the upright Silver Fir. 5*s.*

Evergreen Trees with Needle Leaves, less conical in Shape, but peculiarly suitable for Churchyards and Cemeteries.

Táxus baccàta *E. of T.* p. 939. *A. B.* p. 2066., the common Yew. Height 20—30 ft. 1*s.* 6*d.* A very suitable cemetery tree where a spreading head is not an objection.

Táxus baccàta argéntea, the Silver Yew. 2*s.* 6*d.*

Táxus baccàta aúrea, the Golden Yew. 3*s.* 6*d.*

A'bies canadénsis *E. of T.* p. 1035. *A. B.* p. 2322., the Hemlock Spruce Fir. Height 30—60 ft. 2*s.* 6*d.*

Evergreen Trees with Needle Leaves, of conical Shape, the Branches horizontal, but of larger Growth than the preceding Kinds.

A'bies excélsa *E. of T.* p. 1026. *A. B.* p. 2293., the common Spruce. Height 60—80 ft. 6*d.* The cemetery tree of Sweden and Norway. The twigs are strewed over the corpse before the coffin lid is closed, and also over the floor of the room containing the corpse, and on the grave after the interment has been completed. The tree admits of being cut or clipped into any form. It is the principal tree in the large mountain cemetery at Rouen. (See *Gard. Mag.* for 1841, p. 291.)

A'bies Smithiàna *E. of T.* p. 1032. *A. B.* p. 2317., the Khutrow Spruce Fir. Height 50 ft. 5*s.*

A'bies Douglàsii *E. of T.* p. 1033. *A. B.* p. 2319., Douglas's Spruce Fir. Height 100—180 ft. 10*s.* 6*d.*

A'bies Menzièsii *E. of T.* p. 1034. *A. B.* p. 2321., Menzies's Spruce Fir. 5*s.*

Pícea pectinàta *E. of T.* p. 1037. *A. B.* p. 2329., the Comb-like-leaved Silver Fir. Height 80—100 ft. 1*s.*

Pícea cephalónica *E. of T.* p. 1039. *A. B.* p. 2325., the Mount Enos Fir. Height 50—60 ft. 2*s.* 6*d.*

Pícea Pinsàpo *E. of T.* p. 1041., the Pinsapo, or Malaga Silver Fir. Height 60—70 ft. 5*s.*

Pìnus Cémbra *E. of T.* p. 1016. *A. B.* p. 2274., the Cembran Pine. Height 50—80 ft. 2*s.* 6*d.* A slow-growing, narrow, conical tree; very hardy; and not unsuitable for small burying-grounds, when the Irish yew or Swedish juniper cannot be got.

Evergreen Trees with Needle Leaves, of conical Shapes, the Branches horizontal, but attaining a large Size, which nevertheless admit of being cut in so as to form narrow conical Trees suitable for large Cemeteries.

Pìnus sylvéstris *E. of T.* p. 951. *A. B.* p. 2153., the Scotch Pine, or Scotch Fir. Height 60—100 ft. *6d.* The tree of death and mourning in Russia is the pine, which may be called the Northern Cypress. The poor strew the coffin, at the time of exhibiting the corpse, with pine twigs; and, at the funerals of the wealthy, the whole way from the house to the churchyard is thickly strewed with branches of the same tree. Hence those streets of Petersburg through which funerals frequently pass are almost always covered with this sign of mourning. (*Kohl's Russia*, vol. i. p. 214.) The badge of the Highland clan M'Gregor.

Pìnus Larício *E. of T.* p. 956. *A. B.* p. 2200., the Corsican, or Larch, Pine. Height 60—150 ft. *1s. 6d.*

Pìnus austrìaca *E. of T.* p. 958. *A. B.* p. 2205., the Austrian, or Black, Pine. Height 60—80 ft. *6d.* Dark foliage, very hardy, and bears cutting in.

Pìnus taúrica *E. of T.* p. 959. *A. B.* p. 2206., the Tartarian Pine. Height 60—70 ft. *2s. 6d.* A dark-foliaged tree, very hardy, and admitting of being clipped or cut into narrow conical forms. Altogether the noblest of the European pines.

Pìnus Stròbus *E. of T.* p. 1018. *A. B.* p. 2280., the Weymouth Pine. Height 50—80 ft. *9d.*

Cèdrus Libàni *E. of T.* p. 1057. *A. B.* p. 2402., the Cedar of Lebanon. Height 50—80 ft. *5s.*

Cèdrus *Deodàra* E. of T. p. 1059. A. B. p. 2428., the Deodar, or Indian Cedar. Height 50—100 ft. *7s. 6d.*

* Of the same Kind, attaining a less Size.

Pìnus Pínea *E. of T.* p. 965. *A. B.* p. 2224., the Stone Pine. Height 15—20 ft. *2s. 6d.* More frequently seen as a bush than as a tree, but very ornamental, and its associations are classical.

Pìnus ìnops *E. of T.* p. 970. *A. B.* p. 2192., the Jersey, or poor, Pine. Height 40—50 ft. *2s. 6d.*

Pìnus mìtis *E. of T.* p. 974. *A. B.* p. 2195., the soft-leaved, or yellow, Pine. Height 50—60 ft. *2s. 6d.*

Pìnus pumílio *E. of T.* p. 955. *A. B.* p. 2186., the dwarf, or Mountain, Pine. Height 10—20 ft. *2s. 6d.* The foliage dark, and the tree very hardy, and suitable for a burial-ground of limited extent.

Evergreen Tree with Chaff-like Leaves, of a singular Appearance, and well adapted for Churchyards and Cemeteries.

Araucària imbricàta *E. of T.* p. 1062. *A. B.* p. 2432., the Chili Pine. Height 50—100 ft. *5s.* A very singular tree, of slow growth, and, as it is certain of attracting general attention, when planted in a cemetery, it ought to be surrounded with a wire fence for five or six years to protect it from accidental injury.

Evergreen Trees with Needle Leaves and pendent Branches, peculiarly well adapted for being used in Cemeteries so as to droop over Monuments.

Juníperus recúrva *E. of T.* p. 1089. *A. B.* p. 2504., the recurved Nepal Juniper. Height 5—10 ft. *2s. 6d.* A weeping tree, and on that account peculiarly suitable for cemeteries. Very hardy.

Juníperus virginiàna péndula (*Rivers*) *Gard. Mag.* for 1843, p. 61., the pendulous red Cedar. Hitherto rare. *10s.*

H

Juniperus commùnis péndula (Rivers) Gard. Mag. for 1843, p. 60., the pendulous common Juniper. Rare. 5*s.*
Thùja péndula E. of T. p. 1071. *A. B.* p. 2461., the drooping Arbor Vitæ. 21*s.* Said to be a hybrid between the red cedar and the Occidental arbor vitæ, raised by accident in Messrs. Loddiges's nursery. There is a fine specimen in the gardens at Kew. Rare, but quite hardy.

The foregoing kinds may all be considered as cemetery trees, *par excellence.* Those which follow are for the sake of variety in cemetery gardens of considerable extent, say fifty acres, and for cemetery arboretums.

Evergreen Trees with broad Leaves, of small Size and narrow conical Forms, which may be used in Cemeteries.

Cérasus Laurocérasus strícta *(Rivers), Gard. Mag.* 1843, p. 57., the upright-growing common Laurel, 2*s.* 6*d.*
Quércus *I'lex* Fórdii, Ford's Evergreen Oak. 3*s.* 6*d.* A very handsome low tree or shrub, and one of the best broad-leaved evergreens for a cemetery.

* Of less fastigiate Forms, and small Size.

Búxus baleárica *E. of T.* p. 704. *A. B.* p. 1341., the Minorca Box. Height 15—20 ft. 1*s.* 6*d.*
Búxus sempervìrens arboréscens *E. of T.* p. 703. *A. B.* p. 1333., the Tree Box. Height 15—30 ft. 9*d.* The badge of the Highland clan Macintosh.
Búxus sempervìrens variegàta. 6*d.* The badge of the clan Macpherson.

** Of the same Kind, less fastigiate, and of larger Size.

I'lex Aquifòlium *E. of T.* p. 157. *A. B.* p. 505., the common Holly. Height 20—30 ft. 6*d.* Decidedly the best broad-leaved evergreen tree for a cemetery.
I'lex baleárica *E. of T.* p. 160. *A. B.* p. 516., the Minorca Holly. Height 10—20 ft. 2*s.* 6*d.*
I'lex opàca *E. of T.* p. 160. *A. B.* p. 516., the opaque-leaved, or American, Holly. Height 10—20 ft. 3*s.* 6*d.*
Cérasus Laurocérasus *E. of T.* p. 295. *A. B.* p. 716., the common Laurel. Height 6—20 ft. 6*d.*
Cérasus lusitánica *E. of T.* p. 294. *A. B.* p. 714., the Portugal Laurel. Height 10—20 ft. 1*s.* 6*d.*
Quércus *I'lex E. of T.* p. 880. *A. B.* p. 1899., the common Evergreen Oak. Height 15—30 ft. Several varieties. From 2*s.* to 5*s.* each.
Quércus Sùber *E. of T.* p. 884. *A. B.* p. 1800. and 1911., the Cork Tree. Height 20—30 ft. 2*s.* 6*d.*
Quércus Túrneri *E. of T.* p. 885. *A. B.* p. 1922., Turner's Oak. Height 40—50 ft. 2*s.* 6*d.*

Evergreen Trees with broad Leaves and Shoots more or less pendulous, adapted for being planted singly to hang over Graves.

Cérasus Laurocérasus cólchica *(Rivers) Gard. Mag.* 1843, p. 57., the pendulous-branched common Laurel. 5*s.*
I'lex Aquifòlium péndulum *E. of T.* p. 1113., the drooping-branched common Holly. Rare; not yet to be purchased in the nurseries; but capable of being easily and extensively propagated by budding on the common holly. The badge of the clan Drummond.
Quércus Cérris fulhaménsis péndula *(Rivers) Gard. Mag.* 1843, p. 59., the weeping Fulham Oak.
Quércus *I'lex* péndula, the drooping-branched Evergreen Oak.

DECIDUOUS TREES.

Deciduous Needle-leaved Trees of fastigiate Shapes, which may be used in Churchyards.

Làrix americàna *E. of T.* p. 1056. *A. B.* p. 2399., the American Larch. Height 80—100 ft. 1*s.*

Làrix europæ'a commùnis *E. of T.* p. 1054. *A. B.* p. 2350., the common Larch. Height 80—100 ft. 6*d.*

Taxòdium dístichum *E. of T.* p. 1078. *A. B.* p. 2481., the deciduous Cypress. Height 50—80 ft. 2*s.* 6*d.*

* With pendulous Branches.

Làrix europæ'a péndula *E. of T.* p. 1054. *A. B.* p. 2350., the weeping Larch. 7*s.* 6*d.*

Taxòdium dístichum péndulum *E. of T.* p. 1078. *A. B.* p. 2481., the weeping deciduous Cypress. 5*s.*

Deciduous broad-leaved Trees of fastigiate Forms and small Size.

Amelánchier flórida *E. of T.* p. 414. *A. B.* p. 876., the flowery Amelanchier. Height 10—20 ft. 2*s.* 6*d.*

Amelánchier sanguínea *E. of T.* p. 413. *A. B.* p. 875., the blood-coloured Amelanchier. Height 10—20 ft. 2*s.* 6*d.*

Cotoneáster acuminàta *E. of T.* p. 409. *A. B.* p. 872., the acuminated-leaved Cotoneaster. Height 10—15 ft. 1*s.* 6*d.*

Cratæ'gus Oxyacántha strícta *E. of T.* p. 375. *A. B.* p. 832., the upright Hawthorn. 2*s.* 6*d.* Very hardy, and very suitable for a cemetery where deciduous trees are admitted.

Cratæ'gus tanacetifòlia *E. of T.* p. 372. *A. B.* p. 828., the Tansy-leaved Thorn. Height 20—30 ft. 2*s.* 6*d.*

Gymnócladus canadénsis *E. of T.* p. 255. *A. B.* p. 656., the Kentucky Coffee Tree. Height 30—60 ft. 2*s.* 6*d.*

* Of larger Size.

Pópulus balsamífera *E. of T.* p. 830. *A. B.* p. 1673., the Balsam-bearing Poplar. Height 40—50 ft. 1*s.*

Pópulus fastigiàta *E. of T.* p. 827. *A. B.* 1660., the Lombardy Poplar. Height 50—150 ft. 3*d.*

Quércus pedunculàta fastigiàta *E. of T.* p. 849. *A. B.* p. 1731., the pyramidal Oak. 3*s.* 6*d.* Very suitable from its decidedly fastigiate mode of growth, and narrow conical shape. The common oak, of which this is a variety, is the badge of the clan Cameron.

U'lmus montàna fastigiàta *E. of T.* p. 721. *A. B.* p. 1398., the fastigiate Elm. 1*s.* 6*d.*

Deciduous low Trees with round compact Heads.

A'cer O'palus *E. of T.* p. 89. *A. B.* p. 421., the Opal, or Italian, Maple. Height 8—12 ft. 1*s.* 6*d.*

A'cer monspessulànum *E. of T.* p. 92. *A. B.* p. 427., the Montpelier Maple. Height 15—40 ft. 1*s.* 6*d.*

A'cer créticum *E. of T.* p. 94. *A. B.* p. 430., the Cretan Maple. Height 10—30 ft. 2*s.* 6*d.*

Cérasus Mahàleb E. of T. p. 288. A. B. p. 707., the perfumed Cherry Tree. Height 10—20 ft. 2*s.* 6*d.*

Liquidámbar imbérbe *E. of T.* p. 933. *A. B.* p. 2053., the beardless Liquidambar. Height 10—20 ft.

O'rnus europæ'a *E. of T.* p. 651. *A. B.* p. 1241., the European flowering Ash. Height 20—30 ft. 2s. 6d.
O'strya vulgàris *E. of T.* p. 920. *A. B.* p. 2015., the Hop Hornbeam. Height 30—40 ft. 1s.
Pỳrus A'ria *E. of T.* p. 432. *A. B.* p. 910., the White Beam Tree. 1s. 6d.
Pỳrus aucupària *E. of T.* p. 439. *A. B.* p. 916., the Mountain Ash. Height 20—30 ft. 6d. The badge of the clan M'Lachlan.

Deciduous Trees of small Size, with Heads more or less irregular, most of which are remarkable for the Beauty of their Flowers or Fruit.

A'cer campéstre *E. of T.* p. 93. *A. B.* p. 428., the Field Maple. Height 15—30 ft. 1s.
A'cer spicàtum *E. of T.* p. 80. *A. B.* p. 406., the spike-flowered Maple. Height 18—20 ft. 1s. 6d.
A'cer striàtum *E. of T.* p. 81. *A. B.* p. 407., the striped-barked Maple. Height 10—20 ft. 1s. 6d.
A'cer tatáricum *E. of T.* p. 80. *A. B.* p. 406., the Tartarian Maple. Height 20—30 ft. 1s. 6d.
Amýgdalus commùnis *E. of T.* p. 263. *A. B.* p. 674., the common Almond Tree. Height 20—30 ft. 2s. 6d.
Amýgdalus commùnis macrocárpa *E. of T.* p. 264. *A. B.* p. 675., the large-flowered Almond. 2s. 6d.
Armeniaca vulgàris *E. of T.* p. 267. *A. B.* p. 682., the common Apricot Tree. Height 20—30 ft. 2s. 6d.
Bétula nìgra *E. of T.* p. 843. *A. B.* p. 1710., the black Birch. Height 60—70 ft.
Bétula populifòlia *E. of T.* p. 841. *A. B.* p. 1707., the Poplar-leaved Birch. 1s. 6d.
Bétula populifòlia laciniàta *E. of T.* p. 841. *A. B.* p. 1707., the cut-leaved Poplar Birch. 1s. 6d.
Broussonètia papyrífera *E. of T.* p. 710. *A. B.* p. 1361., the Paper Mulberry. Height 10—20 ft. 1s. 6d.
Caragàna arboréscens *E. of T.* p. 237. *A. B.* p. 629., the Siberian Pea Tree. Height 15—20 ft. 1s. 6d.
Cérasus Pàdus *E. of T.* p. 289. *A. B.* p. 709., the Bird-Cherry Tree. Height 12—40 ft. 9d.
Cérasus virginiàna *E. of T.* p. 291. *A. B.* p. 710., the Virginian Bird-Cherry Tree. Height 30—40 ft. 1s. 6d.
Cércis Siliquástrum *E. of T.* p. 257. *A. B.* p. 657., the common Judas Tree. Height 20—30 ft. 1s. 6d. Abundant in the Protestant cemetery at Lisbon, and in the Turkish cemeteries at Constantinople. (*Yacht Voyage*, vol. i. p. 20. and p. 37.)
Córylus Colúrna *E. of T.* p. 923. *A. B.* p. 2029., the Constantinople Hazel, Height 50—60 ft. 2s. 6d.
Cratæ'gus *E. of T.* p. 352. *A. B.* p. 813., the Thorn. Fifty species, all beautiful. 2s. 6d. each.
Cydònia vulgàris *E. of T.* p. 450. *A. B.* p. 929., the common Quince Tree. Height 15—20 ft. 2s. 6d.
Cýtisus alpìnus *E. of T.* p. 215. *A. B.* p. 591., the Alpine, or Scotch, Laburnum. Height 20—30 ft. 1s. 6d.
Cýtisus Labúrnum *E. of T.* p. 214. *A. B.* p. 590., the common Laburnum, Height 20 ft. 1s.
Diospỳros Lòtus *E. of T.* p. 625. *A. B.* p. 1194., the European Lotus, or common Date Plum. Height 20—30 ft. 2s. 6d.
Elæágnus horténsis *E. of T.* p. 696. *A. B.* p. 1321., the garden Elæagnus, Oleaster, or Wild Olive Tree. Height 15—20 ft. 1s. 6d.
Gledítschia sinénsis *E. of T.* p. 252. *A. B.* p. 654., the Chinese Gleditschia. Height 30—50 ft. 2s. 6d.

Halèsia tetráptera *E. of T.* p. 620. *A. B.* p. 1190., the common Snowdrop
Tree. Height 15—30 ft. 2s. 6d.
Hippóphae Rhamnöïdes fémina *E. of T.* p. 698. *A. B.* p. 1324., the female
Sea Buckthorn. Height 15—20 ft. 1s. 6d.
Kölreutèria paniculàta *E. of T.* p. 135. *A. B.* p. 475., the panicled-flower-
ing Kolreuteria. Height 20—40 ft. 1s. 6d.
Magnòlia acuminàta *E. of T.* p. 29. *A. B.* p. 273., the pointed-leaved Mag-
nolia. Height 30—50 ft. 5s.
Méspilus germánica *E. of T.* p. 415. *A. B.* p. 877., the common Medlar.
2s. 6d.
Méspilus Smíthii E. of T. p. 416. A. B. p. 878., Smith's Medlar. Height
15—20 ft. 2s. 6d.
Mòrus nìgra *E. of T.* p. 706. *A. B.* p. 1343. 3s. 6d.; and *M.* álba *E. of T.*
p. 707. *A. B.* p. 1348. 1s.; the common-fruited and white-fruited Mul-
berry Tree. Height 20—30 ft.
Ptèlea trifoliàta *E. of T.* p. 144. *A. B.* p. 489., the three-leafleted Ptelea,
or shrubby Trefoil. Height 6—10 ft. 1s. 6d.
Pỳrus *E. of T.* p. 417. *A. B.* p. 879., the Pear Tree. Ten species. 2s. 6d.
Quércus Æ'gilops *E. of T.* p. 860. *A. B.* p. 1861., the great prickly-cupped
Oak. Height 20—50 ft. 2s. 6d.
Quércus E'sculus *E. of T.* p. 853. *A. B.* p. 1844., the Italian Oak. Height
20—30 ft. 2s. 6d.
Sambùcus nìgra laciniàta *E. of T.* p. 513. *A. B.* p. 1027., the common, or
black-fruited, Elder. 1s.
Sambùcus racemòsa *E. of T.* p. 515. *A. B.* p. 1031., the racemose-flowered
Elder. Height 10—12 ft. 1s. 6d.
Sophòra japónica *E. of T.* p. 196. *A. B.* p. 563., the Japan Sophora. Height
40—50 ft. 1s. 6d.
Virgília lùtea *E. of T.* p. 198. *A. B.* p. 565., the yellow-wooded Virgilia.
Height 10—20 ft. 5s.

*Deciduous Trees of larger Size, remarkable for the Beauty of their Flowers, or
the Singularity or Fragrance of their Leaves.*

A'cer Pseùdo-Plátanus purpùrea *E. of T.* p. 86. *A. B.* p. 415., the purple-
leaved Sycamore Maple. 1s. The maple is the badge of the clan
Oliphant.
Æ'sculus rubicúnda *E. of T.* p. 126. *A. B.* p. 467., the reddish-flowered
Horsechestnut. Height 20—30 ft. 2s. 6d.
Ailántus glandulòsa *E. of T.* p. 145. *A. B.* p. 490., the glandulous-leaved
Ailanto. Height 50—60 ft. 1s. 6d.
A'lnus cordifòlia *E. of T.* p. 835. *A. B.* p. 1689., the heart-leaved Alder.
Height 15—20 ft. 1s. 6d.
A'lnus incàna *E. of T.* p. 834. *A. B.* p. 1687., the hoary-leaved Alder. Height
50—70 ft. 1s. 6d.
Céltis austràlis *E. of T.* p. 727. *A. B.* p. 1414., the European Nettle Tree.
Height 30—40 ft. 2s. 6d.
Fàgus sylvática purpùrea *E. of T.* p. 905. *A. B.* p. 1950., the common purple
Beech. 2s. 6d.
Liquidámbar Styracíflua *E. of T.* p. 932. *A. B.* p. 2049., the Sweet-Gum
Liquidambar. Height 30—50 ft. 1s. 6d.
Liriodéndron Tulipífera *E. of T.* p. 36. *A. B.* p. 284., the Tulip Tree. Height
50—90 ft. 2s. 6d.
Maclùra aurantìaca *E. of T.* p. 711. *A. B.* p. 1362., the Osage Orange. Height
30—60 ft. 3s. 6d.
Negúndo fraxinifòlium *E. of T.* p. 122. *A. B.* p. 460., the Ash-leaved Ne-
gundo. Height 15—30 ft. 1s.
Pàvia díscolor *E. of T.* p. 133. *A. B.* p. 472., the two-coloured-flowered
Pavia. Height 3—10 ft. 2s. 6d.

Pàvia flàva *E. of T.* p. 130. *A. B.* p. 471., the yellow-flowered Pavia. Height
   30—40 ft. 1*s.* 6*d.*
Plánera Richárdi *E.* of *T.* p. 726. A. B. p. 1409., Richard's Planera. Height
   50—70 ft. 1*s.* 6*d.*
Plátanus orientàlis *E. of T.* p. 928. *A. B.* p. 2033., the Oriental Plane.
   Height 60—80 ft. 1*s.* 6*d.*
Pópulus balsamífera *E. of T.* p. 830. *A. B.* p. 1673., the Balsam-bearing
   Poplar. Height 40—50 ft. 1*s.*
Quércus coccínea *E. of T.* p. 869. *A. B.* p. 1879., the Scarlet Oak. Height
   80 ft. 1*s.* 6*d.*
Quércus palústris *E. of T.* p. 872. *A. B.* p. 1887., the Marsh, or Pin, Oak.
   Height 80 ft. 1*s.* 6*d.*
Quércus rùbra *E. of T.* p. 868. *A. B.* p. 1877., the red, or Champion, Oak.
   Height 80—90 ft.
Robínia Pseùd-Acàcia *E. of T.* p. 233. *A. B.* p. 609., the common Robinia,
   or false Acacia. Height 70—80 ft. 1*s.*
Robínia viscòsa *E. of T.* p. 235. *A. B.* p. 626., the clammy-barked Robinia.
   Height 15—20 ft. 2*s.* 6*d.*
Salisbùria adiantifòlia *E. of T.* p. 945. *A. B.* p. 2094., the Maiden-hair-leaved
   Salisburia. Height 60—80 ft. 3*s.* 6*d.*
Sàlix aurìta *E. of T.* p. 776. *A. B.* p. 1560., the round-eared Sallow, or Willow.
   1*s.* 6*d.* The badge of the clan Cumming.
Sàlix càprea *E. of T.* p. 776. *A. B.* p. 1561., the Goat Sallow, or Willow.
   Height 15—30 ft. 1*s.* 6*d.*
Sàlix pentándra *E. of T.* p. 754. *A. B.* p. 1503., the Sweet Willow, or Bay-
   leaved Willow. Height 18—20 ft. 1*s.* 6*d.*
Sàlix vitellìna *E. of T.* p. 763. *A. B.* p. 1528., the yellow Willow, or Golden
   Osier. Height 30—50 ft. 1*s.* 6*d.*

*Deciduous Trees with pendulous Branches, adapted for being planted singly by
   Monuments, or over Graves as Substitutes for Monuments (Trauerbäume,
   or Trees of Sorrow, Ger.).*

Amýgdalus Pérsica péndula (*Rivers*) *G. M.* 1843, p. 57., the pendulous-
   branched Peach.
Bétula álba péndula *E. of T.* p. 838. *A. B.* p. 1691., the weeping Birch. 1*s.*
   The birch is the badge of the clan Buchanan.
Cérasus Pàdus bracteòsa *E. of T.* p. 290. *A. B.* p. 702., the bracteolate
   weeping Bird-Cherry. 1*s.* 6*d.*
Cérasus Pàdus péndula (*Rivers*) *G. M.* 1843, p. 57., the weeping Bird-Cherry.
Cérasus semperflòrens *E. of T.* p. 281. *A. B.* p. 701., the ever-flowering
   Cherry Tree. Height 10—20 ft. 1*s.* 6*d.*
Cratæ`gus Oxyacántha péndula *E. of T.* p. 376. *A. B.* p. 832., the weeping
   Hawthorn.
Cýtisus Labúrnum péndulum *E. of T.* p. 215. *A. B.* p. 590., the weeping La-
   burnum. 2*s.* 6*d.*
Cýtisus alpìnus péndulus *E. of T.* p. 216. *A. B.* p. 791., the weeping Scotch
   Laburnum. Height 20—30 ft. 2*s.* 6*d.*
Fàgus sylvática péndula *E. of T.* p. 906. *A. B.* p. 1876., the weeping Beech.
   3*s.* 6*d.*
Fàgus sylvática purpùrea péndula (*Rivers*) *G. M.* 1843, p. 60., the purple
   weeping Beech.
Fráxinus excélsior péndula *E. of T.* p. 641. *A. B.* p. 1214., the weeping
   Ash. 3*s.* 6*d.*
Fráxinus lentiscifòlia péndula *E. of T.* p. 645. *A. B.* p. 1231., the weeping
   Lentiscus-leaved Ash. 3*s.* 6*d.*
Pàvia rùbra péndula, the weeping Horsechestnut. 2*s.* 6*d.*
Pópulus trémula péndula *E. of T.* p. 822. *A. B.* p. 1509., the weeping
   Poplar. 1*s.* 6*d.* The poplar is the badge of the clan Ferguson.

P*j̀rus* sp*ù*ria p*é*ndula *E. of T.* p. 445. *A. B.* p. 925., the spurious Service Tree. Height 10—12 ft. 2*s*. 6*d*.

Qu*é*rcus peduncul*à*ta p*é*ndula *E. of T.* p. 849. *A. B.* p. 1731., the weeping Oak.

Rob*í*nia Pse*ù*d-Ac*à*cia p*é*ndula *E. of T.* p. 234. *A. B.* p. 609. *Gard. Mag.* 1843, p. 56., the false Acacia.

*Sà*lix babyl*ó*nica *E. of T.* p. 757. *A. B.* p. 1507., the weeping Willow. Height 30—50 ft. 1*s*.

*Sà*lix americ*à*na p*é*ndula (*Rivers*) *Gard. Mag.* 1843, p. 59., the American weeping Willow.

*Soph*ò*ra* jap*ó*nica p*é*ndula *E. of T.* p. 196. *A. B.* p. 563., the weeping Sophora. Height 30—40 ft. 10*s*. 6*d*.

*T*ì*lia *á*lba p*é*ndula, the white Hungarian Lime. 3*s*. 6*d*.

U'lmus mont*à*na p*é*ndula *E. of T.* p. 721. *A. B.* p. 1398., the weeping Elm. 2*s*. 6*d*.

EVERGREEN SHRUBS.

Evergreen Shrubs with Needle Leaves, and the Plants of great Duration, all well adapted for Cemeteries where Shrubs are introduced.

*C*upr*é*ssus *t*hy*ö*ïdes *E. of T.* p. 1074. *A. B.* p. 2475., the white Cedar. Height 10—15 ft. 2*s*. 6*d*.

Jun*í*perus comm*ù*nis *E. of T.* p. 1081. *A. B.* p. 2489., the common Juniper. Height 3—5 ft. 1*s*. The badge of the clan Murray.

Jun*í*perus d*aü*rica *E. of T.* p. 1082. *A. B.* p. 2489., the Da*ü*rian Juniper.

Jun*í*perus Ox*ý*cedrus *E. of T.* p. 1083. *A. B.* p. 2494., the brown-berried Juniper. Height 10—12 ft. 3*s*. 6*d*.

Jun*í*perus Sab*ì*na *E. of T.* p. 1085. *A. B.* p. 2499., the common Savin. Height 7—8 ft. 1*s*. 6*d*. Several varieties.

*T*à*xus bacc*à*ta microph*ý*lla (*Rivers*) *Gard. Mag.* 1843, p. 60.

*T*à*xus canad*é*nsis *E. of T.* p. 942. *A. B.* p. 2093., the Canada, or North American, Yew. 3*s*. 6*d*.

Evergreen Shrubs with broad Leaves, and the Plants of great Duration.

A'rbutus *U*'nedo *E. of T.* p. 573. *A. B.* p. 1117., and several other species. From 6*d*. to 5*s*. The arbutus is the badge of the clan Ross.

*Aú*cuba* jap*ó*nica *E. of T.* p. 511. *A. B.* p. 1026., the Japan Aucuba. Height 6—10 ft. 1*s*. 6*d*.

*B*é*rberis* d*ú*lcis *E. of T.* p. 47. *A. B.* p. 305., the sweet-fruited Berberry. Height 2—5 ft. 1*s*. 6*d*.

*B*ú*xus semperv*ì*rens myrtif*ò*lia *E. of T.* p. 704. *A. B.* p. 1333., the Myrtle-leaved Box Tree. 9*d*.

Coll*è*ti*a h*ó*rrida *E. of T.* p. 176. *A. B.* p. 541., the bristly Colletia. Height 3—4 ft. 3*s*. 6*d*.

Cotone*á*ster *b*uxif*ò*lia *E. of T.* p. 411. *A. B.* p. 873., the Box-leaved Coto-neaster. 1*s*. 6*d*.

Cratæ'gus *P*yrac*á*ntha *E. of T.* p. 385. *A. B.* p. 844., the fiery Thorn. Height 4—6 ft. 1*s*. 6*d*.

*D*á*phne Laur*è*ola *E. of T.* p. 688. *A. B.* p. 1309., the Spurge Laurel. Height 3—4 ft. 6*d*.

*D*á*phne p*ó*ntica *E. of T.* p. 688. *A. B.* p. 1310., the twin-flowered Spurge Laurel. Height 4—5 ft. 1*s*. 6*d*.

G*á*rrya ell*í*ptica *E. of T.* p. 926. *A. B.* p. 2032., the elliptic-leaved Garrya. Height 8—10 ft. 2*s*. 6*d*.

I'lex *A*quif*ò*lium *E of T.* p. 157. *A. B.* p. 505., the common Holly: most of the variegated sorts. Height 20—30 ft. 1*s*. to 5*s*.

*L*ig*ú*strum vulg*à*re semperv*ì*rens *E. of T.* p. 629. *A. B.* p. 1199., the evergreen Privet. 6*d*.

Phillýrea mèdia *E. of T.* p. 632. *A. B.* p. 1204., the lance-leaved Phillyrea. Height 10—15 ft. 2s. 6d.

Quércus hýbrida nàna *E. of T.* p. 886. *A. B.* p. 1924., the dwarf hybrid Oak.

Rhámnus Alatérnus E. of T. p.171. *A. B.* p. 529., the Alaternus. Height 10—20 ft. 1s. 6d.

Rhámnus hýbridus *E. of T.* p. 172. *A. B.* p. 531., the hybrid Alaternus. Height 10—12 ft. 1s. 6d.

U'lex europæ'a fl. plèno *E. of T.* p. 200., *A. B.* p. 571., the double-blossomed Furze. 1s.

Vibúrnum Tìnus E. of T. p. 516. *A. B.* p. 1032., the Laurustinus. Height 8—10 ft. 1s.

DECIDUOUS SHRUBS.

Deciduous broad-leaved Shrubs, the Plants of compact Growth and of long Duration, adapted for Cemeteries.

A'lnus víridis *E. of T.* p. 836. *A. B.* p. 1689., the green-leaved Alder. Height 5—6 ft.

Bérberis aristàta *E. of T.* p. 49. *A. B.* p. 307., the bristled-tooth-leaved Berberry. Height 6—10 ft. 1s. 6d.

Bérberis asiática *E. of T.* p. 49. *A. B.* p. 306., the Asiatic Berberry. Height 6—8 ft. 3s. 6d.

Bérberis crética *E. of T.* p. 44. *A. B.* p. 304., the Cretan Berberry. Height 3—4 ft. 2s. 6d.

Bérberis ibérica *E. of T.* p. 45. *A. B.* p. 304., the Iberian Berberry. Height 3—5 ft. 1s. 6d.

Bérberis sibírica *E. of T.* p. 42. *A. B.* p. 301., the Siberian Berberry. Height 2—3 ft. 2s. 6d.

Bérberis sinénsis *E. of T.* p. 46. *A. B.* p. 304., the Chinese Berberry. Height 3—5 ft. 2s. 6d.

Bérberis vulgàris *E. of T.* p. 42. *A. B.* p. 301., the common Berberry. Height 6—10 ft. 1s. 6d.

Bétula nàna *E. of T.* p. 840. *A. B.* p. 1705., the dwarf Birch. Height 6—8 ft. 1s. 6d.

Bétula pùmila *E. of T.* p. 840. *A. B.* p. 1705., the hairy dwarf Birch. Height 2—3 ft. 1s. 6d.

Caragàna arboréscens *E. of T.* p. 237. *A. B.* p. 629., the Siberian Pea Tree. Height 15—20 ft. 1s. 6d.

Cérasus hyemàlis *E. of T.* p. 285. *A. B.* p. 704., the Winter Cherry Tree. Height 3—4 ft. 1s. 6d.

Cérasus nìgra *E. of T.* p. 284. *A. B.* p. 704., the black Cherry Tree. Height 6—10 ft. 2s. 6d.

Chimonánthus fràgrans *E. of T.* p. 445. *A. B.* p. 938., the fragrant-flowered Chimonanthus. Height 6—8 ft. 3s. 6d.

Chionánthus virgínica *E. of T.* p. 634. *A. B.* p. 1206., the Fringe Tree. Height 10—30 ft. 2s. 6d.

Córnus álba *E. of T.* p. 503. *A. B.* p. 1011., the white-fruited Dogwood. Height 4—10 ft. 9d.

Córnus álba strícta *E. of T.* p. 503. *A. B.* p. 1012., the straight-branched Dogwood. Height 6—10 ft. 1s. 6d.

Córnus alternifòlia *E. of T.* p. 501. *A. B.* p. 1010., the alternate-leaved Dogwood. Height 15—20 ft. 1s.

Córnus más *E. of T.* p. 505. *A. B.* p.1014., the Cornelian Cherry Tree. Height 12—20 ft. 1s. 6d.

Córnus sanguínea *E. of T.* p. 502. *A. B.* p. 1010., the common Dogwood. Height 4—15 ft. 9d.

Córylus Avellàna E. of T. p. 921. *A. B.* p. 2017., the common Hazel. Height 20 ft. 9d. The badge of the clan Colquhoun.

Córylus Avellàna purpùrea, the purple-leaved Hazel. 1s. 6d.

Cotoneáster frígida *E. of T.* p. 407. *A. B.* p. 871., the frigid Cotoneaster. Height 10—20 ft. 2*s. 6d.*

Cotoneáster frígida affínis *E. of T.* p. 408. *A. B.* p. 871., the related Cotoneaster. Height 10—20 ft. 1*s. 6d.*

Cotoneáster nummulària *E. of T.* p. 409. *A. B.* p. 872., the money-like-leaved Cotoneaster. Height 10—15 ft. 1*s. 6d.*

Cotoneáster vulgàris *E. of T.* p. 406. *A. B.* p. 870., the common Cotoneaster. Height 4—5 ft. 1*s. 6d.*

Cratæ'gus parvifòlia *E. of T.* p. 383. *A. B.* p. 841., the small-leaved Thorn. Height 4—6 ft. 3*s. 6d.*

Cratæ'gus virgínica *E. of T.* p. 384. *A. B.* p. 842., the Virginian Thorn. Height 4—5 ft.

Cydònia japónica *E. of T.* p. 452. *A. B.* p. 931., the Japan Quince Tree. Height 5—6 ft. 1*s. 6d.*

Cydònia sinénsis *E. of T.* p. 451. *A. B.* p. 931., the China Quince Tree. Height 10—12 ft. 2*s. 6d.*

Dáphne *Mezèreum* E. of T. p. 687. *A. B.* p. 1307., the common Mezereon. Height 3—4 ft. 1*s.*

Euónymus europæ'us *E. of T.* p. 149., *A. B.* p. 496., the Spindle Tree. Height 6—12 ft. 9*d.*

Euónymus latifòlius *E. of T.* p. 150. *A. B.* p. 498., the broad-leaved Euonymus, or Spindle Tree. Height 10—20 ft. 1*s. 6d.*

Gledítsch*ia* sinénsis purpùrea *E. of T.* p. 252. *A. B.* p. 654., the Chinese Gleditschia. 2*s. 6d.*

*H*amamèlis virgínica *E. of T.* p. 499. *A. B.* p. 1007., the Wych Hazel. Height 20—30 ft. 2*s. 6d.*

Ligústrum vulgàre *E. of T.* p. 629. *A. B.* p. 1198., the common Privet. Height 6—10 ft. 4*d.*

Paliùrus aculeàtus *E. of T.* p. 168. *A. B.* p. 527., Christ's Thorn. Height 15—20 ft. 1*s. 6d.*

Pàv*ia* macrostàchya *E. of T.* p. 133. *A. B.* p. 473., the long-racemed Pavia. Height 10—15 ft. 2*s. 6d.*

*P*hiladélphus coronàrius *E. of T.* p. 460. *A. B.* p. 951., the Mock Orange. Height 10—12 ft. 9*d.*

*P*rìnos decíduus *E. of T.* p. 164. *A. B.* p. 520., the deciduous Winter Berry. Height 3—5 ft. 1*s. 6d.*

Prùnus marítima *E. of T.* p. 275. *A. B.* p. 691., the sea-side-inhabiting Plum Tree. Height 6—8 ft. 2*s. 6d.*

Prùnus spinòsa *E. of T.* p. 271. *A. B.* p. 684., the common Sloe Thorn. Height 10—15 ft. 1*s. 6d.*

Pỳrus *a*rbutifòlia *E. of T.* p. 446. *A. B.* p. 925., the Arbutus-leaved Aronia. Height 4—6 ft. 2*s. 6d.*

*P*ỳrus Chamæméspilus *E. of T.* p. 449. *A. B.* p. 928., the dwarf Medlar. Height 5—6 ft. 1*s. 6d.*

Pỳrus pùbens *E. of T.* p. 448. *A. B.* p. 927., the downy-branched Aronia. Height 4—5 ft. 3*s. 6d.*

Pỳrus spùria *E. of T.* p. 444. *A. B.* p. 924., the spurious Service Tree. Height 10—20 ft. 2*s. 6d.*

Quércus Banísteri E. of T. p. 876. A. B. p. 1893., the Holly-leaved, or Bear, Oak. Height 3—10 ft.

*R*hámnus alpìnus *E. of T.* p. 175. *A. B.* p. 536., the Alpine Buckthorn. Height 5—10 ft. 1*s.*

*R*hámnus cathárticus *E. of T.* p. 172. *A. B.* p. 531., the purging Buckthorn. Height 10—12 ft. 1*s.*

*R*hámnus Frángula *E. of T.* p. 177. *A. B.* p. 539., the breaking Buckthorn, or Berry-bearing Alder. Height 8—10 ft. 1*s. 6d.*

*R*hámnus latifòlius *E. of T.* p. 177. *A. B.* p. 538., the broad-leaved Buckthorn. Height 10—15 ft. 1*s. 6d.*

Rhús Cótinus E. of T. p. 187. A. B. p. 549., the Venetian Sumach. Height
4—6 ft. 1s. 6d.
Rhús glàbra E. of T. p. 188. A. B. p. 551., the Scarlet Sumach. Height
5—18 ft. 1s. 6d.
Rhús typhìna E. of T. p. 187. A. B. p. 550., the Stag's Horn Sumach.
Height 20 ft. 9d.
Rhús venenàta E. of T. p. 189. A. B. p. 552., the poisonous Rhus, Poison
Wood, or Swamp Sumach. Height 15—20 ft. 1s. 6d.
Sambùcus racemòsa E. of T. p. 515. A. B. p. 1031., the racemose-flowered
Elder. Height 10—12 ft. 1s. 6d.
Shephérdia argéntea E. of T. p. 700. A. B. p. 1327., the silver-leaved Shep-
herdia. Height 12—18 ft. 1s. 6d.
Shephérdia canadénsis E. of T. p. 700. A. B. p. 1327., the Canadian Shep-
herdia. Height 6—8 ft. 2s. 6d.
Spiræ`a ariæfòlia E. of T. p. 309. A. B. p. 731., the White-Beam-tree-
leaved Spiræa. Height 6—8 ft. 1s.
Spiræ`a chamædrifòlia E. of T. p. 300. A. B. p. 724., the Germander-leaved
Spiræa. Height 2—8 ft. 9d.
Spiræ`a hypericifòlia E. of T. p. 303. A. B. p. 726., the Hypericum-leaved
Spiræa. Height 4—6 ft. 9d.
Spiræ`a opulifòlia E. of T. p. 299. A. B. p. 723., the Virginian Guelder
Rose. Height 8—10 ft. 9d.
Staphylèa trifòlia E. of T. p. 147. A. B. p. 493., the Bladder-nut Tree.
Height 6—12 ft. 1s.
Symphoricárpos montànus E. of T. p. 542., the Mountain St. Peter's Wort.
Height 5—6 ft. 1s.
Symphoricárpos vulgàris E. of T. p. 541. A. B. p. 1058., the common St.
Peter's Wort. Height 3—6 ft. 9d.
Syrínga Josikæ`a E. of T. p. 637. A. B. p. 1201., Josika's Lilac. Height
6—12 ft. 1s. 6d.
Syrínga pérsica E. of T. p. 637. A. B. p. 1211., the Persian Lilac. Height
4—6 ft. 9d.
Syrínga rothomagénsis E. of T. p. 637. A. B. p. 1212., the Rouen Lilac.
Height 6—8 ft. 9d.
Syrínga vulgàris E. of T. p. 636. A. B. p. 1209., the common Lilac. Height
8—10 ft. 9d.
Syrínga vulgàris álba E. of T. p. 636. A. B. p. 1209., the common White
Lilac. 9d.
Vibúrnum dentàtum E. of T. p. 521. A. B. p. 1038., the toothed-leaved Vi-
burnum. Height 4—6 ft. 1s.
Vibúrnum Lantàna E. of T. p. 520. A. B. p. 1035., the Wayfaring Tree.
Height 12—15 ft. 1s.
Vibúrnum Lentàgo E. of T. p. 517. A. B. p. 1033., the Lentago, or pliant-
branched Viburnum. Height 6—10 ft. 1s. 6d.
Vibúrnum O'pulus E. of T. p. 522. A. B. p. 1039., the Guelder Rose. Height
6—12 ft. 9d.
Xanthóxylum *fraxíneum* E. of T. p. 142. A. B. p. 488., the common Tooth-
ache Tree. Height 10—15 ft. 2s. 6d.

LOW TREES AND SHRUBS FOR WALLS.

*Select low Trees or Shrubs for a Cemetery or Churchyard Wall, where the
Expense of Training is not an Object.*

* Evergreen or Subevergreen.

A'rbutus Andráchne E. of T. p. 575. A. B. p. 1120., the Strawberry Tree.
Height 20—30 ft. 5s.
Aristotélia *Mácqui* E. of T. p. 183. A. B. p. 543., the Macqui Aristotelia.
Height 6 ft. 1s. 6d.

Ceanòthus azùreus E. of T. p. 180. *A. B.* p. 539., the Red Root. Height 6—10 ft. 2*s.* 6*d.*

Cratæ'gus mexicàna E. of T. p. 384. *A. B.* p. 843., the Mexican Thorn. Height 10—15 ft. 2*s.* 6*d.*

Escallònia rùbra E. of T. p. 490. *A. B.* p. 993., the red-flowered Escallonia. Height 3—6 ft. 1*s.* 6*d.*

Euónymus japónicus E. of T. p. 153. *A. B.* p. 501. 1*s.* 6*d.*

Laùrus nóbilis E. of T. p. 681. *A. B.* p. 1297., the Sweet Bay. Height 30—60 ft. 1*s.* 6*d.*

Ligústrum lùcidum E. of T. p. 630. *A. B.* p. 1201., the shining-leaved Privet, or Wax Tree. Height 10—20 ft. 1*s.* 6*d.*

Magnòlia grandiflòra E. of T. p. 22. *A. B.* p. 261., the large-flowered Magnolia. Height 20—30 ft. 3*s.* 6*d.*

Mahònia fasciculàris E. of T. p. 50. *A. B.* p. 309., the Ash Berberry. Height 5—8 ft. 7*s.* 6*d.*

Photínia serrulàta E. of T. p. 404. *A. B.* p. 868., the serrulated-leaved Photinia. Height 12—15 ft. 2*s.* 6*d.*

Yúcca gloriòsa E. of T. p. 1101. *A. B.* p. 2521., the glorious Adam's Needle. Height 5 ft. 5*s.*

** Deciduous.

Amýgdalus orientàlis E. of T. p. 265. *A. B.* p. 679., the Eastern Almond Tree. Height 8—10 ft. 2*s.* 6*d.*

Búddlea globòsa E. of T. p. 670. *A. B.* p. 1276. the globe-flowered Buddlea. Height 12—15 ft. 1*s.* 6*d.*

Deùtzia scàbra E. of T. p. 466. *A. B.* p. 950, the scabrous Deutzia. Height 4—6 ft. 1*s.* 6*d.*

Hibíscus syrìacus E. of T. p. 62. *A. B.* p. 362., the Althæa Frutex. Height 6 ft. Nine varieties. From 6*d.* to 1*s.*

Magnòlia conspícua E. of T. p. 33. *A. B.* p. 278., the Yulan, or conspicuous-flowered Magnolia. Height 20—30 ft. 5*s.*

Magnòlia c. Soulangeàna E. of T. p. 33. *A. B.* p. 272., Soulange's Magnolia. Height 15—20 ft. 5*s.*

Magnòlia cordàta E. of T. p. 30. *A. B.* p. 275., the heart-leaved Magnolia. Height 20—30 ft. 3*s.* 6*d.*

* *Magnòlia purpùrea E. of T.* p. 35. *A. B.* p. 282., the purple-flowered Magnolia. Height 3—5 ft. 2*s.* 6*d.*

Rìbes aùreum præ'cox E. of T. p. 487. *A. B.* p. 989., the golden-flowered Currant. 1*s.*

Rìbes Menzièsii E. of T. p. 475. Menzies's Gooseberry. Height 4—5 ft. 1*s.* 6*d.*

Rìbes sanguíneum E. of T. p. 486. *A. B.* p. 988., the bloody, or red-flowered, Currant. Height 4—8 ft. 9*d.*

Rìbes speciòsum E. of T. p. 474. *A. B.* p. 974., the showy-flowered Gooseberry. Height 4—8 ft. 1*s.* 6*d.*

Robínia híspida E. of T. p. 236. *A. B.* p. 627., the Rose Acacia. Height 6—20 ft. 1*s.* 6*d.*

Robínia macrophýlla E. of T. p. 237. *A. B.* p. 628., the large-leaved Rose Acacia. 1*s.* 6*d.*

Robínia ròsea E. of T. p. 237. *A. B.* p. 627., the rosy-flowered Rose Acacia. 1*s.* 6*d.*

CLIMBERS.

Climbing Shrubs adapted for a Wall where the Ground is not dug.

* Evergreen.

Hédera Hèlix E. of T. p. 497. *A. B.* p. 1000., the common Ivy. Height 20—60 ft. Seven varieties, all beautiful. From 6*d.* to 1*s.* 6*d.* The badge of the clan Gordon.

** Deciduous.

Ampelópsis *hederàcea* E. of T. p. 139. A. B. p. 482., the five-leaved Ivy. Height 30—50 ft. 1s. 6d.

Aristolòchia sìpho E. of T. p. 701. A. B. p. 1329., the tube-flowered Birthwort. Height 15—30 ft. 2s. 6d.

Clématis Flámmula E. of T. p. 3. A. B. p. 233., the sweet-scented Virgin's Bower. Height 10—15 ft. 1s. 6d.

Clématis Vitálba E. of T. p. 5. A. B. p. 235., the Traveller's Joy. Height 15—30 ft. 1s.

Jasmìnum officinàle E. of T. p. 656. A. B. p. 1250., the common Jasmine. Height 40—50 ft. 1s.

Lonícera E. of T. p. 526. A. B. p. 1042., the Honeysuckle. Ten sorts. From 6d. to 1s. 6d.

Lýcium bárbarum E. of T. p. 666. A. B. p. 1270., the Barbary Box Thorn. Height 20—30 ft. 9d.

Menispérmum canadénse E. of T. p. 40. A. B. p. 296., male and female, the Canadian Moonseed. Height 8—12 ft. 1s. 6d.

Períploca græ\ca E. of T. 659. A. B. p. 1257., the Greek Periploca. Height 20—30 ft. 2s. 6d.

Physiánthus álbicans E. of. T. p. 659. A. B. p. 2581. 2s. 6d.

Rhús radìcans E. of T. p. 190. A. B. p. 555., the rooting-branched Sumach. Height 10—20 ft. 1s. 6d.

Rhús suavèolens E. of T. p. 191. A. B. p. 557., the sweet-scented Sumach. Height 1—4 ft. 1s. 6d.

Rhús Toxicodéndron E. of T. p. 190. A. B. p. 556., the Poison-tree Rhus, or Sumach. Height 10—20. 1s. 6d.

Ròsa arvénsis E. of T. p. 344. A. B. p. 772. Several varieties, quite hardy. From 6d. to 2s. 6d.

Vìtis cordifòlia E. of T. p. 138. A. B. p. 480., the Chicken Grape. Height 10—20 ft.

Vìtis Labrúsca E. of T. p. 137. A. B. p. 479., the Fox Grape. Height 10—30 ft. 2s. 6d.

Vìtis ripària E. of T. p. 138. A. B. p. 480., the river-side, or sweet-scented, Vine. Height 20—30 ft. 2s. 6d.

Vìtis vinífera *apiifòlia* E. of T. p. 137. A. B. p. 478., the Parsley-leaved Grape Vine. 2s. 6d.

Vìtis vinífera fòliis incànis E. of T. p. 137. A. B. p. 478., the hoary-leaved Grape Vine. 2s. 6d.

Vìtis vinífera fòliis rubescéntibus E. of T. p. 137. A. B. p. 478., the Claret Grape. 2s. 6d.

Wistària frutéscens E. of T. p. 249. A. B. p. 647., the shrubby Wistaria. Height 20—30 ft. 1s. 6d.

Wistària chinénsis E. of T. p. 249. A. B. p. 648., the Chinese Wistaria. Height 50—120 ft. 2s. 6d.

Climbing Shrubs where there is a dug Border.

* Evergreen or Subevergreen.

Bignònia capreolàta E. of T. p. 660. A. B. p. 1259., the tendriled Bignonia, or Trumpet Flower. Height 15—20, 2s. 6d.

Lonícera gràta E. of T. p. 531. A. B. p. 1048., the pleasant, or evergreen, Honeysuckle. Height 15—20 ft. 1s. 6d.

Lonícera sempervìrens E. of T. p. 531. A. B. p. 1049., the evergreen Trumpet Honeysuckle. Height 6—10 ft. 1s.

Ròsa sempervìrens E. of T. p. 345. A. B. p. 773., the evergreen (Field) Rose. Height 20—40 ft. 1s.

** Deciduous.

Lonícera E. of T. p. 526. A. B. p. 1042., the Honeysuckle. Several species and varieties.

Ròsa E. of T. p. 321, A. B. p. 748., the Rose Tree. Several species. From 4d. to 2s.

UNDERSHRUBS.

Undershrubs of very small Size, frequently planted over Graves.

* Evergreen.

Vínca màjor and mìnor, the greater and lesser Perrywinkle, 6d. Common in burying-grounds in the Tyrol, and probably used there in consequence of the notice of the plant by Rousseau: *"Voilà la Pervenche!"*

Hypéricum calycìnum, the Tutsan St. John's Wort. 4d.

Rosmarìnus officinàlis, the common Rosemary. 4d.

Rùta gravèolens, the common Rue. 4d.

Thỳmus vulgàris, the common Thyme. 2d.

Lavándula Spìca, the common Lavender. 3d.

Oxycóccus palústris, the common Cranberry. 6d. The badge of the clan Grant.

Vaccínium Vìtis idæ'a, the red Whortleberry, or Cowberry. 6d. The badge of the clan Macleod.

E'mpetrum nìgrum, the Crowberry. 6d. The badge of the clan M'Lean.

Callùna vulgàris, the Ling. 6d. The badge of the clan Macdonell.

Erìca Tétralix, the cross-leaved Heath. 6d. The badge of the clan Macdonald.

Erìca cinèrea, the fine-leaved Heath. 6d. The badge of the clan Macalister.

** Deciduous.

Artemísia Absínthium, the common Southernwood. 3d.

Sàlix herbàcea, the herbaceous Willow. 6d.

Hypéricum Kalmiànum, Kalm's St. John's Wort. 6d. Common in the cemeteries at Carlsruhe, and in other parts of Baden and Würtemberg.

Hypéricum elàtum, hircìnum, and prolíficum. 6d. each.

Androsæ'mum officinàle, the common Tutsan. 6d.

Myrìca Gàle, the sweet Gale. 6d. The badge of the clan Campbell.

Rùbus saxátilis, the Roebuck-berry. 6d. The badge of the clan Macnab.

SHRUBS FOR GRAFTING STANDARD HIGH.

List of Shrubs which, when grafted standard high, form ornamental Plants of singular Shapes and Habits of Growth, well adapted for planting singly beside Graves or Tombstones, for marking any particular Spot, or for creating Variety in a Shrubbery Walk, or in the Glades of a Pleasure-Ground. The price varies from 2s. 6d. to 7s. 6d.

* Evergreen.

Arctostáphylos U'va úrsi.

A'rbutus alpìna.

Cotoneáster rotundifòlia, microphýlla, and buxifòlia.

Phillýrea, all the sorts on the Evergreen Privet.

Thùja péndula, on the common Arbor Vitæ.

Pìnus Pínea, on P. sylvéstris.

Pìnus pumílio, on P. sylvéstris.

Pìnus Banksiàna, on P. sylvéstris.

Pìnus ìnops, on P. sylvéstris.

** Deciduous.

Calóphaca wolgárica.

Caragàna pygmæ'a.

Caragàna spinòsa.

Caragàna tragacanthoìdes.

Caragàna Chamlàgu.
Cérasus Chamæcérasus.
Cérasus prostràta.
Cérasus pùmila.
Cérasus depréssa.
Cérasus pygmæ'a.
Cýtisus sessilifòlius.
Cýtisus alpìnus, on *C.* Labúrnum.
Cýtisus scopàrius, the common Broom, on *C.* Labúrnum.
Cýtisus scopàrius álbus.
Cýtisus purpùreus, on *C.* Labúrnum.
Fráxinus excélsior aúrea, and other varieties.
Genísta tríquetra.
Halimodéndron argénteum.
Jasmìnum officinàle, and other species, on the common Ash, or on the common Lilac.

Pàvia díscolor.
Pàvia rùbra hùmilis.
Pàvia macrostàchya.
Pýrus spùria.
Pýrus spùria péndula.
Pýrus arbutifòlia.
Pýrus arbutifòlia serótina.
Pýrus melanocárpa.
Pýrus floribúnda.   *P.* depréssa.
Robínia Pseud-Acàcia umbraculífera.
Robínia Pseud-Acàcia tortuòsa.
Sàlix purpùrea.   *S.* herbàcea.
Spártium júnceum, on the Laburnum.
Syrínga pérsica, and its varieties, on the common Ash.
Syrínga vulgàris, on the common Ash.
Técoma radìcans, on the Catalpa.

PERENNIAL HERBACEOUS PLANTS.

Perennial herbaceous Plants adapted for Cemeteries and Churchyards.

For planting in dug ground, whether in beds or over graves, every description of herbaceous plant, except those which require peat soil, is eligible ; but for planting on turf to form single specimens, or what gardeners call "lawn plants," a selection requires to be made of such as have peculiar properties. These are : considerable bulk above ground ; great natural hardiness of stem and foliage and durability of root ; under-ground buds, or strong surface stocks, that will be secure from injury during the winter or dormant season ; a compact habit of growth both of the roots and top ; and sufficient natural vigour not to be injured by the compact texture of a grassy surface. The common pæony, the rhubarb, and the asparagus, are good examples of the kind of plant required ; and the following list includes such plants, and a few others which may be procured in the principal botanic gardens and nurseries. The prices, when a single plant is ordered, vary from 3*d.* to 1*s.* 6*d.*

Herbaceous Perennials with strong under-ground Buds, and compact Heads that do not require the Support of Stakes.

Clématis ochroleùca, the yellowish white Virgin's Bower.   Height 2 ft.
Thalíctrum màjus, the greater Meadow Rue.   Height 3 ft.
Aconìtum variegàtum, the variegated Aconite.   Height 5 ft.
Actæ'a spicàta, the spiked Bane-berry.   Height 3 ft.   The berries are poison.
Pæònia albiflòra, *P.* officinàlis, *P.* tenuifòlia, and others ; the white-flowered, common, and slender-leaved pæonies.   Height 2 ft.
Macleàya cordàta, the cordate Macleaya.   Height 6 ft.   The stems require support in exposed situations.
Crámbe marítima and *C.* cordifòlia, the common and the heart-leaved Sea-kale.   Height 1 ft. 6 in. and 6 ft.   The latter is a noble plant.
Lunària redivìva, the revived Honesty.   Height 3 ft.
Datísca cannàbina, the Hemp-like Datisca.   Height 4 ft.
Althæ'a officinàlis, the officinal Marsh Mallow.   Height 4 ft.
Ge[`e]ranium ibéricum, the Iberian Crane's Bill.   Height 1 ft. 6 in.
Dictámnus Fraxinélla, the Fraxinella.   Height 3 ft.
O'robus niger, the black Bitter Vetch.   Height 3 ft.
O'robus vérnus, the spring Bitter Vetch.   Height 1 ft.

Spiræ'a Arúncus, the Goat's-beard. Height 4 ft.
Lýthrum virgàtum, the twiggy Lythrum. Height 3 ft.
Erýngium plànum, the flat-leaved Eryngo. Height 3 ft.
Erýngium alpìnum, the alpine Eryngo. Height 2 ft.
Erýngium amethýstinum, the amethystine Eryngo. Height 3 ft.
Aràlia racemòsa, the racemose Aralia. Height 4 ft.
Echìnops sphærocéphalus, the round-headed Globe Thistle. Height 5 ft.
Echìnops *Rì*tro, the Ritro Globe Thistle. Height 3 ft.
*A'*ster sibíricus, the Siberian Starwort. Height 2 ft.
Solidàgo bícolor, the two-coloured Golden Rod. Requires a stake in exposed
   situations.
Stenáctis speciòsa, the showy-flowered Stenactis. Height 2 ft.
Solidàgo flexicaúlis, the crook-stalked Golden Rod. Height 2 ft.
*I'*nula *H*elèni*um*, the Elecampane. Height 4 ft.
Telèkia cordifòlia, the showy Telekia. Height 4 ft.
Heliánthus multiflòrus, the many-flowered Sunflower. Height 6 ft.
Campánula latifòlia, C. macrántha, C. *T*rachèlium. and C. glomeràta ; the broad-
   leaved, large-flowered, Throatwort, and clustered, Bellflower. Height
   from 2 ft. to 3 ft. These plants, in exposed situations, require stakes.
Phlóx paniculàta, P. corymbòsa, and P. acuminàta, the panicled-flowered,
   corymbose-flowered, and pointed-leaved Phlox. Height 3 ft. to 5 ft. ; in
   exposed situations requiring stakes.
Gentià*na* lùtea, the yellow Gentian. Height 4 ft. Requires an open airy si-
   tuation, and a stake if it be much exposed.
Phlóx glabérrima, the smoothest Phlox. Height 3 ft.
*S*ýmphytum bohémicum, the Bohemian Comfrey. Height 3 ft.
Scopòli*a* carniólica, the Carniolan Scopolia. Height 1 ft.
Betónica grandiflòra, the great-flowered Betony. Height 1 ft. 6 in.
*S*álvia glutinòsa, the glutinous Sage. Height 3 ft.
Lysimàchia vulgàris, the common Loose-strife. Height 3 ft.
Lysimàchia verticillàta, the whorled Loose-strife. Height 1 ft.
Lysimàchia thyrsiflòra, the thyrse-flowered Loose-strife. Height 1½ ft.
*St*átice latifòlia, the broad-leaved Sea Lavender. Height 1 ft.
*R*ùmex alpìnus, the alpine Dock. Height 4 ft.
*R*hèum palmàtum, the palmated Rhubarb. Height 5 ft.
*R*hèum Emòdi, the Southern Rhubarb. Height 8 ft.
*E*uphórbia hibérnica, the Irish Spurge. Height 1 ft.
*U*rtìca nívea, the snow-white-leaved Nettle. Height 6 ft. Requires a stake
   in exposed situations.
I'ris sibírica, and *I.s.* flòre álbo, the common and white-flowered Siberian Iris.
   Height 3 ft. and 2½ feet.
*A'*rum *D*racúnculus, the common Dragon Arum. Height 3 ft.
Fúnki*a* subcordàta, the subcordate-leaved Funkia. Height 1 ft.
Fúnki*a* ovàta, the ovate-leaved Funkia. Height 1½ ft.
*A'*llium Victoriàlis, the Victorialis Garlic. Height 2 ft.
*A*spáragus officinàlis, the common Asparagus. Height 4 ft.
*V*eràtrum nìgrum, the dark-flowered Veratrum, or black Hellebore. Height
   3 ft.
*V*eràtrum álbum, the white Veratrum, or white Hellebore. Height 5 ft.
Uvulària grandiflòra, the large-flowered Uvularia. Height 1 ft.

*Herbaceous Plants with the same Properties, except that the Roots are less
   compact, though still not creeping.*

*Sì*da Napæ'a, the Napæa Sida. Height 4 ft. Requires a stake in exposed
   situations.
Baptísia austràlis, the Southern Baptisia. Height 2½ ft.
Galèga orientàlis, the Oriental Goat's Rue. Height 4 ft.
Epilóbium angustíssimum, the narrowest-leaved Willow Herb. Height 2 ft.

Astrántia máxima, the greatest Masterwort. Height 2 ft. In very mild
    winters does not die quite down to the ground.
Phyteùma campanuloìdes, the Campanula-like Rampion. Height 1 ft.
Cynánchum Vìncetóxicum, the Vincetoxicum Cynanchum. Height 2 ft.
Boràgo orientàlis, the Oriental Borage. Height 2 ft. In mild winters does
    not die quite down. .
Acánthus móllis, A. spinòsus, and A. spinosíssimus, the soft, prickly, and most
    prickly, Bear's-breech. Height 3 ft. In sheltered situations these plants
    sometimes retain a little foliage through the winter. They are interest-
    ing on account of their foliage, which, according to some, gave rise to that
    of the Corinthian capital; but the adherent petioles of palm leaves are
    much more likely to have been the original type.
Hemerocállis flàva and H. fúlva, the yellow and copper-coloured Day Lily.
    Height 2 ft.

*Herbaceous Plants of vigorous Growth and compact Habit, but which do not lose
    the Whole of their Foliage in Winter.*

Aconìtum Napéllus, the Monk's-hood Aconitum. Height 4 ft.
Papàver orientàlis and P. bracteàta, the Oriental and bracteate Poppy.
    Height 3—4 ft. In exposed situations these may require to be staked.
Gerànium sanguíneum, the bloody Crane's Bill. Height 1 ft.
Gerànium lívidum, the livid-flowered Crane's Bill. Height 1½ ft.
Gerànium refléxum, the reflexed-flowered Crane's Bill. Height 1½ ft.
Lupìnus polyphýllus, the many-leaved Lupine. Height 2 ft.
Astrántia màjor, the greater Masterwort. Height 2 ft.
A'ster Améllus, the Amellus Starwort. Height 2 ft.
Agrimònia Æupatòria, the Eupatoria Agrimony. Height 3 ft.
Phlòmis gigantèa and P. sàmia, the gigantic and Samian Jerusalem Sage.
    Height 3 ft.
Làmium Orvàla, the Orvala, or Balm-leaved, Archangel. Height 1¾ ft.
Betónica strícta, the strict Betony. Height 1½ ft.
Melíssa officinàlis, the officinal Balm. Height 1 ft.

*Evergreen herbaceous Plants of compact Habit, which will grow on a grassy
    Surface.*

Helléborus fœ'tidus, the fetid Bear's-foot Hellebore. Height 1½ ft.
Helléborus nìger, the black Christmas Rose. Height 1 ft.
Helléborus olýmpicus, the Olympian Hellebore. Height 1 ft.
Málva moschàta, the Musk Mallow. Height 2 ft.
Saxífraga crassifòlia, the thick-leaved Saxifrage. Height 1 ft.
Saxífraga cordifòlia, the heart-leaved Saxifage. Height 1 ft.
Valeriàna rùbra (Centránthus rùber Dec.), the red Valerian; and C. r. flòre
    álbo, the white-flowering Valerian. Height 1½ ft.
Férula commùnis, the common Giant Fennel. Height 10 ft.
Verbáscum ferrugíneum, the rust-coloured Mullein. Height 3 ft.
Potèrium Sanguisórba, the Sanguisorba Burnet. Height 2 ft.
Ròhdea japónica, the Japan Rohdea. Height 2 ft.
Íris fœtidíssima and I. f. variegàta, the common and variegated Gladiolus Iris.
    Height 1½ ft.
Státice latifòlia and stellulàta, the broad-leaved and the stellulate Sea Laven-
    der. Height 1 ft.
Asphódelus lùteus, the yellow Asphodel. Height 3 ft.
Anthéricum Liliástrum and A. Liliàgo, the Liliaster and the Liliago Antheri-
    cum. Height 1½ ft. and 1 ft.
Yúcca filamentòsa, the filamentose Adam's Needle. Height 2 ft.

Herbaceous Plants, of bold Growth, which produce many upright Stems ; and, in exposed Situations, will require Stakes from the Middle of June till September or October.

Clématis erécta, the upright Virgin's Bower. Height 3 ft.
Clématis integrifòlia, the entire-leaved Virgin's Bower. Height 2 ft.
Thalíctrum glaúcum, the glaucous-leaved Meadow Rue. Height 5 ft.
Delphínium elàtum, the tall Bee Larkspur. Height 6 ft.
Delphínium azùreum, the azure Larkspur. Height 6 ft.
Lýchnis chalcedónica, the Chalcedonian Lychnis. Height 2 ft.
Sìda dioíca, the diœcious Sida. Height 6 ft.
Sanguisórba canadénsis, the Canadian great Burnet. Height 3 ft.
Sanguisórba officinàlis, the officinal great Burnet. Height 4 ft.
Ligústicum Levísticum, the common Lovage. Height 6 ft.
Scabiòsa leucántha, the white-flowered Scabious. Height 3 ft.
Rudbéckia purpùrea, the purple Rudbeckia. Height 5 ft.
Sìlphium perfoliàtum, the perfoliate Silphium. Height 7 ft.
Sìlphium laciniàtum, the jagged-leaved Silphium. A splendid plant, which attains the height of 10 or 12 feet on a lawn.
Sýmphytum aspérrimum, the roughest Comfrey. Height 6 ft.

Herbaceous Plants with creeping Roots, which will thrive on a grassy Surface, and may therefore be introduced in Burying-Grounds or on Lawns.

Monárda dídyma, the twin, or Oswego Tea, Monarda. Height 3 ft.
Tanacètum vulgàre, the common Tansy. Height 2 ft.
Gnaphàlium margaritàceum, the pearly Everlasting. Height 1½ ft.
Gàlium Mollùgo, the great hedge Bed-straw. Height 2 ft.
Convallària Polygónatum, Solomon's Seal. Height 2 ft.
Convallària majàlis, the Lily of the Valley. Height 6 in.
Epilòbium angustifòlium, the narrow-leaved Willow Herb. Height 4 ft.
Erýngium campéstre, the field Eryngo. Height 2 ft.
Centaurèa montàna, the mountain Centaurea. Height 1½ ft.
Myosòtis palústris, the Forget-me-not. Height 6 in.

BULBS.

The genera Eránthis, Galánthus, Cròcus, Scílla, Hyacínthus, Erythrònium Cólchicum, and some others of low growth, which flower in early spring or late in autumn, may be planted on graves, or at the base of gravestones, where their foliage, after they have done flowering, will be out of the way of the scythe. The following may be planted singly on a grassy surface.

Adònis vernàlis, the spring-flowering Adonis. Height 9 in.
Lílium cándidum, the white Lily. A favourite flower in Catholic countries. Height 3 ft.
Lílium. Most of the other species in sheltered situations.
Fritillària imperiàlis, the Crown-Imperial Fritillary. Height 4 ft.
Scílla esculénta, the Quamash Squill. Height 1 ft.
Gladìolus commùnis, natalénsis, and other species of the Corn Flag. Height 2—4 ft.
Amarýllis formosíssima, the Jacobæa Lily. The lily of Turkish cemeteries, and the badge of the Knights of St. James of Spain.
Narcíssus. All the species.
Sternbérgia lùtea, the yellow Sternbergia. Height 6 in. Supposed by Sir J. E. Smith to be the lily alluded to by our Saviour in his sermon on the Mount.
Leucòjum æstìvum, the summer Snowflake. Height 1½ ft.

I

Ornithógalum. All the species.
Tùlipa sylvéstris, the wild Tulip. Height 1 ft.

FERNS.

Struthiópteris germánica, the German Struthiopteris. Height 2 ft.
Struthiópteris pennsylvánica, the Pennsylvanian Struthiopteris. Height 2 ft.
Osmúnda regàlis, the royal Osmunda. Height 2 ft.
Ptèris aquilìna, the common Brake. The badge of the clan Robertson.
  Height 3—4 ft.
Asplènium Filix más, and *A. Filix fœ'mina,* the male and female Fern.
  Height 2—3 ft.
Aspídium aculeàtum, A. lobàtum, and A. rígidum; the common prickly, the
  lobed-leaved, and the rigid Shield Fern. Height 6 in. to 2 ft.

PLANTS USED AS BADGES.

Plants which form national Badges.

Countries.	Names of Plants.
ENGLAND.	The Rose, *Ròsa* sp.
SCOTLAND.	The Thistle, *Cnicus* lanceolàtus.
IRELAND.	The Shamrock, *O'xalis* Acetosélla *L.,* according to Mr. Bicheno; but commonly considered to be the white clover, *Trifòlium rèpens L.*
FRANCE.	The Fleur-de-lis, *I'ris* sp.

List of Plants which form the Badges of the Highland Clans.

These plants, many of which are trees or shrubs, are frequently planted over graves by Highland families settled abroad; they are also occasionally planted in gardens both abroad and at home, and in some cases they are sculptured on tombs. Our authority for the following list is *Blackwood's Magazine,* vol. xii. p. 271.

Names of the Clans.	Names of the Plants used as Badges.
BUCHANAN.	*Bétula álba L.,* the common Birch.
CAMERON.	*Quércus* pedunculàta *W.* (Q. *Ròbur L.*), the common British Oak.
CAMPBELL.	*Myrìca Gàle L.,* the Sweet Gale, or Dutch Myrtle.
CHISHOLM.	*A'lnus* glutinòsa, the Alder.
COLQUHOUN.	*Córylus Avellàna L.,* the common Hazel.
CUMMING.	*Sàlix càprea L.,* the great round-leaved Sallow; or any other native species.
DRUMMOND.	*I'lex Aquifòlium L.,* the common Holly.
FARQUHARSON.	*Digitàlis purpùrea L,* the purple Foxglove.
FERGUSON.	*Pópulus álba L.,* the great white Poplar, or Abele.
FORBES.	*Cýtisus scopàrius L.,* the common Broom.
FRAZER.	*Táxus baccàta L.,* the Yew.
GORDON.	*Hédera Hèlix L.,* the common Ivy.
GRAHAM.	*Dáphne* Laurèola, Spurge Laurel.
GRANT.	*Vaccínium* Oxycóccus *L.,* the Marsh Whortleberry, or Cranberry.
GUNN.	Rhodìola ròsea *L.,* the Rose Root.
LAMONT.	*Pỳrus Màlus L.,* the Crab-Apple Tree.
MACALISTER.	*Erìca* cinèrea *L.,* the fine-leaved Heath.

MACDONALD.	Erìca Tétralix L., the cross-leaved Heath.
MACDONELL.	Callùna vulgàris Salisb., the common Ling.
M'DOUGALL.	Cupréssus sempervìrens L., the Cypress.
MACFARLANE.	Rùbus Chamæmòrus L., the Cloudberry.
M'GREGOR.	Pìnus sylvéstris L., the Scotch Pine.
MACINTOSH.	Búxus sempervìrens L., the common Box Tree.
M'KENZIE.	Lìchen rangiferìnus L., the Reindeer Lichen.
M'KINNON.	Hypéricum púlchrum, St. John's Wort.
McLACHLAN.	Pỳrus aucupària Gært., the Quicken Tree, Mountain Ash, or Rowan Tree.
McLEAN.	E'mpetrum nìgrum L., the black Crowberry, or Crake-berry.
MACLEOD.	Vaccínium Vìtis idæ'a L., the red Whortleberry, or Cow-berry.
MACNAB.	Rùbus saxátilis, Roebuck-berry.
M'NEILL.	Fùcus vesiculòsus, the Sea Ware.
MACPHERSON.	Búxus sempervìrens variegàta L., the variegated Box Tree.
M'QUARRIE.	Prùnus spinòsa L., the Black Thorn.
MACRAE.	Lycopòdium alpìnum L., the Savin-leaved Club Moss.
M'RAY.	Scírpus lacústris L., the Bulrush.
MENZIES.	Fráxinus excélsa L., the Ash.
MUNRO.	Eagle's Feathers; or, according to the Vestiarium Scoticum, the Juniper.
MURRAY.	Juníperus commùnis L., the common Juniper.
OGILVIE.	Cratæ'gus Oxyacántha L., the Hawthorn.
OLIPHANT.	A'cer campéstre, common Maple.
ROBERTSON.	Ptèris aquilìna L., the common Brake.
ROSE.	Ròsa canìna L., the Briar Rose.
ROSS.	A'rbutus alpìna L., the black Bearberry.
SINCLAIR.	Lycopòdium clavàtum, common Club Moss.
STEWART.	Cnìcus lanceolatus, Spear Plume-thistle.
SUTHERLAND.	Phlèum praténse L., the Cat's-tail Grass, or Timothy Grass.

SUPPLEMENTARY ENGRAVINGS.

THIS lodge (*fig. 55.*) is referred to in p. 25. We consider it as peculiarly appropriate for a cemetery, on account of its church-like towers; one of which

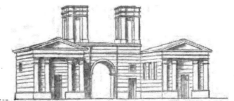

Fig. 55. *Entrance Lodge to the Newcastle Cemetery.*

is used as a belfry, and the other contains a clock. The design is by John Dobson, Esq., of Newcastle upon Tyne, the contributor of several beautiful cottage villas to the *Supplement* to our *Encyclopædia of Cottage Architecture.*

The tiles represented in *fig.* 56. are the invention of Mr. Reed, tile - maker, at Bishop Stortford, and have only lately come into use. They are formed and put together exactly on the same principle as the new French roofing tiles, described and figured in the *Supplement* to the *Encyclopædia of Cottage Architecture*, p. 1260.; and, like them, they are completely weather-tight, even when used with little or no cement. They

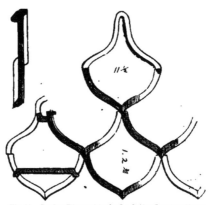

Fig. 56. *Roofing Tiles used in the Cambridge Cemetery Chapel.*

are the handsomest English tiles that we know of, and peculiarly suitable for ornamental cottages, lodges, &c., in the old English style.

APPENDIX.

Before publishing the preceding sheets, we sent a copy of them to a much esteemed correspondent at Leeds, Thomas Wilson, Esq., in whose taste and judgement we have the greatest confidence, and the following are his criticisms and suggestions. We have preferred giving them in his own words, although we are aware they were written rather as hints for ourselves, than with the expectation that they would be published in the form in which they were sent us.

There is nothing that is so little creditable to the national taste as the mode of conducting funerals. It is easy to account for it however. We are a trade-ridden people; and allow, from habit and indolence, tailors to be judges of taste in our dress, and milliners in that of ladies; and yet, in the present state of education in this country, how is it possible that the former, at any rate, should have the knowledge and the cultivation necessary to qualify them to judge in such matters? So with our undertakers: except in the metropolis, they are men of very limited cultivation; and, besides, the subject is one on which people are so sensitive, in those cases where they are individually concerned as directors of funerals, that no man likes to go out of the beaten path; and we remain, therefore, with parcels and patches of ceremonies and costumes as unsuitable to that which is associated with them, as bag wigs and court dresses with our ordinary attire. The reform in this, as in all other cases, must come out of the people themselves, when they are more enlightened; and especially when they are trained to comprehend the nature of their own minds, and to reason logically, instead of being governed by conventional practices; and particularly when correct principles of taste are established and acted upon, and deduced from the nature of things and from optical principles, and not regarded as a peculiar subject to be comprehended only by a few gifted individuals. I incline to believe that they are susceptible of mathematical demonstration, within limits nearly as rigid as any other branch of human enquiry.

Page 11. "*The ancients contemplated death without terror,*" &c. I do not at all agree with the writer quoted, as to the feelings of the ancients respecting death; but I have not time to seek for instances to support my views. I would, however, just allude to their constant and guarded avoidance of the term death, by the use of the euphemismi, sleep, or repose, fallen asleep, departed, &c.

P. 12. "*The influence of cemeteries and churchyards in improving the taste,*" &c. I should rather consider the cemetery as the result of the taste of the community, than the cause of it ; and I think, on reflection, you will admit that your suggestions, as to making it a place of instruction, are only applicable to the transition state of society in which we live.

P. 14. The "*situation*" should not be fixed on without reference to the geology of the country ; for instance, if all risk of injury to springs is to be avoided, it should be placed somewhere between *a, b,* and *c,* in *fig.* 57.; and drains should be made, as at *a d,* to pre-

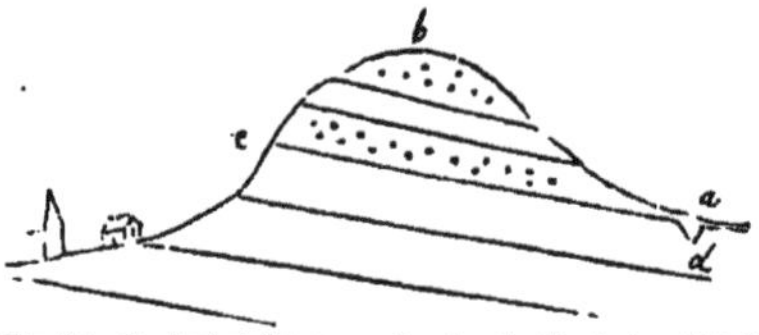

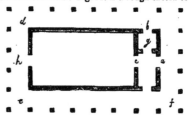

Fig. 57. *Geological Diagram, showing the Strata in which Interments may be made, without injuring the Springs and Wells.*

vent any moisture from the porous strata descending lower, and there should be no habitations on these strata.

P. 15. line 9. from the bottom. "*One main road, so as to allow of a hearse,*" &c. I should prefer an arrangement like the following. Let the entrance to the chapel be under an extensive portico, which would admit of the whole procession being under cover : here the coffin should be taken out, and the hearse admitted no farther. If the grave be at a distance from the chapel, a somewhat low bier on wheels might be provided, which would move without much exertion on flagged or macadamised roads. *Fig. 58.* is a rough sketch of

the way in which I would arrange a cemetery chapel, and conduct the procession. The porch would be a protection to the whole train in wet weather. Let the procession enter at *d,* and the hearse proceed to *a,* the first carriage stopping at *b.* When the coffin arrived at *c,* the mourners would enter from *g ;* and they would thus be spared all risk of seeing or hearing the arrange-

Fig. 58. *Plan for a Cemetery Chapel.*

ments attendant on removing so heavy a weight as a coffin, which often cause alarm lest any accident should occur, and which, however carefully managed, are so trying to the feelings of those whose thoughts should not be rudely disturbed. By rollers fixed in the floor of the hearse, the coffin might be more easily withdrawn, and placed on a frame so contrived that the bearers might take their places, while the coffin was suspended shoulder height. After the service, it might proceed, without turning, through *h.*

P. 17. last line. "*Requires no mapping.*" How am I to find any person's grave, if there is not a plan of the cemetery kept ? If the friends of the deceased know it, how are his grandchildren to discover it ?

P. 19. last paragraph. "*A mason's yard, with the sheds,*" &c. By no means admit workshops within the cemetery at any rate ; nor a mason's or statuary's within hearing. There should be no sound of tools, giving " dreadful note of preparation," to disturb the silence of the place.

P. 25. "*Entrance Lodge to the Tower Hamlets Cemetery,*" &c. In fig. 11. *a*, the substitution of folding doors for one swing door would be a great improvement ; as it is now, you must shut yourself into the vestibule *b*, before you can see the door leading to *c*.

P. 35. "*The Grave-Box,*" &c. Why should not the grave-boxes be constructed, like contractor's waggons, to tilt up ; and, like them, be placed on wheels ?

P. 38. "*Sixthly, . . . and therefore we would render it expensive,*" &c. Upon reflection, I think you will allow that we ought not to do that indirectly, which public opinion will not support us in doing directly. If a practice be admitted to be wrong, then prohibit it altogether. To check it by taxing it is tyranny : it is admitting passion, and not reason, into legislation ; and it is also false, on the same principles as the old sumptuary laws are admitted to be wrong. Let acts of parliament stop outside the grave : all on this side of it, in this act of parliament nation, is governed by statute. No sooner, in these days, does a kind and benevolent spirit detect a hardship or a wrong, than it flies to parliament for a remedy ; forgetting that, if we are to deal with effects, we must have millions of laws ; but, if we deal with causes, very few will suffice, and those few will soon be superfluous.

"*Interments in catacombs or vaults.*" With respect to interments in vaults or catacombs, as they will probably be continued, it is worth while considering whether there should not be provided some outlet for the gas, by a drain running at the back, and communicating with a chimney in which a current of warm air would aid the draught, or with a chamber in which it might be absorbed or decomposed. In *fig.* 59., *a a* are catacombs ; *b b*, channels com-

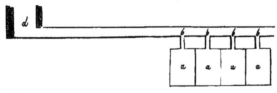

Fig. 59. *Diagram showing how the Mephitic Gas may be collected and carried off from Catacombs.*

municating with a drain *c ; d*, a chimney or chamber, in which there may be a fire for rarefying the air and creating a draught.

"*Seventhly. . . . We would allow individual taste,*" &c. There should be a veto somewhere, to exclude inscriptions improper, inaccurate, or ludicrous.

"*Monuments.*" It appears not to come within the scope of your work to give designs for monuments ; and, perhaps, it would render it more costly than you purpose ; but, if this work should, as I feel sure it ought and must, attract great attention, you might follow it up by a dissertation on the style of monuments, with examples. Such a manual would be a great boon to many a wounded spirit, that has now no other means of satisfying its desire to perpetuate some beloved object, than by consulting some rude village or town marble-mason, whose business-like ideas and technical expressions are in sad contrast with the thoughts of his employer.

P. 42. "*Order Book.*" If this work is to be a manual, at least for directors of cemeteries, if not for the managers, it might be useful, in the Appendix, to give the best forms of these books. Most of the books so used are susceptible of great improvement. If the present modes were thus made public, you might, through the *Gardener's Magazine*, from time to time, receive and record various suggestions for their improvement.

"*Register Book.*" I have expressed an opinion that the books in use might be improved ; and, as an instance, I offer the following arrangement as much superior to the one you have given, because grouping together facts that are of the same kind or time. I have not considered whether it contains all that is desirable; I merely take it as it is, and rearrange it thus. No. of interment; name, description, and residence of the deceased; age; disease (this will, however, be of no value unless it be certified by a medical man); date and hour of burial; officiating clergyman; sexton; undertaker: all these relate to the past. The following refer to the future: No. of grave; in what part of cemetery; monumental distinction, purchaser, and date; amount for interment; sum paid for keeping in order the grave, &c., and time during which, &c.

P. 43. "*Ledger.*" I think there ought to be a corresponding ledger, showing what duties are to be performed towards each grave, in double form. First, classed numerically. No. 1. Stone to be kept in order for ten years; date at which the liability commences and ceases. No. 5. Flowers to be planted, &c. &c.

Again, in another form. Gravestones to be kept in order: Nos. 7. 12., &c., &c. Flowers to be planted: Nos. 5. 9. 13., &c. &c. Or, perhaps, the same end might be obtained by having a map with a distinctive colour for each kind of duty, so that the attendants and managers might see at a glance that the whole was correctly performed.

"*Map Book.*" The scales adopted should be uniform, and should be some multiple of the scale used in the township plan or government survey.

"*Rules and regulations,*" &c. If you propose to make your work a manual, then add a code of these rules, compiled from the best existing codes, with additions. Perhaps these details might accompany the collection of monuments which I before suggested.

P. 49. "*Temporary cemeteries,*" &c. The best purpose to apply what you have designated temporary cemeteries to, would be to plant them and keep them in timber, and so insure that the ground need not be disturbed, at any rate not to a depth that would interfere with the interments.

P. 50. "*Shillibeer's hearse*" was introduced here [Leeds] a few weeks since, and struck me as a great boon to those who wish to reduce the cost of funerals, and yet fear to do what may be considered not respectful towards the deceased. I cannot say whether it has been much used or not, but I have no doubt of its soon being employed when it is fully known.

"*Mr. Jukes's truck-hearse*" would, I suppose, answer within the cemetery, as I have already suggested. I should think it is susceptible of very great improvement. The retarding ought to be effected by some mode more consistent with the solemnity required.

P. 51. "*Funeral processions,*" &c. I wish you had enlarged more on the subject of funeral processions and attendants. It would be improper to treat the subject with levity; but it may be safely asserted that the whole of the arrangements are suitable only to a barbarous age. The dresses and decorations are even childish, and many of the accompaniments any thing but appropriate. The heavy and ponderous ornaments are intended to convey an idea at once of solemnity and magnificence; but how badly are they supported by the appearance of the jaded and foundered horses, and the uncouthness of the drivers! This is a part of the subject that I hope you will take up, and illustrate it by drawings contrasting the present modes with others more consistent with good taste. It is in vain, at present and at once, to advise the middle classes to retrench in these expenses; but it may be possible to persuade them to adopt more rational modes of proceeding.

P. 53. "*The soil of the Cambridge Cemetery,*" &c. I think borings should have been taken, to the depth of 10 or 12 feet at the least, and the result stated, as well as the direction of the dip, if any, of the strata.

P. 57. line 5. "*Steps to the chapel,*" &c. I should object to a flight of steps, even at the risk of injuring the appearance of the building, as unsuitable to the purpose and inconvenient to those who carry the body; if it must be elevated, let the ground rise gently: but, if you will have steps, let them be not less than 7 ft. broad, that the bearers may have room to stand at each rise.

P. 67. line 31. "*No evil results,*" &c. That is, of course, no appreciable evil; but I incline to think that the gas will still escape, and, though in small quantities, be injurious: now, could not some substance be found, that might be placed round the coffin, which, having a greater affinity for some of the elements of the gas than the other elements have, would decompose it, and render it innocuous? The next consideration is, at what expense could this be done? I need not say this is a very different matter from putting lime *into* the coffin (p.48.); the object here is not to decompose, but, when the products of decomposition are formed, to render them harmless. As to expense, I believe that is, in all cases, only a question of time. I mean that, if we can once accomplish an object at any cost, we shall ultimately, by some means or other, do it economically. Expense depends on modes, not on principles, in these matters.

P. 67. "*Graves as deep as wells,*" except that the cost would soon be such as to defeat the object. This object might be attained where there had been quarries excavated, by filling the ground up gradually; but this would also be an expensive process.

P. 72. line 4. "*Mnemata, or the tombs.*" Is it not the Greek word μνη-μαρα? and, if so, it means recollections, remembrances, memories; and forms a beautiful instance of their euphemismi, as applied to the tomb.

P. 80. "*The practice of admitting cattle into churchyards*" has arisen out of an abuse of the law. When a church was founded, as almost all our churches were, by the great landowners of the time for the use of their tenants, a church-yard was added for interment. By legal construction, the incumbent is con-sidered as a corporation sole, and the freehold vested in him to preserve it for the uses of the church; but he has gradually come to look upon it as if it were as much his, for any purposes, as any other freehold, subject only to the limit of the right of interments. Hence his claim (which is good in law but not in justice, nor consonant to the feelings of these times,) to stock it as well as any part of the glebe. It ought not to require an enactment to remove this encroachment: the bishops or archdeacons have only to discourage it; and the public has only to direct attention quietly and generally, but not offen-sively and personally, to it, and it will be prohibited. It is quite clear that this practice must be discontinued, before any useful attempt can be made to beautify our churchyards.

P. 81. line 36. "*The enlargement of churchyards*" should be provided for by forming them at first, or on their first alteration, so as to admit of additions at the least cost. It would seem to be the best way, to provide for the addition on one side, and that the narrowest, so as to destroy the shortest possible length of fence. To enable this to be done, building within certain limits of a churchyard should be prohibited, and a power given to certain per-sons to take land for the purpose.— *T. W. Crimbles House, March* 24. 1843

Fig. 60. *Hand-bier referred to in* p. 51.

LONDON: Printed by A. SPOTTISWOODE, New-Street-Square.

Lightning Source UK Ltd.
Milton Keynes UK
UKHW022032260421
382682UK00003B/221